ANIMALS AS PERSONS

Animals as Persons

Essays on the Abolition of Animal Exploitation

GARY L. FRANCIONE

Columbia University Press *New York*

Columbia University Press
Publishers Since 1893
New York   Chichester, West Sussex
Copyright © 2008 Gary L. Francione
All rights reserved

Library of Congress Cataloging-in-Publication Data
Francione, Gary L. (Gary Lawrence), 1954–
Animals as persons : essays on the abolition of animal exploitation / Gary L.
Francione.
p.   cm.
Includes bibliographical references and index.
ISBN 978-0-231-13950-2 (cloth : alk. paper) — ISBN 978-0-231-13951-9 (pbk. : alk. paper)
ISBN 978-0-231-51156-8 (ebook)
1. Animal rights.   2. Animal welfare—Law and legislation.
3. Animals—Law and legislation.   I. Title.
K3620.F73 2008
344.04'9—dc22
2007053043

Columbia University Press books are printed
on permanent and durable acid-free paper.

This book is printed on paper with recycled content.
Printed in the United States of America

References to Internet Web sites (URLs) were accurate at the time of writing.
Neither the author nor Columbia University Press is responsible for URLs
that may have expired or changed since the manuscript was prepared.

To the two hamsters and twelve dogs
who taught me the meaning of personhood

CONTENTS

FOREWORD
Gary Steiner

Paradigm shifts in human thought always depend on iconoclasts who are not afraid to challenge conventional wisdom. Although our thinking in the past generation about the moral status of animals has advanced in certain respects, its fundamental presuppositions have suffered from a debilitating stagnation. In contemporary thought no individual has been doing more to challenge these presuppositions in a fruitful way than Gary Francione.

The past generation of thinking about animals has been dominated by the thought of Peter Singer and Tom Regan. Indeed, Singer's and Regan's work on animals has been so influential that few thinkers have been willing to question their basic assumptions. Singer takes a utilitarian approach derived from Bentham and Mill, while Regan takes a deontological approach inherited from Kant. Both seek to refine and improve the views of their historical forebears, and both have done a great deal to draw attention to the plight of animals. But as Francione has shown through his meticulous and critical examination of their work, neither Singer nor Regan has succeeded in overcoming the anthropocentric limitations of traditional Western philosophical thinking about the moral status of animals. Nonetheless, Francione has succeeded in rethinking the tenets of utilitarianism and deontology so as to develop an entirely new approach that identifies sentience as the necessary and sufficient condition for the possession of rights. Specifically, he argues that all sentient beings, those capable of experiencing pleasure and pain, have a fundamental interest in avoiding suffering and continuing to exist. We protect (at least in theory) the right of all humans not to have to suffer the deprivation of their fundamental interests by being used as the resources of others. In other words, all humans have the right not to be treated as the property of others. Francione contends that there is no reason not to accord this right to nonhuman animals as well. Once we recognize this right, we must abolish our institutionalized exploitation of animals, which rests on their status as economic commodities.

Francione has argued for this conclusion at length in numerous essays and in his books, *Animals, Property, and the Law* (1995) and *Introduction to Animal Rights: Your Child or the Dog?* (2000). Central to Francione's critique of Singer and Regan is his rejection of "similar-minds theory," the view that animals must be cognitively like human beings in order to possess inherent moral worth (see "Taking Sentience Seriously" in this volume). The dominant assumption in the history of Western philosophy has been that only those beings capable of reason and language can have full moral worth. Thus animals would have to be rational and linguistic in the same sense as humans in order to merit moral respect and to have the right not to be mere resources. Like Bentham and Mill before him, Singer proceeds from the idea that sentience is the only capacity relevant to considerations of moral worth, and concludes that human beings enjoy certain moral prerogatives over animals on the ground that our superior cognitive capacities make it possible for the future to matter to us in ways that it cannot matter to animals. Humans, like nonhumans, have an interest in how they are treated, but unlike animals, humans also have an interest in life per se. Thus Singer ultimately reinforces an anthropocentric hierarchy that subordinates animals to the interests of human beings and accordingly focuses on the treatment, not the use, of animals. Similarly, Regan argues that animals (at least mammals over one year of age and perhaps other animals as well) have inherent moral worth equal to that of humans but concludes that in unavoidable conflicts of interest between humans and animals, the interest of humans should prevail because our superior cognitive abilities give us greater opportunities for future satisfaction than animals can have. Francione challenges the basic assumptions behind these conclusions and rejects the idea that the inherent worth of human beings is any greater than that of animals (see "Comparable Harm and Equal Inherent Value: The Problem of the Dog in the Lifeboat" in this volume).

The crux of Francione's challenge to Singer and Regan is the proposition that any being that is sentient necessarily has an interest in life because sentience is a means to the end of continued existence, an idea expressed in a number of essays in this book. Once we acknowledge that a being has an interest in life, we must recognize that this being also has a right to life and the avoidance of suffering that is equal in principle to the right to life enjoyed by any other sentient being. We may not make quantitative or qualitative distinctions among sentient beings in regard to their right to life. If a being has a right to life, then that being also has a right not to be property. This right is basic in the sense that it gives rise to important subsidiary rights, such as the right not to be killed for food, experimented upon, or used for entertainment. As Francione argues in the essays in this volume, these rights are shared equally by human and nonhuman animals; they have a categorical force that forbids us to subordinate the interests and fortunes of animals to those of humans.

A related aspect of Francione's iconoclasm is his absolute rejection of animal welfarism. In *Rain Without Thunder: The Ideology of the Animal Rights Movement* (1996) and in "Reflections on *Animals, Property, and the Law* and *Rain Without Thunder*" in this volume, Francione distinguishes between animal welfarism and abolitionism. Welfarists take the view that using animals to satisfy human desires is acceptable, and they emphasize the need to treat animals well in the process of using them. Welfarists often argue that killing and eating animals is permissible as long as we raise them in comfortable and healthy circumstances. For example, we are entitled to kill and eat chickens as long as they are allowed free-range living conditions. Abolitionists, on the other hand, see any such uses of animals as a fundamental violation of their right not to be property, and they argue that all uses of animals to satisfy human desires must cease altogether. Francione argues that we have no moral justification for continuing to bring domestic animals into existence for human use. One focal point of his work has been his effort to demonstrate that there are now more animal welfare regulations in place than ever before, and yet there is more exploitation inflicted on more animals today than ever before. In effect, animal welfare regulation simply permits human beings to feel better about exploiting animals.

Recognizing that abolition will not occur immediately, Francione focuses on the incremental eradication of the status of animals as property and on the importance of veganism, the complete rejection of the use of animals for food or other purposes. As he describes it, veganism is the application of the principle of abolition to the life of the individual. For Francione, perhaps more than any other contemporary figure since Donald Watson, who founded the Vegan Society in Britain in 1944, veganism must be the guiding conviction in all discussion of animal ethics.

I have often heard it said that the kind of radical change in the moral and legal status of animals envisioned by Francione will never take place. What Francione shows us, however, is that animals have the same *right* as human beings to live their lives, free from ownership and exploitation, quite apart from speculations about what may or may not come to pass. The fact that we humans tend to be comfortable with a regime of animal exploitation dating back thousands of years is not a justification for our continued subjugation of animals. It is an obstacle that we urgently need to overcome. To this end, what we need more than anything else is thinkers with the courage and the determination to break the images in the temple. Gary Francione is doing exactly that.

Department of Philosophy
Bucknell University
Lewisburg, Pennsylvania
October 17, 2007

ACKNOWLEDGMENTS

My animal rights scholarship is controversial.

Unlike most other authors in this field, I maintain that we ought to abolish animal use altogether and not seek to regulate our exploitation of animals to make it more "humane." In this sense, my analysis differs from that of Peter Singer who, in *Animal Liberation,* maintains that our use of nonhumans may be morally acceptable if we ensure that animals have reasonably pleasant lives and relatively painless deaths. I maintain that we have no moral justification for treating animals as replaceable resources—as our property—however "humanely" we may treat them or kill them.

Moreover, I link the moral significance of nonhumans with sentience alone, and I explicitly reject the notion that humanlike cognitive characteristics are required for full membership in the moral community. In this sense, I differ not only from Singer who, although he focuses on sentience, does not believe that sentience alone is sufficient to create at least a prima facie reason not to use animals at all, but also from Tom Regan who, in *The Case for Animal Rights,* links rights and full moral significance with characteristics beyond sentience.

I have long been critical of the efforts of animal protection organizations to approach the problem of animal exploitation by seeking to make that exploitation more "humane" through improved animal welfare laws or industry standards. I have argued that the property status of animals means that the level of protection provided by these laws and standards generally does not go beyond what is necessary to exploit the animals efficiently. We generally protect animal interests only to the extent we derive an economic benefit from doing so. I reject the position that supposedly better regulation will lead to abolition; on the contrary, animal welfare reform tends to facilitate social acceptance of continued use and militates against abolition in a number of ways. Almost all the large animal organizations in the United States and Europe pursue these welfarist reforms, and as a result, my work has not been embraced by these organizations, which are understandably more comfortable with Singer's welfarist theory. Indeed, many of these organizations have expressed considerable hostility to my work over the years.

This is by way of background to my expression of appreciation to Wendy Lochner, Christine Mortlock, Anne McCoy, Roy Thomas, and their colleagues at Columbia University Press for publishing a book of essays that is not likely to be received warmly by large segments of the "animal rights" community. I am grateful that they realize that there is a substantial and ever-increasing number of scholars and animal advocates who are interested in thinking about the issue of animal exploitation in a different way that requires that we challenge the property status of animals and not perpetuate it. Columbia University Press is quickly emerging as a major source of scholarship in this area, and I am grateful to be among its authors.

The introduction to the book presents an analysis of the distinction between animal use and animal treatment. I argue that the animal rights position focuses primarily on the use of animals and rejects the notion that "humane" animal use is morally acceptable. The animal welfare position assumes that animal use per se is not the primary problem and that animal advocates should pursue more "humane" animal treatment either as a good in itself or as a means to the end of the abolition of animal use. I discuss why the welfare position is problematic. Five of the following essays are published recent articles. The final two essays are older but focus on topics of contemporary relevance. The essays are reprinted as originally published, including the citation styles used by the particular journal, with known errors corrected. Those essays that had endnotes in the original were changed to have footnotes for consistency and convenience.

I want to express appreciation to Stuart Deutsch, Dean of the Rutgers University School of Law—Newark, for his support of my work and to the excellent library staff at Rutgers for helping me obtain materials for writing these essays, as well as to my research assistants at Rutgers and the various editors who worked on these essays. Special thanks to Erika Navarro and Aleksandra Fayer, who helped with the final preparation of the manuscript.

I am grateful to Taimie L. Bryant, James Crump, Julian Franklin, Valéry Giroux, Karin Hilpisch, David Langlois, Wendy Lochner, Joanna Lucas, Maria Luisa Arenzana Magaña, Mary Martin, Jeff Perz, Rupert Read, Gary Steiner, Bob Torres, Roger Yates, and Alan Watson for helpful comments on the introduction. I deeply appreciate the kind words in the foreword by Professor Steiner. Randy Sandberg not only commented on the introduction but, along with Toni Sandberg and Jeff Parisi, helped me develop a Web site that promotes my abolitionist theory. Interested readers may access the Web site at *www.AbolitionistApproach.com.*

I want to express my profound gratitude to my life partner, Anna E. Charlton, who has been my ally in this endeavor from the very beginning of our involvement more than twenty-five years ago. Anna was the director of the Animal Rights Law Clinic at Rutgers Law School, which operated from 1990 until 2000 and was the first and only academic enterprise of its kind in the United States. Students enrolled in the Clinic received academic credit for working on actual cases involving animal issues and learning animal rights theory in our weekly seminar. Anna, who is a scholar in this field in her own right, has read multiple drafts of everything I have ever written, and she has discussed things with me to such an extent that I should probably cite her as my coauthor. I love her dearly, and I am grateful to her in ways that I cannot express.

Finally, I want to thank the nonhuman members of my family—the two hamsters and twelve dogs Anna and I have adopted over the years. They have taught me so very much, including that we humans really do suffer from moral schizophrenia in the way we think about nonhumans. We treat some nonhumans as persons, as members of our families; we treat some as things that we eat or use in other ways. And we seek to justify human superiority on the basis of our supposed rationality.

ANIMALS AS PERSONS

INTRODUCTION / THE ABOLITION OF ANIMAL USE VERSUS THE REGULATION OF ANIMAL TREATMENT

In order to understand how we think about animals as a moral and a legal matter—both historically and at the present time—it is necessary to consider two different aspects of our relationship with other animals: our *use* of animals and our *treatment* of animals. These aspects are different because *whether* we use animals at all for a particular purpose is a different question from *how* we treat them pursuant to that purpose. For example, whether it is morally acceptable to kill and eat animals at all is a different question from how we treat the animals we eat and whether, for instance, we raise them in intensive "factory farms" or in "free-range" conditions, or how we slaughter them. Our use of animals is a separate matter from whether our treatment of them is "humane" or "cruel."

Based on this distinction between use and treatment, we can identify four primary ways in which we have conceptualized our moral and legal obligations to nonhuman animals:

- Before the nineteenth century, we generally regarded animals as *things* both in moral theory and under the law. According to this view, neither use nor treatment raised a moral or legal concern because animals simply did not matter at all.
- The animal welfare position, which became popular in the nineteenth century and represents the prevailing contemporary paradigm, separates use and treatment and holds that it is acceptable to use animals for our purposes. We do, however, have a moral and legal obligation to treat them "humanely" and to avoid imposing "unnecessary" suffering on them. The primary focus of animal welfare is the *regulation* of animal treatment.

- The animal rights position, which maintains that our use of animals cannot be justified, seeks to *abolish* all animal use. The abolitionist position rejects regulation on theoretical grounds (even "humane" animal use cannot be justified morally) as well as practical grounds (regulation does not sufficiently protect animal interests and even facilitates the continued social acceptance of animal use).
- The "new welfarist" position, of which there are multiple versions, is more or less critical of traditional welfarist regulation but continues to promote regulation as a means to achieve abolition or significantly reduce animal use and exploitation in the future. Most large animal advocacy organizations promote some version of the new welfarist position.

At each stage, our views about supposed cognitive or spiritual differences between humans and nonhumans and the perceived moral significance of those differences have informed our views about the use and treatment of nonhumans.

I will now briefly examine these four positions in very general terms and then describe the essays in this book, which discuss these topics in greater detail.

ANIMALS AS THINGS: NEITHER USE NOR TREATMENT RAISES A MORAL ISSUE

Until the nineteenth century, the Western view was, with few exceptions, that nonhumans were completely outside the moral and legal community, and that neither our use nor our treatment of them raised any moral or legal concern. We could use them for whatever purpose we wanted, and we could inflict pain and suffering on them pursuant to those uses without violating any obligations that we owed to them. That is, nonhumans were regarded as *things* that were indistinguishable from inanimate objects and toward which we thus could have no moral or legal obligations. Although we might have a legal obligation that concerned animals—such as an obligation not to injure our neighbor's cow—this was an obligation that we owed to our neighbor not to damage her property but not an obligation that we owed to the cow. To the limited extent that the cruel treatment of animals was thought to raise a moral issue, it was only because of a concern that humans who abused animals were more likely to ill treat other humans. Again, the obligation concerned animals but was owed to other humans and did not recognize that nonhuman animals had any moral significance.

Various reasons were offered to justify the status of animals as things. Some people, such as René Descartes (1596–1650), apparently believed that animals were, as a factual matter, indistinguishable from inanimate objects in that animals were not *sentient*—they were simply not beings who were conscious, had subjective and perceptual awareness, or were able to experience pain and suffering. As a result, they were not beings who had *interests;* that is, they did not have preferences, wants, or desires. According to Descartes, animals were "machines" that God created and therefore were no more conscious than the machines that humans created. If Descartes were correct and nonhumans are not sentient and have no interests, then it would not, of course, make sense to talk about having moral or legal obligations to animals concerning our use or treatment of them any more than it would to talk about our obligations to alarm clocks.

Some scholars dispute whether Descartes really believed that animals were not sentient, but if he did, he would have been unusual. At that time, most people did not doubt that animals were sentient and had interests. Rather, they maintained that humans were morally justified in ignoring animal interests and treating animals *as if* they were inanimate objects because animals were inferior to humans. This inferiority had two forms.

The first is what we might regard as "spiritual" inferiority. Western civilization has long entertained the notion that humans (or at least some of them) are created in the image of God and have greater value—with some people referring to souls—that justifies excluding animals from the moral community altogether. The creation story in the book of Genesis talks about God giving "dominion" to humans, a notion interpreted to mean that God authorized the *domination* of nonhumans by humans. Indeed, the English philosopher John Locke (1632–1704), who was central to the development of the modern theory of private property, based the exclusive ownership of property on the supposedly absolute control that God gave us over animals, as described in Genesis.

The second form of inferiority is what we might consider "natural" inferiority, based on the purported lack in nonhumans of some special mental characteristic regarded as uniquely human. According to this view, although animals are similar to us in that they are sentient or consciously aware, their minds are otherwise different from ours. That is, they lack cognitive characteristics possessed by all or most humans, such as rationality, abstract thought, language ability, reflective self-awareness, or the ability to engage in reciprocal moral relations. This qualitative difference between humans and animals, it was claimed, allowed us to ignore animal interests and to treat animals as things. For example, the German philosopher Immanuel Kant (1724–1804) recognized that animals were sentient and could suffer but denied that we had any direct moral obligations to animals because they were neither rational nor self-aware. Kant maintained that our treatment of animals was morally relevant only to the extent that it made us more likely to treat other humans in the same callous way.

A hybrid version of this doctrine regarded animals as things combining natural and spiritual inferiority. For example, St. Thomas Aquinas (ca. 1225–1274) linked rationality with having a soul and saw nonhumans both as naturally and spiritually inferior. Although Locke believed that God had given animals to humans for the latter to use, he also maintained that animals were not capable of abstract thought. Indeed, it is accurate to say that during this period, many people linked natural and spiritual inferiority and maintained that animals lacked some supposed uniquely human characteristic, such as rationality or the ability to think abstractly, because they, unlike humans, were not made in the image of God.

Therefore, in this first phase, which continued through the beginning of the nineteenth century, we viewed both the use and the treatment of animals as not presenting any sort of moral or legal issue. Animals were considered indistinguishable from machines and not sentient or, alternatively, sentient but spiritually or naturally inferior to humans. In any case, humans could use nonhumans for whatever purpose they wanted and treat them as they wanted pursuant to those uses, as long as they did not damage the property of others or engage in conduct toward animals that might make them likely to act in a similarly unkind manner toward other humans. Humans may have had obligations that concerned nonhumans, but they did not have any obligations that they owed to them.

ANIMAL WELFARE: WE CAN USE ANIMALS BUT MUST TREAT THEM "HUMANELY"

In the nineteenth century, as part of the progressive movements in favor of women's rights and in opposition to human slavery, our thinking shifted to the animal welfare position, which purported to reject the notion that animals were merely things of no moral or legal consequence. Not everyone rejected the Cartesian view that animals were not sentient or the notion that nonhumans, even if sentient, were completely outside the moral community because of some natural or spiritual inferiority. Rather, these notions continued to inform thinking about our obligations to nonhumans, but the view that animals were at least partial members of the moral community emerged, enjoyed widespread social acceptance, found its way into the law, and remains the prevailing contemporary view.

The animal welfare position maintains, for the most part, that we may use animals for our purposes because they are our spiritual or natural inferiors but that there are limitations on our treatment of them. That is, animals are able to suffer whether or not they have souls or some human-like cognitive characteristic. Therefore, we may use animals because they are different from us, but we nonetheless are obligated to treat them "humanely" and not to cause them "unnecessary" suffering. We must use animals "gently." Moreover, this is a moral obligation that we owe directly to the animals and is not one that merely concerns animals but is really owed to other humans.

Among people who were influential in the development of the animal welfare position was the British lawyer and philosopher Jeremy Bentham (1748–1832), who maintained that animals had been "degraded into the class of *things,*" with the result that humans "torment" them in various ways. Bentham made clear that nonhumans shared to some degree the characteristics regarded as unique to humans and that in any event, the absence of these characteristics did not grant people a license to treat animals in any way that they wished:

> A full-grown horse or dog is beyond comparison a more rational, as well as a more conversable animal, than an infant of a day, or a week, or even a month, old. But suppose the case were otherwise, what would it avail? the question is not, Can they *reason?* nor, Can they *talk?* but, Can they *suffer?*

As long as an animal is sentient, the animal's interests and particularly interests in not suffering, must be given appropriate consideration.

Although Bentham suggested that some animals might be more rational than some humans, he certainly did not reject the position that human minds were qualitatively different from animal minds. On the contrary, Bentham believed that such differences existed and he maintained that although these differences did not permit us to "torment" animals, they did allow us to use animals as long as we took care to minimize their suffering.

Bentham discussed this in the context of why it was morally permissible to eat animals. He certainly was aware that we did not have to eat animals to survive but thought that it was morally permissible for us to eat them because they were not self-aware and had no sense of the future. Animals do not have an interest in not being killed and eaten; that is, animals do not care about *whether* we use them but only *how* we use them. According to Bentham,

> [i]f the being eaten were all, there is very good reason why we should be suffered to eat such of them as we like to eat: we are the better for it, and they are never the worse. They have none of those long-protracted anticipations of future misery which we have.

He maintained that animals are "never the worse for being dead." Therefore, because Bentham believed that cognitive differences between humans and nonhumans meant that the latter did not have an interest in their lives, he did not challenge our use of animals, but only our treatment of them.

There was a religious dimension to the welfarist position that emerged in the nineteenth century, in that the "dominion" that God supposedly granted us over animals was reinterpreted by some as being a stewardship of some sort and not domination. Although our spiritual superiority meant that we could continue to use them for our purposes, God did not give us an unrestricted license to their treatment, and thus we had a moral obligation to treat animals kindly.

The animal welfare view was eventually incorporated into the law. Great Britain and the United States (as well as other nations) enacted various laws, such as anticruelty statutes, which purported to require the "humane" treatment of animals. For the first time, we recognized that we had legal obligations that we owed directly to animals. This is not to say that these laws did not also reflect the concern that the cruel treatment of animals would have the effect of making humans treat one another badly. But it is also clear that for the first time, animals were seen not merely as things but as partial members of the moral community who were inherently deserving of some legal protection. Animal welfare laws therefore allow us to use animals but require that we balance human and nonhuman interests in order to ascertain whether animal suffering is justified.

Even though the animal welfare position ostensibly represented a dramatic departure from the view that animals are merely things, the laws that were enacted in Britain, the United States, and other nations have, for the most part, failed to significantly protect animals. Although the animal welfare position supposedly prohibits the infliction of "unnecessary" suffering on animals, we do not ask whether particular institutional uses are themselves necessary because we assume that these uses are acceptable and because our only concern is treatment. It is clear, however, that most of our animal uses are transparently frivolous and cannot be described as involving any "necessity." For example, we kill billions of animals every year for food. It is certainly not necessary for us to eat animal flesh, dairy, eggs, or other animal products; indeed, the evidence is mounting that animal foods are detrimental to human health. Moreover, animal agriculture is an ecological disaster. The only justification that we have for using animals in this way is that we are accustomed to and enjoy the taste of meat and animal products. The welfare position does not challenge our use of animals for food and says only that we should not inflict more suffering than is necessary when we use animals for this unnecessary purpose. But what does "necessary" mean in this context, given that *no* suffering is necessary because we have no need to eat meat or animal products?

The central theme of my 1995 book, *Animals, Property, and the Law,* is that because animals are *property*—they are commodities with only extrinsic or conditional value—the level of "humane" treatment required under animal welfare laws will, for the most part, be limited to what is required to exploit animals in an efficient manner. We generally protect animal interests only to the extent that we also derive an economic benefit from doing so. For example, we may require that a cow be stunned so that she is unconscious during slaughter, but stunning also reduces damage to the carcass and injuries to workers from a large, moving animal. Although cows have many other interests at various stages of their life and at the time of their death, we do not protect these other interests because we do not derive an economic benefit from doing so. The "suffering" of producers who make less profit, or of consumers who have to pay more for animal products, generally outweighs the suffering of the animals, who almost always lose the supposed balance of interests. The result is that even the most "humane" nations treat animals who are used for food in ways that would be considered torture if humans were so treated. The same analysis applies to our other animal uses.

In order to determine what constitutes "humane" treatment, the law often looks to those who engage in the animal use because we assume that animal users are rational economic actors who would not impose more pain and suffering than is required for a particular use. This, however, reduces animal welfare laws to directives not to treat animals in ways that do not comply with industry or customary standards. Animal welfare laws generally require only that we act as rational property owners and prohibit only those actions that reduce the value of animal property or that have no economic benefit for humans. Just as a rational person would not smash her car with a hammer, a rational farmer would not impose more suffering than necessary on her cow, as both are valuable pieces of property. But as long as pain and suffering are regarded as providing economic benefits to humans and occur within generally recognized institutions of animal use, animal welfare laws usually are silent. Animal exploiters often offer token opposition to welfare legislation and initiatives but ultimately support such regulation because they have little or nothing to lose and everything to gain; indeed, their support is usually required for these measures to be successful. If all animal users were perfectly rational and had full information about how particular practices affected animal productivity, we would probably not even need animal welfare laws because rational users would not impose more suffering than needed for a particular purpose.

In certain respects, the regulation of animal exploitation is similar to the regulation of human slavery in North America. Although many laws supposedly required the "humane" treatment of slaves and prohibited the infliction of "unnecessary" punishment, these laws offered almost no protection for slaves. In conflicts between slave owners and slaves, the latter almost always lost. Slave welfare laws, like animal welfare laws, generally required that slave owners merely act as rational property owners but did not recognize the inherent value of the slaves. Slave owners were, of course, free to treat their slaves, or particular slaves, better. But as far as the law was concerned, slaves were merely economic commodities with only extrinsic or conditional value, and slave owners were essentially free to value their slaves' interests as they chose, just as we are free to value the interests of our dogs and cats and treat them as members of our families or abandon them at a shelter or have them killed because we no longer want them.

In sum, the animal welfare position, which is the common contemporary paradigm for thinking about our moral and legal obligations to animals, does not question our use per se of animals but focuses only on the treatment of animals we use. Most of us agree with Bentham and the fundamental premise of the animal welfare position that it is acceptable to use animals as long as we treat them in a "humane" manner. But because animals are property, the standard of "humane" treatment is generally limited to what can be justified in light of their property status. Although the animal welfare paradigm has prevailed for some two hundred years, we are using more animals than ever before in human history and we still "torment" them. Animal welfare separates use and treatment and claims to take treatment seriously but clearly fails on its own terms to protect animal interests in a meaningful way.

ANIMAL RIGHTS: THE PRIMARY PROBLEM IS USE, NOT TREATMENT

The animal rights position—as I have developed it in my *Introduction to Animal Rights: Your Child or the Dog?* and in my other work—is that the principal problem is not *how* we use animals but *that* we use animals for human purposes at all. We have no moral justification for using nonhumans, however "humanely" we treat them. To the extent that we do use animals, it is, of course, always better to cause less pain than more pain. It is better that a rapist not torture the victim in addition to committing the rape. But just as it is not morally acceptable to commit rape even if you do not torture the victim, it is not morally acceptable to use nonhumans as human resources despite how we treat them.

The animal rights position rejects the notion that serves as the foundation of the welfarist distinction between use and treatment: that as an empirical matter, animals do not have an interest in whether or not they continue to exist and have an interest only in being treated well. Nonhumans may have a different sense of what it means to have a life than normal human adults do, but this does not mean that they have no interest in continuing to exist, that they are not self-aware and indifferent to whether we use them and kill them for our purposes, or that death is any less a harm to them than it is to us.

Consider a human who has transient global amnesia, in which the person has a sense of herself only in the present and no recollection of her past and no thoughts about her future. This is more or less how Bentham viewed the minds of nonhumans—as rooted in a continuing present. Can we conclude that a human with this sort of amnesia has no interest in continuing to live because her mind is different from that of normal humans, who can recall the past and anticipate the future beyond the present instance? Surely not. Although such a characteristic may justify differential treatment for some purposes, it would not justify forcing such a person to be an organ donor as long as we removed her organs with minimal pain or suffering on her part.

Similarly, even if nonhumans have a sense of themselves only in the present, we cannot assume that they do not value their lives and are concerned only with how we treat them. Sentience, or subjective awareness, is only a means to the end of continued survival for certain beings who have evolved in particular ways that have made sentience a characteristic to help them adapt to their environment and survive. A sentient being *is* a being with an interest in continuing to live, who desires, prefers, or wants to continue to live. When a nonhuman with subjective and perceptual awareness sees another nonhuman engaged in some activity, the former is aware that it is the latter, and not she, who is engaged in the activity. A sentient being is self-aware in that she knows that it is she, and not another, who is feeling pain and suffering. There is no basis for saying that only those who possess the sort of self-awareness that we associate with normal humans have an interest in continuing to live.

Just as the purported cognitive differences between humans and nonhumans cannot justify our cruel treatment of nonhuman animals, they also cannot justify our use of animals as our resources, however "humanely" we treat them. There probably are significant differences between the minds of humans and those of nonhumans given that human cognition is linked so closely to abstract language and, with the possible exception of the nonhuman great apes, nonhumans presumably do not use symbolic communication. It may well be that nonhumans do not have intentional states that are predicative in the way that human intentional states are. But we cannot conclude from these differences that nonhumans do not have cognitive states that are at least equivalent to those of humans. Indeed, it is difficult to explain plausibly a great deal of animal behavior without attributing equivalent cognitive states to animals.

There is, however, a great deal of controversy about the nature of animal minds and there will always be those who deny that nonhumans have any cognitive ability beyond being sentient and subjectively aware. But we do not need to resolve this perhaps unresolvable debate. Sentience is necessary to have interests at all. If a being is not sentient, then it may be alive but does not have interests in that there is nothing that it prefers, desires, or wants. But if a being is sentient, this is sufficient to be self-aware and to have an interest in continued existence. Although whether a being is sentient may not be clear in all cases, such as those involving insects or mollusks, the overwhelming number of nonhuman animals we exploit are unquestionably subjectively aware and have an interest in continuing to exist, even if they do not have the same reflective self-awareness that we associate with normal humans.

The position that cognitive characteristics beyond sentience or humanlike versions of these characteristics are morally more important than other characteristics begs the question from the outset. Why is the ability to do calculus morally better than the ability to fly with your wings? Why is the ability to recognize yourself in a mirror morally better than your ability to recognize yourself in a scent that you left on a bush? Moreover, there is no logical relationship between differences in cognitive characteristics and the issue of animal use, although these differences may be relevant for some purposes. Consider the case of a severely mentally disabled human. We may not want to give such a person a driver's license because of her inability to drive. But is her impairment relevant to whether we use her as an unwilling subject in a biomedical experiment or force her to become an organ donor? No, of course not. Indeed, many of us would argue that her particular disability means that we have a greater moral obligation to her, but it certainly does not mean that we have a lesser one. Similarly, the fact that a dog's mind is different from ours means that we do not give the dog a driver's license but it does not mean that we can use the dog for purposes for which we would not use humans.

In sum, we cannot rely on any cognitive differences between humans and nonhumans as a basis for treating animals as our property and continuing to use them for our purposes, however "humanely" we do so. We do not regard it as acceptable to treat any humans as the property of other humans. Although there is a great deal of controversy about what rights humans do or do not have, and we may argue about the moral status of human fetuses, we all agree that every person, irrespective of her particular mental characteristics, must be accorded the basic right not to be treated as the property of others. We do not question that every human, whether intelligent, gifted, ordinary, or mentally challenged, has the right not to be treated as the resource of others. This is not, of course, to deny that human slavery still exists; it does, but no one defends it. This is also not to say that we treat everyone equally. Clearly, we do not. We may, for instance, compensate a brilliant musician at a higher level than we do someone with a severe mental disability. But whether or not we agree whether we should allocate resources equally to both, we all agree that neither should be used exclusively as a means to the ends of others. If, as we claim, animals matter morally, then we must apply the principle of equal consideration—the moral rule that we treat similar cases similarly—and ask whether there is a good reason to accord the right not to be treated as property to nonhumans as well.

The answer is clear. There is no rational justification for our continuing to deny this one right to nonhumans, however "humanely" we treat them. We can, of course, fall back on religious superstition and claim that animal use is justified because animals do not have souls, are not created in God's image, or are otherwise inferior spiritually. Alternatively, we can claim that our use of animals is acceptable because we are human and they are not, which is like saying we are white and they are black; we are men and they are women; we are straight and they are gay.

The animal rights position does not mean releasing our domesticated nonhumans to run wild in the street. If we took animals seriously and recognized our obligation not to treat them as things, then we would stop producing and facilitating the production of domestic animals altogether. We would care for the ones whom we have here now, but we would stop breeding more for human consumption. And with respect to nondomesticated nonhumans, we would simply leave them alone.

In *The Case for Animal Rights,* Tom Regan also argues against animal welfare and regulation and in favor of animal rights and abolition. But my view and Regan's differ. Regan links moral significance with the concept of being a "subject-of-a-life," a notion focusing on cognitive characteristics beyond mere sentience and requiring a sort of preference autonomy, or the ability to satisfy preferences and not merely to have interests. Although Regan says that being a subject-of-a-life is a sufficient and not necessary condition for being morally significant, his theory is based in important respects on cognitive characteristics beyond sentience.

Furthermore, although Regan does not deny that nonhumans have an interest in continuing to live, he maintains that because of the cognitive differences between humans and nonhumans, humans have a qualitatively greater interest in continuing to live than animals do. That is, Regan believes that in the normal case death is a greater harm for humans than for nonhumans because it forecloses more opportunities for human satisfaction. Regan's position is problematic, however, because if death is a qualitatively greater harm to humans than to nonhumans, then there is a nonarbitrary way to distinguish humans from nonhumans for the purpose of treating the latter as human resources, which Regan ostensibly rejects. At the very least, if we favor humans over nonhumans in situations of conflict according to a morally relevant distinction between the harm of death to humans and nonhumans, we risk resolving all such conflicts against the latter solely on the basis of species.

In fact, as a result of our own cognitive limitations, we may not be able to understand the mental processes of other species, including how nonhumans regard death. In situations of true conflict—and not when we have manufactured the conflict by bringing animals into existence to use as our resources—we may decide to break a difficult tie and choose the human over the nonhuman because we simply do not know what death means to the nonhuman. Conversely, we may also choose the nonhuman over the human in a situation of genuine conflict. Either choice, or a coin flip, is morally acceptable. We cannot say, however, that death is a lesser harm to nonhumans any more than we can say that death is a lesser harm to a person with global amnesia than it is to a person without it, or that death is a greater harm to a highly intelligent person than it is to a less intelligent person. Regan's position on this point is thus problematic for a theory that proposes the abolition of all animal use, and my approach rejects it.

NEW WELFARISM: A COMPROMISE BETWEEN REGULATION AND ABOLITION?

In the 1980s, animal advocates in the United States and Great Britain attempted to formulate a position recognizing the limitations of traditional animal welfare regulation but avoiding a direct acceptance of the rights or abolitionist position. This "new welfarism," which I first identified in 1996 in *Rain Without Thunder: The Ideology of the Animal Rights Movement,* has several different versions.

Regulation as Leading to Abolition

The first version of new welfarism claims to seek the abolition of animal exploitation as a long-term goal but nonetheless advocates the improved regulation of animal use in the short term as a supposed means to the end of abolishing (or significantly reducing animal use) by raising consciousness about the moral significance of nonhuman animals. Although this position has been promoted by many of the large animal protection organizations in the United States and Europe, it has both theoretical and practical problems.

As a theoretical matter, if our use of animals is not morally justifiable, promoting more "humane" exploitation as a means to the end of abolition is unacceptable as a matter of moral theory. For example, if we believe that any form of pedophilia is morally wrong, we cannot, consistent with that position, campaign for "humane" pedophilia. In the struggle against human slavery in the United States, many of those who favored abolition refused to campaign for the reform of slavery because they considered reform as inconsistent with the basic moral principle that slavery was an inherently unjust institution. Similarly, the promotion of more "humane" animal use is inconsistent with the idea that we do not have a moral right to exploit animals in the first place.

As a practical matter, this first version of the new welfarist position—that improved regulation will lead to abolition or a significant reduction in use—also is problematic for at least three reasons. First, animal welfare regulation simply does not provide any significant protection for animal interests in the short term. As I discussed earlier, welfarist regulation generally protects animal interests only to the extent that there is an economic benefit for humans. Regulation that extends beyond this and requires animal interests to be protected when there is no economic benefit involves some recognition that animals have value that exceeds their extrinsic value as property and, depending on how far the regulation goes, represents an incremental diminution of the property status of nonhumans. Such regulation is fiercely resisted by both producers, who want to keep costs as low as possible, and consumers, who want to feel good about consuming animal products but who are generally unwilling to pay for significantly improved animal welfare, particularly when they have been reassured that animals are being treated in ways that do not cause "unnecessary" suffering.

Second, there is no evidence that making exploitation more "humane" advances toward the abolition of that exploitation. Indeed, the contrary appears to be true. We have had animal welfare laws for nearly two hundred years, and yet we now exploit more animals in more horrible ways than at any time in the past. To the extent that animal welfare reform raises consciousness about animals, it merely reinforces the notion that animals are things that we are entitled to use if our treatment of them is "humane" and facilitates the continued acceptance of exploitation, which is characterized as meeting that standard.

Third, the phenomenon of new welfarism has resulted in a curious partnership between those who claim to endorse animal rights and institutional animal exploiters who claim to seek mutually acceptable welfare reforms that the former believes will lead to abolition and the latter believes will further reassure the public that animal treatment is at a morally acceptable level. But because animals are property, these reforms are necessarily limited to minor changes in animal welfare that, in many cases, do nothing more than improve animal productivity and increase producer profit. In effect, animal advocates have become advisers to institutional exploiters regarding how they can achieve greater profits by making these minor changes. To the extent that these changes offer any benefits to animals, they are offset by the fact that exploiters can point to the support of animal advocates, which in turn promotes the continued social acceptance of animal exploitation. Indeed, many large animal advocacy organizations actively advertise animal products that supposedly have been produced in a "humane" manner. Such promotion may actually increase consumption by people who had stopped eating animal products because of concerns about treatment and will certainly provide as a general matter an incentive for continued consumption of animal products.

New welfarism presents a false dichotomy: even if we embrace abolition as the ultimate goal, we have no choice but to pursue welfarist regulation in the short term because that is the only realistic strategy that we can pursue, given that animal use will not be abolished anytime soon. Putting aside that welfarist regulation does not significantly protect nonhumans in the short term, does not lead to abolition in the long term, and only facilitates social comfort with and acceptance of animal use as a general matter, this position neglects other choices that are arguably not only more consistent with a theory that rejects animal use as immoral but whose practical strategy is more effective.

A central tenet of my theory is that the rights position offers clear normative guidance for incremental change. On an individual level, the rights position prescribes incremental changes in the form of veganism. Veganism means not eating meat, dairy, eggs, honey, and other animal products, or wearing or using animal products or products tested on animals. Veganism, which results in a decreased demand for animal products, is much more than a matter of diet, lifestyle, or consumer choice; it is a personal commitment to nonviolence and the abolition of exploitation. A person who agrees that animal use is not morally justified but who continues to consume animal products is similar to those in 1830 who opposed slavery but who continued to own slaves. In a society underpinned by animal exploitation, it is extremely difficult—perhaps impossible—not to be at least indirectly complicit in animal exploitation as consumers, but we can nevertheless be clear that if we are not vegans, we certainly *are* animal exploiters.

Just as the decision to become a vegan is the most important incremental change that advocates can make on a personal level, creative vegan education and campaigning are the most important activist incremental activities on a social level. Again, promoting veganism on this level is not merely a matter of influencing consumer choices; rather, the focus is on promoting a vision of justice for nonhumans as well as humans, many of whom are condemned to starvation because of the inefficient use of resources involved in animal agriculture. It involves recognizing that our unjustified exploitation of nonhumans is related to our oppression of other humans and to the discrimination that manifests itself as racism, sexism, heterosexism, and other forms of discrimination. Indeed, the concern about justice for nonhumans makes sense only as part of a progressive social and political view that values human rights and opposes human exploitation.

If we ever hope to shift the paradigm away from the speciesist hierarchy that currently informs our thinking about nonhumans, we must develop a political and social movement in favor of abolishing animal use, with veganism, as both a logical and a moral matter, being the clear baseline of that movement. Many new welfarists, however, reject veganism as a moral baseline. They maintain that it is more "practical" to support welfarist reform and to promote animal uses that are more "humane." But this approach reinforces the prevailing view that animal use is morally acceptable if treatment is "humane," and it makes veganism appear as a radical or extreme response to animal exploitation, which is counterproductive to the goal of abolishing animal use.

I have long argued, and continue to believe, that an afternoon spent distributing literature on veganism at a crowded place or giving a lecture on veganism at a local community college is a much better use of time, as a matter of both moral theory and practical strategy, than spending that time working on a campaign to get battery hens some extra space or to require that vivisectors treat animals used in laboratories more "humanely."

Singer and Animal Liberation

The second form of new welfarism is the position advocated by Peter Singer. Although Singer is often mischaracterized as an "animal rights" advocate, he, like Bentham, is a utilitarian who maintains that normative matters are determined only by consequences, and he rejects the concept of moral rights for humans and nonhumans alike. Singer's view is also and more accurately described as the theory of "animal liberation," presumably reflecting the title of his book, *Animal Liberation.*

Singer agrees with Bentham that sentience is the only characteristic required for animals to be morally significant and that no other characteristic, such as rationality or abstract thought, is needed. Singer maintains that we should apply the principle of equal consideration and should treat animal interests in essentially the same way that we would treat the similar interests of a human and not discount or ignore those interests on the basis of species. But, also like Bentham, Singer regards most nonhumans as living in a sort of eternal present that precludes their having an interest in a continued existence. This position leads Singer to maintain that animal use per se does not raise a moral problem, and so he does not challenge the property status of animals as inherently problematic. Singer therefore accepts the welfarist distinction between use and treatment and claims that the latter is the main issue, in that we should focus more on animal suffering and less (and perhaps not at all) on animal killing except to the degree that it causes suffering.

If Singer is wrong in assuming that animals do not have an interest in their continued existence, then our use of animals in ways in which we do not use humans and our treatment of animals as our property *necessarily* violates the principle of equal consideration. As discussed earlier, humans who lack the reflective self-awareness of normal adults, such as those with particular forms of amnesia or very young children or those with certain mental disabilities, still are self-aware and still have an interest in continuing to live. There may, of course, be a difference between the self-awareness of normal adult humans and that of other animals. But even if that is the case, it does not mean that the latter have no interest in continuing to live, and it does not justify treating the latter as commodities. Singer begs the question from the outset by maintaining that the only self-awareness that matters to having an interest in life is the sort that normal humans possess.

Moreover, even if animals do not have an interest in continued life, the application of the principle of equal consideration to the treatment of animals we use still is problematic for at least two reasons. First, any such endeavor requires that we make interspecies comparisons in order to determine whether the animal interest in question is similar to a human interest and therefore merits similar treatment. This sort of determination is difficult when only humans are involved. Is your interest in not suffering the same as mine? Can you tolerate more pain? It is almost impossible when comparing members of different species. There is an understandable tendency to think that a human interest is always different and more important.

Second, putting aside these considerations, assessments of similarity are particularly difficult given the property status of animals. The fact that an animal is property and has only extrinsic or conditional value automatically prejudices us against perceiving an animal interest as similar to a human one. Given the importance of property rights, it should not be surprising that many humans think that any inability to use their property as they wish is a significant deprivation that leads them to discount heavily any animal interests at stake. Indeed, the fact that we consider ourselves to be a "humane" society, yet we tolerate and support horrible animal suffering for trivial reasons, is proof that the property status of animals is paramount to our perceptions that animal interests are unlike those of humans. If an animal's interest is not considered similar, then the principle of equal consideration does not require similar treatment. And even if we determine that an animal has an interest similar to that of a human, the animal's property status is a good reason not to accord similar treatment to the animal unless doing so would benefit humans.

Because Singer does not challenge the property status of nonhumans and maintains that use per se does not raise a moral issue, his theory is essentially a version of animal welfare. It is arguably more progressive in that it requires that we accord greater weight to animal interests than we currently do, but as a theoretical matter, Singer never explains how to do this, and, as a matter of his individual animal advocacy, he promotes traditional animal welfare reform such as supposedly more "humane" slaughtering processes or larger cages for battery hens. In any event, he does not see animal welfare as a means of abolishing animal use because he does not advocate abolition. Rather, he sees animal welfare as a means of reducing animal suffering. He maintains that we can be "conscientious omnivores" if we take care to eat flesh and other products made from animals who have been raised and killed in a "humane" fashion.

Singer does claim that if nonhumans are sufficiently similar to humans, they may be entitled to greater protection, including not being used as human resources. Singer coedited *The Great Ape Project: Equality Beyond Humanity* in 1993, a collection of essays organized around "A Declaration on Great Apes," which insists that nonhuman great apes be included in the community of equals with humans and given rights to life, liberty, and freedom from torture. Although I was a contributor to *The Great Ape Project,* I maintained then, and do now, that sentience alone is sufficient for the right not to be treated as a human resource. To require that nonhumans have minds similar to humans as a condition for not treating them as things reinforces and perpetuates an unjustifiable speciesist hierarchy.

Feminist Theory and the Rejection of Rights

The third sort of new welfarism may be found in the writings of certain feminist theorists who claim that all rights are patriarchal and reinforce hierarchies and that we must therefore move beyond rights to develop an "ethic of care" for our relationship with nonhumans. Those who adopt this view reject universal rules, such as an absolute prohibition on the use of animals as human resources, in favor of using values such as love, care, and trust to make judgments about animal use in particular situations.

Although rights certainly have been used to establish and reinforce a variety of morally odious hierarchies, rights are not inherently patriarchal. Instead, a right is simply a way of protecting an interest; it treats that interest as inviolable even if the consequences to others of violating it are considerable. Such normative notions are part of feminist theory in that no feminist of whom I am aware believes that the morality of rape is dependent on a case-by-case analysis in light of an ethic of care. On the contrary, a woman's interest in the integrity of her body is correctly treated as inviolable: A woman has a *right* not to be raped, and the ethic of care has nothing to do with this.

Similarly, if a nonhuman is sentient, we have no justification for ignoring the fundamental interests of that nonhuman and treating her as a resource. The feminist ethic of care does not go beyond rights. Rather, it is a form of welfarist theory, which, like Singer's position, seeks to accord greater weight to nonhuman interests but still preserves the hierarchy of humans, who, despite what these theorists claim, are accorded protection of their rights that is denied to nonhumans.

❖ ❖ ❖

The animal advocacy movement is really two vastly different movements. One sees our use of animals as central and seeks the abolition of animal exploitation through the progressive and deliberate eradication of the property status of animals. The other regards treatment as the primary concern and seeks better regulation of animal exploitation through measures that mainly make animal exploitation more efficient but do not effectively challenge property status. The essays in this book focus on the inherent tension between these two approaches, the failure of animal welfare laws to provide significant protection to animal interests, and the idea, present even in the writing of animal advocates Peter Singer and Tom Regan, that issues of use and treatment are properly informed by supposed differences between the minds of humans and those of nonhumans.

The first essay, "Animals—Property or Persons?" presents a version of the abolitionist theory of animal rights that I developed more fully in *Introduction to Animal Rights: Your Child or the Dog?* I argue that our moral thinking about animals is terribly confused and that a large part of the problem is our treatment of animals as property, which cannot be justified morally. I conclude that our acceptance of the right of nonhumans not to be treated as property requires that we abolish institutionalized animal exploitation and stop producing domestic nonhumans for human use.

In the second essay, "Reflections on *Animals, Property, and the Law* and *Rain Without Thunder*," I respond to various critics who argue that the property status of animals is not an insurmountable obstacle to improving animal welfare and that animal welfare regulation is an effective way of moving incrementally toward the recognition that nonhumans have more than extrinsic or conditional value.

In the third essay, "Taking Sentience Seriously," I discuss how our focus on whether animal minds are like ours—what I have called the "similar-minds" approach to the human/nonhuman relationship—has led us to analyze inadequately the moral importance of animal suffering, despite our claim to take it seriously through the prohibition on inflicting "unnecessary" suffering and the requirement that we treat animals "humanely."

In the fourth essay, "Equal Consideration and the Interest of Nonhuman Animals in Continued Existence: A Response to Professor Sunstein," I reply to Professor Cass Sunstein who, in a lengthy review of my *Introduction to Animal Rights* in *The New Republic,* claims that I have failed to justify why we should not focus on better regulating our treatment of animals rather than abolishing animal use.

In the fifth essay, "The Use of Nonhuman Animals in Biomedical Research: Necessity and Justification," I discuss how the discourse on the use of animals in biomedical research usually focuses on two issues. The first issue is empirical and asks whether the use of nonhumans in experiments is required in order to obtain data. The second issue is moral and asks whether the use of nonhumans can be defended as a matter of ethical theory. I argue that although the use of animals in research may involve a plausible necessity claim—indeed, our use of animals in this context is our *only* animal use that is not transparently frivolous—there is no moral justification for using nonhumans in situations in which we would not use humans. And with the exception of Singer and a few other utilitarians, almost no one argues that it is ever permissible to use humans in this way.

In the sixth essay, "Ecofeminism and Animal Rights," I contend that when applied to nonhumans who are property, the feminist ethic of care does not provide protection that extends beyond rights. Rather, when so applied, it is a form of new welfarist theory, which, like Singer's position, seeks to accord greater weight to the interests of nonhumans but still preserves the hierarchy of humans, who have rights protection that is denied to nonhumans.

In the final essay, "Comparable Harm and Equal Inherent Value: The Problem of the Dog in the Lifeboat," I discuss Regan's view that harm is a qualitatively greater loss, and therefore a greater harm, for humans than for nonhumans and that when we must choose to save the life of a human or a nonhuman, we are morally obligated to save the life of the human. I discuss some of the problems that arise from Regan's analysis. I have, since writing this article in 1995, decided that Regan's theory of comparable harm is more problematic for Regan's theory than I thought initially. Accordingly, I have added some comments as a postscript to this essay that reflect my more recent views.

It is my hope that these essays will help sharpen the meaning of the "animal rights," which has come to be used to describe any normative position that vaguely concerns animals, and to make clear that the rights approach means abolishing the exploitation of animals and accepting the personhood of nonhuman animals. By "personhood of nonhuman animals," I do not mean that we are morally obligated to treat nonhumans as human persons. Humans have interests that nonhumans do not have, and vice versa. But just as we regard every human as having inherent value that precludes treating that human exclusively as a resource for others, so, too, do animals have inherent value that precludes our treating them as our property. It is my hope also that my views will inform the debate between the abolitionist and welfare approaches, a debate that is increasingly taking the center stage in our thinking about the moral and legal status of nonhuman animals.

CHAPTER 1 / ANIMALS—PROPERTY OR PERSONS?

When it comes to other animals, we humans exhibit what can best be described as moral schizophrenia. Although we claim to take animals seriously and to regard them as having morally significant interests, we routinely ignore those interests for trivial reasons. In this essay, I argue that our moral schizophrenia is related to the status of animals as property, which means that animals are nothing more than *things* despite the many laws that supposedly protect them. If we are going to make good on our claim to take animal interests seriously, then we have no choice but to accord animals one right: the right not to be treated as our property.

Our acceptance that animals have this one right would require that we abolish and not merely better regulate our institutionalized exploitation of animals. Although this is an ostensibly radical conclusion, it necessarily follows from certain moral notions that we have professed to accept for the better part of 200 years. Moreover, recognition of this right would not preclude our choosing humans over animals in situations of genuine conflict.

This essay was published originally in Cass R. Sunstein and Martha C. Nussbaum eds., *Animal Rights: Current Debates and New Directions* (New York: Oxford University Press, 2004), pp. 108–142.

Copyright © 2003 by Gary L. Francione. Many thanks to Anna Charlton, Cora Diamond, Lee Hall, and Alan Watson for their helpful comments. The ideas and arguments discussed in this essay were developed and are expanded in Gary L. Francione, *Animals, Property, and the Law* (1995), *Introduction to Animal Rights: Your Child or the Dog?* (2000), and *Rain Without Thunder: The Ideology of the Animal Rights Movement* (1996). The notes will direct the reader to further discussion in these books. This essay is dedicated to my seven rescued canine companions, who are undoubtedly persons.

ANIMALS: OUR MORAL SCHIZOPHRENIA

There is a profound disparity between what we say we believe about animals and how we actually treat them. On one hand, we claim to take animals seriously. Two-thirds of Americans polled by the Associated Press agree with the following statement: "An animal's right to live free of suffering should be just as important as a person's right to live free of suffering," and more than 50 percent of Americans believe that it is wrong to kill animals to make fur coats or to hunt them for sport.[1] Almost 50 percent regard animals to be "just like humans in all important ways."[2] These attitudes are reflected in other nations as well. For example, 94 percent of Britons[3] and 88 percent of Spaniards[4] think that animals should be protected from acts of cruelty, and only 14 percent of Europeans support the use of genetic engineering that results in animal suffering, even if the purpose is to create drugs that would save human lives.[5]

On the other hand, our actual treatment of animals stands in stark contrast to our proclamations about our regard for their moral status.[6] Consider the suffering of animals at our hands. In the United States alone, according to the U.S. Department of Agriculture, we kill more than 8 billion animals a year for food; every day, we slaughter approximately 23 million animals, or more than 950,000 per hour, or almost 16,000 per minute, or more than 260 every second. This is to say nothing of the billions more killed worldwide. These animals are raised under horrendous intensive conditions known as "factory farming," mutilated in various ways without pain relief, transported long distances in cramped, filthy containers, and finally slaughtered amid the stench, noise, and squalor of the abattoir. We kill billions of fish and other sea animals annually. We catch them with hooks and allow them to suffocate in nets. We buy lobsters at the supermarket,

---

1. David Foster, "Animal Rights Activists Getting Message Across: New Poll Findings Show Americans More in Tune with 'Radical' Views," *Chicago Tribune,* Jan. 25, 1996, at C8.
2. John Balzar, "Creatures Great and—Equal?," *L.A. Times,* Dec. 25, 1993, at A1.
3. Julie Kirkbride, "Peers Use Delays to Foil Hedgehog Cruelty Measure," *Daily Telegraph,* Nov. 3, 1995, at 12.
4. Edward Gorman, "Woman's Goring Fails to Halt Death in the Afternoon," *Times* (London), June 30, 1995, Home News Section.
5. Malcolm Eames, "Four Legs Very Good," *The Guardian,* Aug. 25, 1995, at 17.
6. For sources discussing the numbers of animals used for various purposes, see Gary L. Francione, *Introduction to Animal Rights: Your Child or the Dog?,* at xx–xxi (2000).

where they are kept for weeks in crowded tanks with their claws closed by rubber bands and without receiving any food, and we cook them alive in boiling water.

Wild animals fare no better. We hunt and kill approximately 200 million animals in the United States annually, not including animals killed on commercial game ranches or at events such as pigeon shoots. Moreover, hunters often cripple animals without killing or retrieving them. It is estimated, for example, that bow hunters do not retrieve 50 percent of the animals hit with their arrows. This increases the true death toll from hunting by at least tens of millions of uncounted animals. Wounded animals often die slowly, over a period of hours or even days, from blood loss, punctured intestines and stomachs, and severe infections.

In the United States alone, we use millions of animals annually for biomedical experiments, product testing, and education. Animals are used to measure the effects of toxins, diseases, drugs, radiation, bullets, and all forms of physical and psychological deprivations. We burn, poison, irradiate, blind, starve, and electrocute them. They are purposely riddled with diseases such as cancer and infections such as pneumonia. We deprive them of sleep, keep them in solitary confinement, remove their limbs and eyes, addict them to drugs, force them to withdraw from drug addiction, and cage them for the duration of their lives. If they do not die during experimental procedures, we almost always kill them immediately afterward, or we recycle them for other experiments or tests and then kill them.

We use millions of animals for the sole purpose of providing entertainment. Animals are used in film and television. There are thousands of zoos, circuses, carnivals, race tracks, dolphin exhibits, and rodeos in the United States, and these and similar activities, such as bullfighting, also take place in other countries. Animals used in entertainment are often forced to endure lifelong incarceration and confinement, poor living conditions, extreme physical danger and hardship, and brutal treatment. Most animals used for entertainment purposes are killed when no longer useful, or sold into research or as targets for shooting on commercial hunting preserves.

And we kill millions of animals annually simply for fashion. Approximately 40 million animals worldwide are trapped, snared, or raised in intensive confinement on fur farms, where they are electrocuted or gassed or have their necks broken. In the United States, 8–10 million animals are killed every year for fur.

For all of these reasons, we may be said to suffer from a sort of moral schizophrenia when it comes to our thinking about animals. We claim to regard animals as having morally significant interests, but our behavior is to the contrary.

ANIMALS AS THINGS

Before the nineteenth century, the foregoing litany of animal uses would not have raised any concern. Western culture did not recognize that humans had any moral obligations to animals because animals did not matter morally at all. We could have moral obligations that concerned animals, but these obligations were really owed to other humans and not to animals. Animals were regarded as things, as having a moral status no different from that of inanimate objects.

As late as the seventeenth century, the view was advanced that animals are nothing more than machines. René Descartes (1596–1650), considered the founder of modern philosophy, argued that animals are not conscious—they have no mind whatsoever—because they do not possess a soul, which God invested only in humans. In support of the idea that animals lack consciousness, Descartes maintained that they do not use verbal or sign language—something that every human being does but that no animal does. Descartes certainly recognized that animals act in what appear to be purposive and intelligent ways and that they seem to be conscious, but he claimed that they are really no different from machines made by God. Indeed, he likened animals to "automatons, or moving machines."[7] Moreover, just as a clock can tell time better than humans can, so some animal machines can perform some tasks better than humans can.

---

7. René Descartes, "Discourse on the Method," pt. V, *in* 1 *The Philosophical Writings of Descartes* III, 139 (John Cottingham, Robert Stoothoff, & Dugald Murdoch trans., Cambridge Univ. Press 1985) (1637). Some scholars have argued that Descartes did recognize animal consciousness in certain respects, and that traditional interpretations of Descartes are incorrect. *See, e.g.,* Daisie Radner & Michael Radner, *Animal Consciousness* (1989). There is, however, no doubt that Descartes regarded animals as morally indistinguishable from inanimate objects and, to the extent that he viewed animals as conscious and as having interests in not suffering, he ignored those interests.

An obvious implication of Descartes's position was that animals are not sentient; they are not conscious of pain, pleasure, or anything else. Descartes and his followers performed experiments in which they nailed animals by their paws to boards and cut them open to reveal their beating hearts. They burned, scalded, and mutilated animals in every conceivable manner. When the animals reacted as though they were suffering pain, Descartes dismissed the reaction as no different from the sound of a machine that is functioning improperly. A crying dog, Descartes maintained, is no different from a whining gear that needs oil.

In Descartes's view, it is as senseless to talk about our moral obligations to animals, machines created by God, as it is to talk about our moral obligations to clocks, machines created by humans. We can have moral obligations that concern the clock, but any such obligations are really owed to other humans and not to the clock. If I smash the clock with a hammer, you may object because the clock belongs to you, or because I injure you when a piece of the clock accidentally strikes you, or because it is wasteful to destroy a perfectly good clock that could be used by someone else. I may be similarly obliged not to damage your dog, but the obligation is owed to you, not to the dog. The dog, like the clock, according to Descartes, is nothing more than a machine and possesses no interests in the first place.

There were others who did not share Descartes's view that animals are merely machines but who still denied that we can have any moral obligations to animals. For example, the German philosopher Immanuel Kant (1724–1804) recognized that animals are sentient and can suffer, but denied that we can have any direct moral obligations to them because, according to Kant, they are neither rational nor self-aware. According to Kant, animals are merely a means to human ends; they are "man's instruments." They exist only for our use and have no value in themselves. To the extent that our treatment of animals matters at all for Kant, it does so only because of its impact on other humans: "[H]e who is cruel to animals becomes hard also in his dealings with men."[8] Kant argued that if we shoot and kill a faithful and obedient dog because the dog has grown old and is no longer capable of serving us, our act violates no obligation that we owe to the dog. The act is wrong only because of our moral obligation to reward the faithful service of other humans; killing the dog

---

8. Immanuel Kant, *Lectures on Ethics* 240 (Louis Infield trans., Harper Torchbooks, 1963).

tends to make us less inclined to fulfill these human obligations. "[S]o far as animals are concerned, we have no direct duties." Animals exist "merely as a means to an end. That end is man."[9]

The view that we have no direct moral obligations to animals was also reflected in Anglo-American law. Before the nineteenth century, it is difficult to find any statutory recognition of legal obligations owed directly to animals.[10] To the extent that the law provided animals any protection, it was, for the most part, couched solely in terms of human concerns, primarily property interests. If Simon injured Jane's cow, Simon's act might violate a malicious mischief statute if it could be proved that the act manifested malice toward Jane. If Simon had malice toward the cow but not toward Jane, then he could not be prosecuted. It was irrelevant whether Simon's malice was directed toward Jane's cow or toward her inanimate property. Any judicial condemnation of animal cruelty was, with rare exceptions, expressed only as concern that such conduct would translate into cruelty to other humans, or that acts of cruelty to animals might offend public decency and cause a breach of the peace. That is, the law reflected the notion expressed by Kant and others that if there were any reason for us to be kind to animals, it had nothing to do with any obligation that we owed to animals, but only with our obligations to other humans.

THE HUMANE TREATMENT PRINCIPLE: A REJECTION OF ANIMALS AS THINGS

Consider the following example. Simon proposes to torture a dog by burning the dog with a blowtorch. Simon's only reason for torturing the dog is that he derives pleasure from this sort of activity. Does Simon's proposal raise any moral concern? Is Simon violating some moral obligation

---

9. *Id.* at 239. There were others, such as Aristotle, St. Thomas Aquinas, and John Locke, who recognized that animals are sentient but who claimed that they lack characteristics such as rationality or abstract thought, and we could, therefore, treat them as things. *See* Francione, *supra* note 6, at 103–29. *See also infra* notes 74–97 and accompanying text.

10. A possible exception is the 1641 legal code of the Massachusetts Bay Colony, which prohibited cruelty to domestic animals. *See* Gary L. Francione, *Animals, Property, and the Law* 121 (1995). It is not clear whether this provision prohibited cruelty at least in part out of concern for the animals themselves, or only because cruelty to animals might adversely affect humans.

not to use the animal in this way for his amusement? Or is Simon's action morally no different from crushing and eating a walnut?

I think that most of us would not hesitate to maintain that blowtorching the dog simply for pleasure is not a morally justifiable act under any circumstances. What is the basis of our moral judgment? Is it merely that we are concerned about the effect of Simon's action on other humans? Do we object to the torture of the dog merely because it might upset other humans who like dogs? Do we object because by torturing the dog Simon may become a more callous or unkind person in his dealings with other humans? We may very well rest our moral objection to Simon's action in part on our concern for the effect of his action on other humans, but that is not our primary reason for objecting. After all, we would condemn the act even if Simon tortures the animal in secret, or even if, apart from his appetite for torturing dogs, Simon is a charming fellow who shows only kindness to other humans.

Suppose that the dog is the companion animal of Simon's neighbor, Jane. Do we object to the torture because the dog is Jane's property? We may very well object to Simon's action because the dog belongs to Jane, but again, that is not our first concern. We would find Simon's action objectionable even if the dog were a stray.

The primary reason that we find Simon's action morally objectionable is its effect on the dog. The dog is sentient; like us, the dog is the sort of being who has the capacity to suffer and has an interest in not being blowtorched.[11] The dog prefers, or wants, or desires not to be blowtorched. We have an obligation—one owed directly to the dog and not merely one that concerns the dog—not to torture the dog. The sole ground for this obligation is that the dog is sentient; no other characteristic, such as humanlike rationality, reflective self-consciousness, or the ability to communicate in a human language, is necessary. Simply because the dog can experience pain and suffering, we regard it as morally necessary to justify

---

11. The neurological and physiological similarities between humans and nonhumans render the fact of animal sentience noncontroversial. Even mainstream science accepts that animals are sentient. For example, the U.S. Public Health Service states that "[u]nless the contrary is established, investigators should consider that procedures that cause pain or distress in human beings may cause pain or distress in other animals." U.S. Department of Health and Human Services, National Institutes of Health, "Public Health Service Policy and Government Principles Regarding the Care and Use of Animals," in *Institute of Laboratory Animal Resources, Guide for the Care and Use of Laboratory Animals* 117 (1996).

our infliction of harm on the dog. We may disagree about whether a particular justification suffices, but we all agree that some justification is required, and Simon's pleasure simply cannot constitute such a justification. An integral part of our moral thinking is the idea that, other things being equal, the fact that an action causes pain counts as a reason against that action, not merely because imposing harm on another sentient being somehow diminishes us, but because imposing harm on another sentient being is wrong in itself. And it does not matter whether Simon proposes to blowtorch for pleasure the dog or another animal, such as a cow. We would object to his conduct in either case.

In short, most of us claim to reject the characterization of animals as things that has dominated Western thinking for many centuries. For the better part of 200 years, Anglo-American moral and legal culture has made a distinction between sentient creatures and inanimate objects. Although we believe that we ought to prefer humans over animals when interests conflict, most of us accept as completely uncontroversial that our use and treatment of animals are guided by what we might call the *humane treatment principle,* or the view that because animals can suffer, we have a moral obligation that we owe directly to animals not to impose unnecessary suffering on them.

The humane treatment principle finds its origins in the theories of English lawyer and utilitarian philosopher Jeremy Bentham (1748–1832). Bentham argued that despite any differences, humans and animals are similar in that they both can suffer, and it is only the capacity to suffer and not the capacity for speech or reason or anything else that is required for animals to matter morally and to have legal protection. Bentham maintained that animals had been "degraded into the class of *things,*" with the result that their interest in not suffering had been ignored.[12] In a statement as profound as it was simple, Bentham illuminated the irrel-

---

12. Jeremy Bentham, *An Introduction to the Principles of Morals and Legislation,* ch. XVII, para. 4, at 282 (footnote omitted) (J.H. Burns & H.L.A. Hart eds., Athlone Press 1970) (1781). I do not mean to suggest that Bentham was the first person ever to express a concern about animal suffering distinct from its effect on human character, nor that he was the only or the first to argue that humans and animals have morally significant interests in not suffering. Several years before Bentham, Rev. Humphry Primatt expressed the view that suffering was an evil irrespective of species. *See* Humphry Primatt, *A Dissertation on the Duty of Mercy and Sin of Cruelty to Brute Animals* (London, T. Cadell 1776). Bentham clearly had a greater impact on both moral and legal thinking concerning the issue.

evance of characteristics other than sentience: "[A] full-grown horse or dog, is beyond comparison a more rational, as well as a more conversible animal, than an infant of a day, or a week, or even a month, old. But suppose the case were otherwise, what would it avail? the question is not, Can they *reason*? nor, Can they *talk*? but, Can they *suffer*?"[13]

Bentham's position marked a sharp departure from a cultural tradition that had never before regarded animals as other than things devoid of morally significant interests. He rejected the views of those, like Descartes, who maintained that animals are not sentient and have no interests. He also rejected the views of those, like Kant, who maintained that animals have interests but that those interests are not morally significant because animals lack characteristics other than sentience, and that our treatment of animals matters only to the extent that it affects our treatment of other humans. For Bentham, our treatment of animals matters because of its effect on beings that can suffer, and our duties are owed directly to them. Bentham urged the enactment of laws to protect animals from suffering.

Bentham's views had a profound effect on various legal reformers, and the result was that the legal systems of the United States and Britain (as well as other nations) purported to incorporate the humane treatment principle in animal welfare laws. These laws are of two kinds: general and specific. General animal welfare laws, such as anticruelty laws, prohibit cruelty or the infliction of unnecessary suffering on animals without distinguishing between various uses of animals. For example, New York law imposes a criminal sanction on any person who "overdrives, overloads, tortures or cruelly beats or unjustifiably injures, maims, mutilates or kills any animal."[14] Delaware law prohibits cruelty and defines as cruel "every act or omission to act whereby unnecessary or unjustifiable physical pain or suffering is caused or permitted," and includes "mistreatment of any animal or neglect of any animal under the care and control of the neglector, whereby unnecessary or unjustifiable physical pain or suffering is caused."[15] In Britain, the Protection of Animals Act of 1911 makes

---

13. Bentham, *supra* note 12, at 282–83 n.b.
14. N.Y. Agric. & Mkts. Law § 353 (Consol. 2002). The first known anticruelty statute in the United States was passed in Maine in 1821. New York passed a statute in 1829, but New York courts held as early as 1822 that cruelty was an offense at common law.
15. Del. Code. Ann. tit. 11, §§ 1325(a)(1) & (4) (2002).

it a criminal offense to "cruelly beat, kick, ill-treat, over-ride, over-drive, over-load, torture, infuriate, or terrify any animal" or to impose "unnecessary suffering" on animals.[16] Specific animal welfare laws purport to apply the humane treatment principle to a particular animal use. For example, the American Animal Welfare Act, enacted in 1966 and amended on numerous occasions,[17] the British Cruelty to Animals Act, enacted in 1876,[18] and the British Animals (Scientific Procedures) Act of 1986[19] concern the treatment of animals used in experiments. The American Humane Slaughter Act, originally enacted in 1958, regulates the killing of animals used for food.[20]

As we saw earlier, if Simon injured Jane's cow, malicious mischief statutes required a showing that Simon bore malice toward Jane. To the extent that courts had any concern about cruelty to animals, this concern was limited to the effect that cruelty might have on public sensibilities or on the tendency of cruelty to animals to encourage cruelty to other humans. The passage of anticruelty laws allowed for Simon's prosecution even if he bore Jane no ill will and instead intended malice only to her cow. Moreover, these laws reflect concern about the moral significance of animal suffering, in addition to the detrimental repercussions of cruelty to animals for humans. Anticruelty laws are often explicit in applying to all animals, whether owned or unowned. Thus, whereas malicious mischief statutes were "intended to protect the beasts as property instead of as creatures susceptible of suffering," anticruelty statutes are "designed for the protection of animals."[21] They are intended "for the benefit of animals, as creatures capable of feeling and suffering, and . . . intended to protect them from cruelty, without reference to their being property."[22] The purpose of these laws is, in part, to instill in humans "a humane regard for the rights and feelings of the brute creation by reproving evil and indifferent tendencies in human nature in its intercourse with ani-

---

16. Protection of Animals Act, 1911, c. 27 § 1(1)(a) (Eng.). British legislation prohibiting cruelty to animals was passed as early as 1822.
17. 7 U.S.C. §§ 2131–2159 (2003).
18. Cruelty to Animals Act, 1876 (Eng.).
19 Animals (Scientific Procedures) Act, 1986 (Eng.).
20. 7 U.S.C. §§ 1901–1907 (2003).
21. State v. Prater, 109 S.W. 1047, 1049 (Mo. Ct. App. 1908).
22. Stephens v. State, 65 Miss. 329, 330 (1887).

mals."[23] They are said to "recognize and attempt to protect some abstract rights in all that animate creation, made subject to man by the creation, from the largest and noblest to the smallest and most insignificant."[24] Anticruelty laws acknowledge that because animals are sentient, we have legal obligations that we owe directly to animals to refrain from imposing unnecessary pain and suffering on them: "Pain is an evil" and "[i]t is impossible for a right minded man . . . to say that unjustifiable cruelty is not a wrong."[25] Other animal welfare laws similarly focus on the suffering of animals as intrinsically undesirable.[26]

Many animal welfare laws, such as anticruelty statutes, are criminal laws. For the most part, only those moral rules that are widely accepted, such as prohibitions against killing other humans, inflicting physical harm on them, or taking or destroying their property, are enshrined in criminal laws. That many animal welfare laws are criminal laws suggests that we take animal interests seriously enough to punish violations of the humane treatment principle with the social stigma of a criminal penalty.

The humane treatment principle and the operation of the animal welfare laws that reflect it purport to require that we balance the interests of animals against our interests as humans in order to determine whether animal suffering is necessary. To balance interests means to assess the relative strengths of conflicting interests. If our suffering in not using animals outweighs the animal interest in not suffering, then our interests prevail, and the animal suffering is regarded as necessary. If no justifiable human interests are at stake, then the infliction of suffering on animals must be regarded as unnecessary. For example, the British law regulating the use of animals in experiments requires, before any experiment is approved, a balancing of "the likely adverse effects on the animals concerned against the benefit likely to accrue."[27]

In sum, the principle assumes that we may use animals when it is necessary to do so—when we are faced with a conflict between animal

---

23. Hunt v. State, 29 N.E. 933, 933 (Ind. Ct. App. 1892).

24. Grise v. State, 37 Ark. 456, 458 (1881).

25. People v. Brunell, 48 How. Pr. 435, 437 (N.Y. City Ct. 1874).

26. *See, e.g.,* Francione, *supra* note 10, at 193 (discussing the federal Animal Welfare Act).

27. Animals (Scientific Procedures) Act, 1986, c. 14, § 5(4) (Eng.).

and human interests—and that we should impose only the minimum amount of pain and suffering necessary to achieve our purpose. If a prohibition against unnecessary suffering of animals is to have any meaningful content, it must preclude the infliction of suffering on animals merely for our pleasure, amusement, or convenience. If there is a feasible alternative to our use of animals in a particular situation, then the principle would seem to proscribe such use.

THE PROBLEM: UNNECESSARY SUFFERING

Although we express disapproval of the unnecessary suffering of animals, nearly all of our animal use can be justified *only* by habit, convention, amusement, convenience, or pleasure.[28] To put the matter another way, most of the suffering that we impose on animals is completely unnecessary, and we are not substantially different from Simon, who proposes to blowtorch the dog for pleasure. For example, the uses of animals for sport hunting and entertainment purposes cannot, by definition, be considered necessary. Nevertheless, these activities are protected by laws that supposedly prohibit the infliction of unnecessary suffering on animals. It is certainly not necessary for us to wear fur coats, or to use animals to test duplicative household products, or to have yet another brand of lipstick or aftershave lotion.

More important in terms of numbers of animals used, however, is the animal agriculture industry, in which billions of animals are killed for food annually. It is not necessary in any sense to eat meat or animal products; indeed, an increasing number of health care professionals maintain that these foods may be detrimental to human health. Moreover, respected environmental scientists have pointed out the tremendous inefficiencies and resulting costs to our planet of animal agriculture. For example, animals consume more protein than they produce. For every kilogram (2.2 pounds) of animal protein produced, animals consume an average of almost 6 kilograms, or more than 13 pounds, of plant protein

---

28. For a discussion about the necessity of various animal uses, see Francione, *supra* note 6, at 9–49. *See also* Stephen R.L. Clark, *The Moral Status of Animals* (1977) (arguing that much animal use cannot be regarded as necessary).

from grains and forage. It takes more than 100,000 liters of water to produce one kilogram of beef, and approximately 900 liters to produce one kilogram of wheat. In any event, our only justification for the pain, suffering, and death inflicted on these billions of farm animals is that we enjoy the taste of their flesh.

Although many regard the use of animals in experiments as involving a genuine conflict of human and animal interests, the necessity of animal use for this purpose is open to serious question as well. Considerable empirical evidence challenges the notion that animal experiments are necessary to ensure human health and indicates that, in many instances, reliance on animal models has actually been counterproductive.

ANIMALS AS PROPERTY: AN UNBALANCED BALANCE

The profound inconsistency between what we say about animals and how we actually treat them is related to the status of animals as our property.[29] Animals are commodities that we own and that have no value other than that which we, as property owners, choose to give them. Although Bentham changed moral thinking and legal doctrine by introducing the idea that sentience is the only characteristic required for animals to matter, neither he nor the reformers interested in incorporating his views into law ever questioned the property status of animals.[30] Under the law, "animals are owned in the same way as inanimate objects such as cars and furniture."[31] They "are by law treated as any other form of movable property and may be the subject of absolute, *i.e.,* complete

---

29. *See generally* Francione, *supra* note 10 (discussing the status of animals as property as a general matter, and in the context of anticruelty laws and the federal Animal Welfare Act). The status of animals as property has existed for thousands of years. Indeed, historical evidence indicates that the domestication of animals is closely related to the development of the concepts of property and money. The property status of animals is particularly important in Western culture for two reasons. First, property rights are accorded a special status and are considered to be among the most important rights we have. Second, the modern Western concept of property, whereby resources are regarded as separate objects that are assigned and belong to particular individuals who are allowed to use the property to the exclusion of everyone else, has its origin in God's grant to humans of dominion over animals. *See id.* at 24–49; Francione, *supra* note 6, at 50–54.

30. *See infra* notes 75–81 and accompanying text.

31. Godfrey Sandys-Winsch, *Animal Law* 1 (1978).

ownership . . . [and] the owner has at his command all the protection that the law provides in respect of absolute ownership."[32] The owner is entitled to exclusive physical possession of the animal, the use of the animal for economic and other gain, and the right to make contracts with respect to the animal or to use the animal as collateral for a loan. The owner is under a duty to ensure that her animal property does not harm other humans or their property, but she can sell or bequeath the animal, give the animal away, or have the animal taken from her as part of the execution of a legal judgment against her. She can also kill the animal. Wild animals are generally regarded as owned by the state and held in trust for the benefit of the people, but they can be made the property of particular humans through hunting or by taming and confining them.

The property status of animals renders meaningless any balancing that is supposedly required under the humane treatment principle or animal welfare laws, because what we really balance are the interests of property owners against the interests of their animal property. It is, of course, absurd to suggest that we can balance human interests, which are protected by claims of right in general and of a right to own property in particular, against the interests of property, which exists only as a means to the ends of humans. Although we claim to recognize that we may prefer animal interests over human interests only when there is a conflict of interests, there is always a conflict between the interests of property owners who want to use their property and the interests of their animal property. The human property interest will almost always prevail. The animal in question is always a "pet" or a "laboratory animal," or a "game animal," or a "food animal," or a "rodeo animal," or some other form of animal property that exists solely for our use and has no value except that which we give it. There is really no choice to be made between the human and the animal interest because the choice has already been predetermined by the property status of the animal; the "suffering" of property owners who cannot use their property as they wish counts more than animal suffering. We are allowed to impose any suffering required to use our animal property for a particular purpose even if that purpose is our mere amusement or pleasure. As long as we use our animal property to gener-

---

32. T. G. Field-Fisher, *Animals and the Law* 19 (1964).

ate an economic benefit, there is no effective limit on our use or treatment of animals.[33]

There are several specific ways in which animal welfare laws ensure that there will never be a meaningful balance of human and animal interests. First, many of these laws explicitly exempt most forms of institutionalized property use, which account for the largest number of animals that we use. The most frequent exemptions from state anticruelty statutes involve scientific experiments, agricultural practices, and hunting.[34] The Animal Welfare Act, the primary federal law that regulates the use of animals in biomedical experiments, does not even apply to most of the animals used in experiments—rats and mice—and imposes no meaningful limits on the amount of pain and suffering that may be inflicted on animals in the conduct of experiments.[35]

Second, even if anticruelty statutes do not do so explicitly, courts have effectively exempted our common uses of animals from scrutiny by interpreting these statutes as not prohibiting the infliction of even extreme suffering if it is incidental to an accepted use of animals and a customary practice on the part of animal owners.[36] An act "which inflicts pain, even the great pain of mutilation, and which is cruel in the ordinary sense of the word" is not prohibited "[w]henever the purpose for which the act is done is to make the animal more serviceable for the use of man."[37] For example, courts have held consistently that animals used for food may be mutilated in ways that unquestionably cause severe pain and suffering and that would normally be regarded as cruel or even as torture. These practices are permitted, however, because animal agriculture is an accepted institutionalized animal use, and those in the meat industry regard the practices as normal and necessary to facilitate that use. Courts often presume that animal owners will act in their best economic interests and will not intentionally inflict more suffering than is necessary on an animal because to do so would diminish the monetary value of the

---

33. To the extent that animal uses, such as certain types of animal fighting, have been prohibited, this may be understood more in terms of class hierarchy and cultural prejudice than in terms of moral concern about animals. *See* Francione, *supra* note 10, at 18.

34. *See id.* at 139–42.

35. *See id.* at 224–25. For a discussion of the Animal Welfare Act, *see id.* at 185–249.

36. *See id.* at 142–56; Francione, *supra* note 6, at 58–63.

37. Murphy v. Manning, 2 Ex. D. 307, 313, 314 (1877) (Cleasby, B.).

animal.[38] For example, in *Callaghan v. Society for the Prevention of Cruelty to Animals,* the court held that the painful act of dehorning cattle did not constitute unnecessary abuse because farmers would not perform this procedure if it were not necessary. The self-interest of the farmer would prevent the infliction of "useless pain or torture," which "would necessarily reduce the condition of the animal; and, unless they very soon recovered, the farmer would lose in the sale."[39]

Third, anticruelty laws are generally criminal laws and the state must prove beyond a reasonable doubt that a defendant engaged in an unlawful act with a culpable state of mind. The problem is that if a defendant is inflicting pain or suffering on an animal as part of an accepted institutionalized use of animals, it is difficult to prove that she acted with the requisite mental state to justify criminal liability.[40] For example, in *Regalado v. United States,*[41] Regalado was convicted of violating the anticruelty statute of the District of Columbia for beating a puppy. Regalado appealed, claiming that he did not intend to harm the puppy and inflicted the beating only for disciplinary purposes. The court held that anticruelty statutes were "not intended to place unreasonable restrictions on the infliction of such pain as may be necessary for the training or discipline of an animal" and that the statute only prohibited acts done with malice or a cruel disposition.[42] Although the court affirmed Regalado's conviction, it recognized that "proof of malice will usually be circumstantial, and the line between discipline and cruelty will often be difficult to draw."[43]

Fourth, many animal welfare laws have wholly inadequate penalty provisions, and we are reluctant, in any event, to impose the stigma of

---

38. *See* Francione, *supra* note 10, at 127–28; Francione, *supra* note 6, at 66–67. This presumption not only insulates customary practices from being found to violate anticruelty laws, but also militates against finding the necessary criminal intent in cases involving noncustomary uses. *See, e.g.,* Commonwealth v. Barr, 44 Pa. C. 284 (Lancaster County Ct. 1916). *See infra* notes 40–43 and accompanying text.

39. 16 L.R.Ir. 325, 335 (C.P.D. 1885) (Murphy, J.). In Britain, the dehorning of older cattle was found to violate the anticruelty statute but only because dehorning had been discontinued and was no longer an accepted agriculture practice. *See* Ford v. Wiley, 23 Q.B.D. 203 (1889). In his opinion, Hawkins, J., noted that the fact that the practice had been abandoned by farmers who were acting in their economic self-interest was proof that the practice was unnecessary. *See id.* at 221–22.

40. *See* Francione, *supra* note 10, at 135–39; Francione, *supra* note 6, at 63–66.

41. 572 A.2d 416 (D.C. 1990).

42. *Id.* at 420.

43. *Id.* at 421.

criminal liability on animal owners for what they do with their property.[44] Moreover, those without an ownership interest generally do not have standing to bring legal challenges to the use or treatment of animals by their owners.[45]

As the foregoing makes clear, because animals are property, we do not balance interests to determine whether it is necessary to use animals at all for particular purposes. We simply assume that it is appropriate to use animals for food, recreation, entertainment, clothing, or experiments—the primary ways in which we use animals as commodities to generate social wealth and most of which cannot be described plausibly as involving any genuine conflict of human and animal interests. Animal welfare laws do not even apply to many of these uses. To the extent that we do ask whether the imposition of pain and suffering is necessary, the inquiry is limited to whether particular treatment is in compliance with the customs and practices of property owners who, we assume, will not inflict more pain and suffering on their animal property than is required for the purpose. The only way to characterize this process is as a "balancing" of the property owner's interest in using animal property against the interest of an animal in not being used in ways that fail to comply with those customs and practices. Although animal welfare laws are intended to protect the interests of animals without reference to their being property, animal interests are protected only insofar as they serve the goal of rational property use.[46]

Our infliction of suffering on animals raises a legal question only when it does not conform to the customs and practices of those institutions—when we intentionally inflict suffering in ways that do not maximize social wealth, or when the only explanation for the behavior can be characterized as "the gratification of a malignant or vindictive temper."[47] For example, in *State v. Tweedie*,[48] the defendant was found to have violated

---

44. *See* Francione, *supra* note 10, at 156; Francione, *supra* note 6, at 67–68. In recent years, many states have amended their anticruelty laws and have increased penalties for at least certain violations. It remains to be seen whether this will make any real difference because most animal uses will remain exempt and there will still be problems with proof of criminal intent.
45. *See* Francione, *supra* note 10, at 65–90, 156–58; Francione, *supra* note 6, at 69–70.
46. *See* Francione, *supra* note 10, at 27–32.
47. Commonwealth v. Lufkin, 89 Mass. (7 Allen) 579, 581 (1863). *See* Francione, *supra* note 10, at 137–38, 153–56; Francione, *supra* note 6, at 70–73.
48. 444 A.2d 855 (R.I. 1982).

the anticruelty law by killing a cat in a microwave oven. *In re William G.*[49] upheld a cruelty conviction where a minor kicked a dog and set her on fire because she would not mate with his dog. In *Motes v. State,*[50] the defendant was found guilty of violating the anticruelty statute when he set fire to a dog merely because the dog was barking. In *Tuck v. United States,*[51] a pet shop owner was convicted of cruelty when he placed animals in an unventilated display window and refused to remove a rabbit whose body temperature registered as high as the thermometer was calibrated—110 degrees Fahrenheit. In *People v. Voelker,*[52] the court held that cutting off the heads of three live, conscious iguanas "without justification" could constitute a violation of the anticruelty law. In *LaRue v. State,*[53] a cruelty conviction was upheld because the defendant collected a large number of stray dogs and failed to provide them with veterinary care; the dogs suffered from mange, blindness, dehydration, pneumonia, and distemper and had to be killed. In *State v. Schott,*[54] Schott was convicted of cruelty to animals when police found dozens of cows and pigs dead or dying from malnutrition and dehydration on Schott's farm. Schott's defense was that bad weather prevented him from caring for his livestock. The jury found Schott guilty of cruelty and neglect, and the appellate court affirmed. These are, however, unusual cases and constitute a minuscule fraction of the instances in which we inflict suffering on animals.

Moreover, the very same act may be either protected or prohibited depending only on whether it is part of an accepted institution of animal exploitation. If someone kills a cat in a microwave, sets a dog on fire, allows the body temperature of a rabbit to rise to the point of heat stroke, severs the heads of conscious animals, or allows animals to suffer untreated serious illnesses, the conduct may violate the anticruelty laws. But if a researcher engages in the exact same conduct as part of an experiment (and a number of researchers have killed animals or inflicted pain on them in the same and similar ways) the conduct is protected by the law because the researcher is supposedly using the animal to generate a benefit. A farmer may run afoul of the anticruelty law if she neglects

---

49. 447 A.2d 493 (Md. Ct. Spec. App. 1982).
50. 375 S.E.2d 893 (Ga. Ct. App. 1988).
51. 477 A.2d 1115 (D.C. 1984).
52. 172 Misc.2d 564 (N.Y. Crim. Ct. 1997).
53. 478 So.2d 13 (Ala. Crim. App. 1985).
54. 384 N.W.2d 620 (Neb. 1986).

her animals and allows them to suffer from malnutrition or dehydration for no reason, but she may mutilate her animals and raise them in conditions of severe confinement and deprivation, if she intends to sell them for food. The permitted actions cause as much if not more distress to animals as does neglecting them, but they are considered part of normal animal husbandry and are, therefore, protected under the law.

Thus, because animals are our property, the law will require their interests to be observed only to the extent that it facilitates the exploitation of the animal. This observation holds true even in countries where there is arguably a greater moral concern about animals. Britain, for instance, has more restrictions on animal use than does the United States, but the differences in permitted animal treatment are more formal than substantive. In discussing British animal welfare laws, one commentator has noted that "much of the animal welfare agenda has been obstructed and it is difficult to think of legislation improving the welfare of animals that has seriously damaged the interests of the animal users."[55] The law may in theory impose regulations that go beyond the minimum level of care required to exploit animals, yet it has rarely done so, for there are significant economic and other obstacles involved.[56] Voluntary changes in industry standards of animal welfare generally occur only when animal users regard these changes as cost-effective.[57]

---

55. Robert Garner, *Animals, Politics and Morality* 234 (1993).

56. *See* Francione, *supra* note 6, at 13, 73–76, 181–82. *See generally* Gary L. Francione, *Rain Without Thunder: The Ideology of the Animal Rights Movement* (1996) [hereinafter, Francione, *Rain Without Thunder*] (discussing unsuccessful efforts by the animal protection movement to obtain animal welfare laws that exceed the minimal standards required to exploit animals). Cass R. Sunstein argues that the property status of animals does not necessarily mean that they will be treated as means to human ends. *See* Cass R. Sunstein, "Slaughterhouse Jive," *The New Republic*, Jan. 29, 2001, at 40, 44. It is unrealistic to think that animal interests will be accorded significant weight when those interests are balanced against the interests of humans in exploiting their animal property. The fact that animal interests have become increasingly commodified despite 200 years of animal welfare law and philosophy is striking proof of the failure of animal welfare. Moreover, Sunstein ignores that animals have an interest in not suffering at all from our instrumental use of them. *See infra* notes 69–74 and accompanying text.

57. For example, McDonald's, the fast-food chain, announced that it would require its suppliers to observe standards of animal welfare that went beyond current standards: "Animal welfare is also an important part of quality assurance. For high-quality food products at the counter, you need high quality coming from the farm. Animals that are well cared for are less prone to illness, injury, and stress, which all have the same negative impact on the condition of livestock as they do on people. Proper animal welfare practices also benefit producers. Complying with our animal welfare guidelines helps ensure efficient production and reduces waste and loss. This enables our suppliers to be highly competitive." Bruce Feinberg & Terry Williams, "Animal

The status of animals as property renders meaningless our claim that we reject the status of animals as things. We treat animals as the moral equivalent of inanimate objects with no morally significant interests. We bring billions of animals into existence annually simply for the purpose of killing them. Animals have market prices. Dogs and cats are sold in pet stores like compact discs; financial markets trade in futures for pork bellies and cattle. Any interest that an animal has represents an economic cost that may be ignored to maximize overall social wealth and has no intrinsic value in our assessments. That is what it means to be property.

TAKING ANIMAL INTERESTS SERIOUSLY: THE PRINCIPLE OF EQUAL CONSIDERATION

We claim to accept that animals are not merely things. We may use animals when there is a conflict between human and animal interests that requires us to make a choice, but we have a moral obligation that we owe directly to animals not to inflict unnecessary suffering on them. Despite what we say, most of our animal use cannot be described as involving any conflict of interests, and we inflict extreme pain and suffering on animals in the process. Even if we treated animals better, that would still leave open the question of our moral justification for imposing any suffering at all if animal use is not necessary. We may, of course, decide to discard the humane treatment principle and acknowledge that we regard animals as nothing more than things without any morally significant interests. This option would at least spare us the need for thinking about our moral obligations to animals. We would not have any.

Alternatively, if we are to make good on our claim to take animal interests seriously, then we can do so in only one way: by applying the *principle of equal consideration*—the rule that we ought to treat like cases alike unless there is a good reason not to do so—to animals.[58] The principle

---

Welfare Update: North America," *at* http://www.mcdonalds.com/content/corp/values/report/archive/progress_report/north_america.html (last visited Dec. 1, 2003). The principal expert advisor to McDonald's states: "Healthy animals, properly handled, keep the meat industry running safely, efficiently and profitably." Temple Grandin, *Recommended Animal Handling Guidelines for Meat Packers* 1 (1991).

58. *See* Francione, *supra* note 6, at 81–102. A reason not to treat similar cases in a similar way must not be arbitrary and thereby itself violate the principle of equal consideration.

of equal consideration is a necessary component of every moral theory. Any theory that maintains that it is permissible to treat similar cases in a dissimilar way would fail to qualify as an acceptable moral theory for that reason alone. Although there may be many differences between humans and animals, there is at least one important similarity that we all already recognize: our shared capacity to suffer. In this sense, humans and animals are similar to each other and different from everything else in the universe that is not sentient. If our supposed prohibition on the infliction of unnecessary suffering on animals is to have any meaning at all, then we must give equal consideration to animal interests in not suffering.

The suggestion that animal interests should receive equal consideration is not as radical as it may appear at first if we consider that the humane treatment principle incorporates the principle of equal consideration. We are to weigh our suffering in not using animals against animal interests in avoiding suffering. If there is a conflict between human and animal interests and the human interest weighs more, then the animal suffering is justifiable. If there is no conflict, or if there is a conflict of interests but the animal interest weighs more, then we are not justified in using the animal. And if there is a conflict of interests but the interests at stake are similar, then we should presumably treat those interests in the same way and impose suffering on neither or both unless there is some nonarbitrary reason that justifies differential treatment. Moreover, the humane treatment principle as it developed historically explicitly included the principle of equal consideration. Bentham recognized that the only way to ensure that animal interests in not suffering were taken seriously was to apply the principle of equal consideration to animals, and Bentham's position therefore "incorporated the essential basis of moral equality . . . by means of the formula: 'Each to count for one and none for more than one.'"[59] Animal suffering cannot be discounted or ignored based on the supposed lack of some characteristic other than sentience if animals are not to be "degraded into the class of *things*." But Bentham never questioned the property status of animals because he mistakenly believed that the principle of equal consideration could be applied to animals even if they are property.[60] Bentham's error was

---

59. Peter Singer, *Animal Liberation* 5 (2d ed. 1990) (quoting Bentham).
60. *See infra* note 81 and accompanying text.

perpetuated through laws that purported to balance the interest of property owners and their property.

The problem is that, as we have seen, there can be no meaningful balancing of interests if animals are property. The property status of animals is a two-edged sword wielded against their interests. First, it acts as blinders that effectively block even our perception of their interests as similar to ours because human "suffering" is understood as any detriment to property owners. Second, in those instances in which human and animal interests are recognized as similar, animal interests will fail in the balancing because the property status of animals is always a good reason not to accord similar treatment unless to do so would benefit property owners. Animal interests will almost always count for less than one; animals remain as they were before the nineteenth century—things without morally significant interests.

The application of the principle of equal consideration similarly failed in the context of North American slavery, which allowed some humans to treat others as property.[61] The institution of human slavery was structurally identical to the institution of animal ownership. Because a human slave was regarded as property, the slave owner was able to disregard all of the slave's interests if it was economically beneficial to do so, and the law generally deferred to the slave owner's judgment as to the value of the slave. As chattel property, slaves could be sold, willed, insured, mortgaged, and seized in payment of the owner's debts. Slave owners could inflict severe punishments on slaves for virtually any reason. Those who intentionally or negligently injured another's slave were liable to the owner in an action for damage to property. Slaves could not enter into contracts, own property, sue or be sued, or live as free persons with basic rights and duties.

It was generally acknowledged that slaves had an interest in not suffering: Slaves "are not rational beings. No, but they are the creatures of God, sentient beings, capable of suffering and enjoyment, and entitled to enjoy according to the measure of their capacities. Does not the voice

---

61. The principle of equal consideration also failed in other systems of slavery, but because of differences among these systems, I confine my description to North American slavery. For a discussion of various systems of slavery and slave law, see Alan Watson, *Slave Law in the Americas* (1989); Alan Watson, *Roman Slave Law* (1987); Alan Watson, "Roman Slave Law and Romanist Ideology," 37 *Phoenix* 53 (1983).

of nature inform every one, that he is guilty of wrong when he inflicts on them pain without necessity or object?"[62] Although there were laws that ostensibly regulated the use and treatment of slaves, they failed completely to protect slave interests. The law often contained exceptions that eviscerated any protection for the slaves. For example, North Carolina law provided that the punishment for the murder of a slave should be the same as for the murder of a free person, but this law "did not apply to an outlawed slave, nor to a slave 'in the act of resistance to his lawful owner,' nor to a slave 'dying under moderate correction.'"[63] A law that prohibits the murder of slaves but permits three general and easily satisfied exceptions, combined with a general prohibition against the testimony of slaves against free persons, cannot effectively deter the murder of slaves. That the law refused to protect the interests of slaves against slave owners is underscored in *State v. Mann,* in which the court held that even the "cruel and unreasonable battery" of one's own slave is not indictable: Courts cannot "allow the right of the master to be brought into discussion in the Courts of Justice. The slave, to remain a slave, must be made sensible, that there is no appeal from his master."[64] To the extent that the law regulated the conduct of slave owners, it had nothing to do with concern for the interests of the slaves. For example, in *Commonwealth v. Turner,* the court determined that it had no jurisdiction to try the defendant slave owner, who beat his slave with "rods, whips and sticks," and held that even if the beating was administered "wilfully and maliciously, violently, cruelly, immoderately, and excessively," the court was not empowered to act as long as the slave did not die.[65] The court distinguished private beatings from public chastisement; the latter might subject the master to liability "not because it was a slave who was beaten, nor because the act was unprovoked or cruel; but, because ipso facto it disturbed the harmony of society; was offensive to public decency, and

---

62. Chancellor Harper, "Slavery in the Light of Social Ethics," *in Cotton Is King, and Pro-Slavery Arguments* 549, 559 (E. N. Elliott ed., 1860).

63. Stanley M. Elkins and Eric McKitrick, "Institutions and the Law of Slavery: Slavery in Capitalist and Non-Capitalist Cultures," *in The Law of American Slavery* 111, 115 (Kermit L. Hall ed., 1987) (quoting William Goodell, *The American Slave Code in Theory and Practice* 180 (1853)). For a discussion of slave law in the context of animal welfare law, see Francione, *supra* note 6, at 86–90; Francione, *supra* note 10, at 110–12.

64. 13 N.C. (2 Dev.) 263, 264, 267 (1829).

65. 26 Va. (5 Rand.) 678, 678 (1827).

directly tended to a breach of the peace. The same would be the law, if a horse had been so beaten."[66]

Slave welfare laws failed for precisely the same reason that animal welfare laws fail to establish any meaningful limit on our use of animal property. The owner's property interest in the slave always trumped any interest of the slave who was ostensibly protected under the law. The interests of slaves were observed only when it provided an economic benefit for the owners or served their whim. Alan Watson has noted that "[a]t most places at most times a reasonably economic owner would be conscious of the chattel value of slaves and thus would ensure some care in their treatment."[67] Any legal limitations on the cruelty of slave owners reflected the concern that they should not use their property in unproductive ways; as expressed by the Roman jurist Justinian, "'it is to the advantage of the state that no one use his property badly.'"[68] Although some slave owners were more "humane" than others and some even treated slaves as family members, any kind treatment was a matter of the master's charity and not of the slave's right, and slavery as a legal institution had the inevitable effect of treating humans as nothing more than commodities. The principle of equal consideration had no meaningful application to the interests of a human whose only value was as a resource belonging to others. Slaves were rarely considered to have any interests similar to slave owners or other free persons; in those instances in which interests were recognized as similar, the property status of the slave was always a good reason not to accord similar treatment unless to do so would benefit the owner.

We eventually recognized that if humans were to have any morally significant interests, they could not be the resources of others and that race was not a sufficient reason to treat certain humans as property.[69] Although we tolerate varying degrees of exploitation, and we may dis-

---

66. *Id.* at 680.

67. Watson, *Slave Law in the Americas, supra* note 61, at xiv.

68. *Id.* at 31 (quoting Justinian).

69. Even after the abolition of slavery, race continued to serve as a reason to justify differential treatment, often on the ground that whites and people of color did not have similar interests and, therefore, did not have to be treated equally in certain respects, and often on the ground that race was a reason to deny similar treatment to admittedly similar interests. But abolition recognized that, irrespective of race, all humans had a similar interest in not being treated as the property of others.

agree about what constitutes equal treatment, we no longer regard it as legitimate to treat any humans, irrespective of their particular characteristics, as the property of others. Indeed, in a world deeply divided on many moral issues, one of the few norms steadfastly endorsed by the international community is the prohibition of human slavery. It matters not whether the particular form of slavery is "humane" or not; we condemn all human slavery. More brutal forms of slavery are worse than less brutal forms, but we prohibit human slavery in general because all forms of slavery more or less allow the interests of slaves to be ignored if it provides a benefit to slave owners, and humans have an interest in not suffering the deprivation of their fundamental interests merely because it benefits someone else, however "humanely" they are treated. It would, of course, be incorrect to say that human slavery has been eliminated from the planet. But the peremptory norms in international law—those few, select rules regarded as of such significance that they admit of no derogation by any nation—include the prohibition of slavery, which humanity deems so odious that no civilized nation can bear its existence.

The interest of a human in not being the property of others is protected by a right. When an interest is protected by a right, the interest may not be ignored or violated simply because it will benefit others. "Rights are moral notions that grow out of respect for the individual. They build protective fences around the individual. They establish areas where the individual is entitled to be protected against the state and the majority *even where a price is paid by the general welfare.*"[70] If we are going to recognize and protect the interest of humans in not being treated as property, then we must use a right to do so; if we do not, then those humans who do not have this protection will be treated merely as commodities whenever it will benefit others. Therefore, the interest in not being treated as property must be protected against being traded away even if a price is paid by the general welfare.

The right not to be treated as the property of others is basic and different from any other rights we might have because it is the grounding for those other rights; it is a prelegal right that serves as the precondition

---

70. Bernard E. Rollin, "The Legal and Moral Bases of Animal Rights," *in Ethics and Animals* 103, 106 (Harlan B. Miller & William H. Williams eds., 1983). *See* Francione, *supra* note 6, at xxvi-xxx. For a general discussion of the concept of rights and rights theory in the context of laws concerning animals, see Francione, *supra* note 10, at 91–114.

for the possession of morally significant interests. The basic right is the right to the equal consideration of one's fundamental interests; it recognizes that if some humans have value only as resources, then the principle of equal consideration will have no meaningful application to their interests. Therefore, the basic right must be understood as prohibiting human slavery, or any other institutional arrangement that treats humans *exclusively* as means to the ends of others and not as ends in themselves.[71]

The protection afforded by the basic right not to be treated as property is limited. The basic right does not guarantee equal treatment in all respects nor protect humans from all suffering, but it protects all humans, irrespective of their particular characteristics, from suffering any deprivation of interests as the result of being used exclusively as the resources of others and thereby provides essential protections. We may not enslave humans nor, for that matter, may we exert total control over their bodies by using them as we do laboratory animals, or as forced organ donors, or as raw materials for shoes, or as objects to be hunted for sport or tortured—irrespective of whether we claim to treat them "humanely" in the process.[72] An employer may treat her employees instrumentally and disregard their interest in a midmorning coffee break, or even their interest in health care, in the name of profit. But there are limits. She cannot force

71. Similar concepts have been recognized by philosophers and political theorists. Kant, for example, maintained that there is one "innate" right—the right of "innate *equality*," or the "independence from being bound by others to more than one can in turn bind them; hence a human being's quality of being *his own master.*" Immanuel Kant, *The Metaphysics of Morals*, §§ 6:237-38, at 30 (Mary Gregor trans. & ed., Cambridge Univ. Press 1996). This innate right "grounds our right to *have* rights." Roger J. Sullivan, *Immanuel Kant's Moral Theory* 248 (1989). The basic right not to be treated as property is different from what are referred to as natural rights insofar as these are understood to be rights that exist apart from their recognition by any particular legal system because they are granted by God. For example, John Locke regarded property rights as natural rights that were grounded in God's grant to humans of dominion over the earth and animals. The basic right not to be treated as property expresses a proposition of logic. If human interests are to have moral significance (i.e., if human interests are to be treated in accordance with the principle of equal consideration), then humans cannot be resources; the interests of humans who are property will not be treated the same as the interests of property owners. For a further discussion of this basic right and the related concept of inherent value, see Francione, *supra* note 6, at 92–100. *See also* Henry Shue, *Basic Rights* (2d ed. 1996).

72. Human experimentation is prohibited by the Nuremberg Code and the Helsinki Declaration. Torture is prohibited by the International Convention against Torture and Other Cruel, Inhuman or Degrading Treatment or Punishment. The notable exception to the protection provided by the basic right is compulsory military service, which is controversial precisely because it does treat humans exclusively as means to the ends of others in ways that other acts required by the government, such as the payment of taxes, do not.

her employees to work without compensation. Pharmaceutical companies cannot test new drugs on employees who have not consented. Food-processing plants cannot make hot dogs or luncheon meats out of workers. To possess the basic right not to be treated as property is a minimal prerequisite to being a moral and legal *person;* it does not specify what other rights the person may have. Indeed, the rejection of slavery is required by any moral theory that purports to accord moral significance to the interests of all humans even if the particular theory otherwise rejects rights.[73]

Animals, like humans, have an interest in not suffering, but, as we have seen, the principle of equal consideration has no meaningful application to animal interests if they are the property of others just as it had no meaningful application to the interests of slaves. The interests of animals as property will almost always count for less than do the interests of their owners. Some owners may choose to treat their animals well, or even as members of their families as some do with their pets, but the law will generally not protect animals against their owners. Animal ownership as a legal institution inevitably has the effect of treating animals as commodities. Moreover, animals, like humans, have an interest in not suffering at all from the ways in which we use them, however "humane" that use may be. To the extent that we protect humans from being used in these ways and we do not extend the same protection to animals, we fail to accord equal consideration to animal interests in not suffering.

If we are going to take animal interests seriously, we must extend to animals the one right that we extend to all humans irrespective of their particular characteristics. To do so would not mean that animals would be protected from all suffering. Animals in the wild may be injured, or become diseased, or may be attacked by other animals. But it would mean that animals could no longer be used as the resources of humans and would, therefore, be protected from suffering at all from such uses. Is there a morally sound reason not to extend to animals the right not to be treated as property, and thereby recognize that our obligation not to impose unnecessary suffering on them is really an obligation not to treat them as property? Or, to ask the question in another way, why do we

---

73. *See* Francione, *supra* note 6, at 94, 131–33. *See also supra* note 71; *infra* note 78 and accompanying text.

deem it acceptable to eat animals, hunt them, confine and display them in circuses and zoos, use them in experiments or rodeos, or otherwise to treat them in ways in which we would never think it appropriate to treat any human irrespective of how "humanely" we were to do so?

The usual response claims that some empirical difference between humans and animals constitutes a good reason for not according to animals the one right we accord to all humans. According to this view, there is some qualitative distinction between humans and animals (all species considered as a single group) that purportedly justifies our treating animals as our property. This distinction almost always concerns some difference between human and animal minds; we have some mental characteristic that animals lack, or are capable of certain actions of which animals are incapable as a result of our purportedly superior cognitive abilities. The list of characteristics that are posited as possessed only by humans includes self-consciousness, reason, abstract thought, emotion, the ability to communicate, and the capacity for moral action.[74] We claimed to reject the relevance of these characteristics 200 years ago when we supposedly embraced the idea that the capacity to suffer was the only attribute needed to ground our moral obligation to animals not to impose unnecessary suffering on them. Yet, the absence of these same characteristics continues to serve as our justification for treating animals as our resources and has been used to keep animals "degraded into the class of *things*" despite our claim to take animal interests seriously.

The problem started with Bentham himself.[75] Although Bentham's analysis of slavery is not entirely clear, he arguably opposed human slavery at least in part because the principle of equal consideration would not apply to humans who are slaves. He acknowledged that a particular slave owner might treat a slave well and that some forms of slavery were better than others, but "slavery once established, was always likely to be the lot of large numbers. 'If the evil of slavery were not great its extent alone

---

74. Some claim that the relevant difference between humans and nonhumans is that the former possess souls and the latter do not. For a discussion of this and other purported differences, see Francione, *supra* note 6, at 103-29. *See also supra* note 9 and accompanying text. I do not mean to suggest that everyone after 1800 who has relied on these differences to justify our treatment of animals as resources acknowledges that animals have any morally significant interests; indeed, some accept and defend the status of animals as things morally indistinguishable from inanimate objects. *See, e.g.,* Peter Carruthers, *The Animals Issue: Moral Theory in Practice* (1992).

75. For a discussion of the views of Bentham and his modern proponent, Peter Singer, see Francione, *supra* 6, at 130-50.

would make it considerable.'"[76] Slavery as an institution would inevitably result in humans being treated as things and "abandoned without redress to the caprice of a tormentor."[77] Slaves would necessarily count for less than did those who were not slaves. Bentham regarded the concept of moral rights as metaphysical nonsense, but he did, in effect, recognize that humans had a right not to be treated as property.[78] He noted that just as the color of skin was an insufficient reason to abandon humans to the caprice of a tormentor, "the number of the legs, the villosity of the skin, or the termination of the *os sacrum,* are reasons equally insufficient for abandoning a sensitive being to the same fate[.]"[79] Why, then, did Bentham not reject the treatment of animals as property as he had rejected the treatment of humans as property?

The answer is related to Bentham's view that animals, like humans, have interests in not suffering but, unlike humans, have no interest in their continued existence. That is, Bentham believed that animals do not have a sense of self; they live moment to moment and have no continuous mental existence. Their minds consist of collections of unconnected sensations of pain and pleasure. On this view, death is not a harm for animals; animals do not care about whether we eat them, or use and kill them for other purposes, as long as we do not make them suffer in the process: "If the being eaten were all, there is very good reason why we should be suffered to eat such of them as we like to eat: we are the better for it, and they are never the worse. They have none of those long-protracted anticipations of future misery which we have."[80]

---

76. H. L. A. Hart, *Essays on Bentham* 97 (1982) (quoting Bentham).

77. Bentham, *supra* note 12, at 282–83 n.b. (further note omitted).

78. I recognize that most Bentham scholars regard Bentham's objections to slavery to be based exclusively on the consequences of slavery and claim that Bentham did not think that slavery violated any moral right. It appears, however, that Bentham, who is generally regarded as an act utilitarian, was at the very least a rule utilitarian when it came to slavery; that is, he thought that the consequences of the institution of slavery were necessarily undesirable and, in effect, he recognized that the human interest in not being treated as a resource should be accorded rights-type protection. Moreover, Bentham did talk in terms of moral rights when he discussed human slavery and the treatment of animals, *see id.,* although he was probably referring to the right to equal consideration in that passage. Bentham may well have recognized on some level that a right to equal consideration is inconsistent with the status of being a slave. *See* Francione, *supra* note 6, at 132–33.

79. Bentham, *supra* note 12, at 282–83 n.b.

80. *Id.* Bentham also claimed that "[t]he death [that animals] suffer in our hands commonly is, and always may be, a speedier, and by that means a less painful one, than that which would await them in the inevitable course of nature." *Id.* Bentham ignored the fact that the domestic

Although Bentham explicitly rejected the position that, because animals lack characteristics beyond sentience, such as self-awareness, we could treat them as things, he maintained that because animals lack self-awareness, we do not violate the principle of equal consideration by using animals as our resources as long as we give equal consideration to their interests in not suffering.

Bentham's position is problematic for several reasons. Bentham failed to recognize that although particular animal owners might treat their animal property kindly, institutionalized animal exploitation would, like slavery, become "the lot of large numbers," and animals would necessarily be treated as economic commodities that were, like slaves, "abandoned without redress to the caprice of a tormentor." Moreover, Bentham never explained how to apply the principle of equal consideration to animals who were the property of humans.[81] But most important, Bentham was simply wrong to claim that animals are not self-aware and have no interest in their lives.

---

animals that we raise for food would not have a death "in the inevitable course of nature," because they are only brought into existence as our resources in the first place. It is, therefore, problematic to defend the killing of domestic animals by comparing their deaths with those of wild animals, saying that the infliction of unnecessary pain on domestic animals that we do not need to eat is less than the pain that may necessarily be suffered by wild animals.

81. Peter Singer, who, like Bentham, is a utilitarian and eschews moral rights, adopts Bentham's position and argues that most animals do not have an interest in their lives, but that the principle of equal consideration can nevertheless be applied to their interests in not suffering even if animals are the property of humans. Singer's argument fails in a number of respects. First, Singer requires that we make interspecies comparisons of pain and suffering in order to apply the principle of equal consideration to animal interests. *See* Singer, *supra* note 59, at 15. Such comparisons would, of course, be inherently difficult if not impossible to make. Second, because most humans are self-aware and most animals are not (in Singer's view), it is difficult to understand how animals and humans will ever be considered as similarly situated for purposes of equal consideration. Singer recognizes that because we are unlikely to regard human and animal interests as similar in the first place, we are also unlikely to find any guidance in the principle of equal consideration. *Id.* at 16. That is, however, tantamount to admitting that animal interests are not morally significant because the principle of equal consideration will never have any meaningful application to animal interests. Singer avoids this conclusion by claiming that even if the principle of equal consideration is inapplicable, it is still clear that much animal suffering is not morally justifiable. He states, for example, that we need not apply the principle of equal consideration in order to conclude that the positive consequences for animals of abolishing intensive agriculture would be greater than any detrimental consequences for humans. It remains unclear how Singer can arrive at this conclusion other than through mere stipulation. The abolition of intensive agriculture would have a profound impact on the international economy and would cause an enormous rise in the price of meat and animal products. If the issue hinges only on consequences, it is not at all clear that the consequences for self-aware humans would not be weightier than the consequences for non-self-aware animals. Third, even if Singer's

Sentience is not an end in itself. It is a means to the end of staying alive. Sentient beings use sensations of pain and suffering to escape situations that threaten their lives and sensations of pleasure to pursue situations that enhance their lives. Just as humans will often endure excruciating pain in order to remain alive, animals will often not only endure but inflict on themselves excruciating pain—as when gnawing off a paw caught in a trap—in order to live. Sentience is what evolution has produced in order to ensure the survival of certain complex organisms. To claim that a being who has evolved to develop a consciousness of pain and pleasure has no interest in remaining alive is to say that conscious beings have no interest in remaining conscious, a most peculiar position to take.

Moreover, the proposition that humans have mental characteristics wholly absent in animals is inconsistent with the theory of evolution. Darwin maintained that there are no uniquely human characteristics: "[T]he difference in mind between man and the higher animals, great as it is, is certainly one of degree and not of kind."[82] Animals are able to think, and possess many of the same emotional responses as do humans: "[T]he senses and intuitions, the various emotions and faculties, such as love, memory, attention, curiosity, imitation, reason, &c., of which man boasts, may be found in an incipient, or even sometimes in a well-developed condition, in the lower animals."[83] Darwin noted that "associated animals have a feeling of love for each other" and that animals "certainly sympathise with each other's distress or danger."[84]

Even if we cannot know the precise nature of animal self-awareness, it appears that *any* being that is aware on a perceptual level must be self-aware and have a continuous mental existence. Biologist Donald Griffin

---

theory would lead to more "humane" animal treatment, it would still permit us to use animals as resources in ways that we do not use any humans. Singer's response to this would be that he would be willing to use similarly situated humans, such as the mentally or physically disabled, as replaceable resources. *Id.; see also* Peter Singer, *Practical Ethics* 186 (2d ed. 1993). For the reasons discussed below, most of us would reject Singer's views on the use of vulnerable humans. *See infra* notes 95–97 and accompanying text. For a discussion of Singer's views, see Francione, *supra* note 6, at 135–48; Francione, *Rain Without Thunder, supra* note 56, at 156–60, 173–76.

82. Charles Darwin, *The Descent of Man, and Selection in Relation to Sex* 105 (Princeton Univ. Press 1981) (1871). *See* James Rachels, *Created From Animals: The Moral Implications of Darwinism* (1990).

83. Darwin, *supra* note 82, at 105.

84. *Id.* at 76, 77.

has observed that if animals are conscious of anything, "the animal's own body and its own actions must fall within the scope of its perceptual consciousness."[85] Yet we deny animals self-awareness because we maintain that they cannot "think such thoughts as 'It is *I* who am running, or climbing this tree, or chasing that moth.'"[86] Griffin maintains that "when an animal consciously perceives the running, climbing, or moth-chasing of another animal, it must also be aware of who is doing these things. And if the animal is perceptually conscious of its own body, it is difficult to rule out similar recognition that it, itself, is doing the running, climbing, or chasing."[87] Griffin concludes that "[i]f animals are capable of perceptual awareness, denying them some level of self-awareness would seem to be an arbitrary and unjustified restriction."[88] Griffin's reasoning can be applied in the context of sentience. Any sentient being must have some level of self-awareness. To be sentient means to be the sort of being who recognizes that it is *that* being, and not some other, who is experiencing pain or distress. When a dog experiences pain, the dog necessarily has a mental experience that tells her "this pain is happening to me." In order for pain to exist, some consciousness—some*one*—must perceive it as happening to her and must prefer not to experience it.

Antonio Damasio, a neurologist who works with humans who have suffered strokes, seizures, and conditions that cause brain damage, maintains that such humans have what he calls "core consciousness." Core consciousness, which does not depend on memory, language, or reasoning, "provides the organism with a sense of self about one moment—now—and about one place—here."[89] Humans who experience transient global amnesia, for example, have no sense of the past or the future but do have a sense of self with respect to present events and objects, and such humans would most certainly regard death as a harm. Damasio maintains that many animal species possess core consciousness. He distinguishes core consciousness from what he calls "extended consciousness," which requires reasoning and memory, but not language, and in-

85. Donald R. Griffin, *Animal Minds: Beyond Cognition to Consciousness* 274 (2001).
86. *Id.*
87. *Id.*
88. *Id.*
89. Antonio R. Damasio, *The Feeling of What Happens: Body and Emotion in the Making of Consciousness* 16 (1999).

volves enriching one's sense of self with autobiographical details and what we might consider a representational sense of consciousness. Extended consciousness, "of which there are many levels and grades," involves a self with memories of the past, anticipations of the future, and awareness of the present.[90] Although Damasio argues that extended consciousness reaches its most complex level in humans, who have language and sophisticated reasoning abilities, he maintains that chimpanzees, bonobos, baboons, and even dogs may have an autobiographical sense of self.[91] Even if most animals do not have extended consciousness, most of the animals we routinely exploit undoubtedly have at least core consciousness, which means that they are self-conscious. In short, the fact that animals may not have an autobiographical sense of their lives (or one that they can communicate to us) does not mean that they do not have a continuous mental existence, or that they do not have an interest in their lives, or that killing them makes no difference to them.

Cognitive ethologists and others have confirmed that animals, including mammals, birds, and even fish, have many of the cognitive characteristics once thought to be uniquely human.[92] Animals possess considerable intelligence and are able to process information in sophisticated and complex ways. They are able to communicate with other members of their own species as well as with humans; indeed, there is considerable evidence that nonhuman great apes can communicate using symbolic language. The similarities between humans and animals are not limited to cognitive or emotional attributes alone. Some argue that animals exhibit what is clearly moral behavior as well. For example, Frans de Waal states that "honesty, guilt, and the weighing of ethical dilemmas are traceable to specific areas of the brain. It should not surprise us, therefore, to find animal parallels. The human brain is a product of evolution. Despite its larger volume and greater complexity, it is fundamentally similar to the central nervous system of other mammals."[93] There

---

90. *Id.*
91. *See id.* at 198, 201.
92. *See, e.g.,* Griffin, *supra* note 85; Marc D. Hauser, *The Evolution of Communication* (1996); Marc D. Hauser, *Wild Minds: What Animals Really Think* (2000); *Readings in Animal Cognition* (Marc Bekoff & Dale Jamieson eds., 1996); Sue Savage-Rumbaugh & Roger Lewin, *Kanzi: The Ape at the Brink of the Human Mind* (1994).
93. Frans de Waal, *Good-Natured: The Origins of Right and Wrong in Humans and Other Animals* 218 (1996).

are numerous instances in which animals have acted in altruistic ways toward unrelated members of their own species and toward other species, including humans.

Although it is clear that animals other than humans possess characteristics purported to be unique to humans, it is also clear that there are differences between humans and other animals. For example, even if animals are self-aware on some level, that does not mean that animals can recognize themselves in mirrors (although some nonhuman primates do) or keep diaries or anticipate the future by looking at clocks and calendars; even if animals have the ability to reason or think abstractly, that does not mean that they can do calculus or compose symphonies. Yet for at least two related reasons, the humanlike varieties of these characteristics cannot serve to provide a morally sound, nonarbitrary basis for denying the right not to be treated as property to animals who may lack these characteristics.[94]

First, any attempt to justify treating animals as resources based on their lack of supposed uniquely human characteristics begs the question from the outset by assuming that certain human characteristics are special and justify differential treatment. Even if, for instance, no animals other than humans can recognize themselves in mirrors or can communicate through symbolic language, no human is capable of flying, or breathing

---

94. There are problems in relying on similarities between humans and animals beyond sentience to justify the moral significance of animals. *See* Francione, *supra* note 6, at 116–19. For example, a focus on similarities beyond sentience threatens to create new hierarchies in which we move some animals, such as the great apes or dolphins, into a preferred group, and continue to treat other animals as our resources. There has for some years been an international effort to secure certain rights for the nonhuman great apes. This project was started by the publication of a book entitled *The Great Ape Project: Equality Beyond Humanity* (Paola Cavalieri & Peter Singer eds., 1993), which seeks "the extension of the community of equals to include all great apes: human beings, chimpanzees, gorillas and orang-utans." *Id.* at 4. I was a contributor to *The Great Ape Project. See* Gary L. Francione, "Personhood, Property, and Legal Competence," *in id.* at 248–57. The danger of *The Great Ape Project* is that it reinforces the notion that characteristics beyond sentience are necessary and not merely sufficient for equal treatment. In my essay in *The Great Ape Project,* I tried to avoid this problem by arguing that although the considerable cognitive and other similarities between the human and nonhuman great apes are sufficient to accord the latter equal protection under the law, these similarities are not necessary for animals to have a right not to be treated as resources. *See id.* at 253. *See also* Lee Hall & Anthony Jon Waters, "From Property to Person: The Case of Evelyn Hart," 11 *Seton Hall Const. L.J.* 1 (2000). For an approach that argues that characteristics beyond sentience are necessary and not merely sufficient for preferred animals to have a right not to be treated as resources in at least some respects, see Steven M. Wise, *Drawing the Line: Science and the Case for Animal Rights* (2002), and Steven M. Wise, *Rattling the Cage: Toward Legal Rights for Animals* (2000).

underwater, without assistance. What makes the ability to recognize oneself in a mirror or use symbolic language better in a moral sense than the ability to fly or breathe underwater? The answer, of course, is that *we* say so. But apart from our proclamation, there is simply no reason to conclude that characteristics thought to be uniquely human have any value that allows us to use them as a nonarbitrary justification for treating animals as property. These characteristics can serve this role only after we have assumed their moral relevance.

Second, even if all animals other than humans lack a particular characteristic beyond sentience, or possess it to a different degree than do humans, there is no logically defensible relationship between the lack or lesser degree of that characteristic and our treatment of animals as resources. Differences between humans and other animals may be relevant for other purposes—no sensible person argues that we ought to enable nonhuman animals to drive cars or vote or attend universities—but the differences have no bearing on whether animals should have the status of property. We recognize this inescapable conclusion where humans are involved. Whatever characteristic we identify as uniquely human will be seen to a lesser degree in some humans and not at all in others.[95] Some humans will have the exact same deficiency that we attribute to animals, and although the deficiency may be relevant for some purposes, most of us would reject enslaving such humans, or otherwise treating such humans exclusively as means to the ends of others.

Consider, for instance, self-consciousness. Peter Carruthers defines self-consciousness as the ability to have a "conscious experience . . . whose existence and content are available to be consciously thought about (that is, available for description in acts of thinking that are themselves made available to further acts of thinking)."[96] According to

---

95. Some argue that although certain humans may lack a particular characteristic, the fact that all humans have the potential to possess the characteristic means that a human who actually lacks it is for purposes of equal consideration distinguishable from an animal who may also lack it. *See, e.g.,* Carl Cohen, "The Case for the Use of Animals in Biomedical Research," 315 *New Eng. J. Med.* 865 (1986). This argument begs the question because it assumes that some humans have a characteristic that they lack and thereby ignores the factual similarity between animals and humans who lack the characteristic. Moreover, in some instances, animals may possess the characteristic to a greater degree than do some humans.

96. Carruthers, *supra* note 74, at 181. Peter Singer also requires this sort of self-consciousness before animals or humans can be considered to have an interest in their lives. *See* Singer, *supra* note 59, at 228–29. *See also supra* note 81.

Carruthers, humans must have what Damasio refers to as the most complex level of extended consciousness, or a language-enriched autobiographical sense of self, in order to be self-conscious. But many humans, such as the severely mentally disabled, do not have self-consciousness in that sense; we do not, however, regard it as permissible to use them as we do laboratory animals, or to enslave them to labor for those without their particular disability. Nor should we. We recognize that a mentally disabled human has an interest in her life and in not being treated exclusively as a means to the ends of others even if she does not have the same level of self-consciousness that is possessed by normal adults; in this sense, she is similarly situated to all other sentient humans, who have an interest in being treated as ends in themselves irrespective of their particular characteristics. Indeed, to say that a mentally disabled person is not similarly situated to all others for purposes of being treated exclusively as a resource is to say that a less intelligent person is not similarly situated to a more intelligent person for purposes of being used, for instance, as a forced organ donor. The fact that the mentally disabled human may not have a particular sort of self-consciousness may serve as a nonarbitrary reason for treating her differently in some respects—it may be relevant to whether we make her the host of a talk show, or give her a job teaching in a university, or allow her to drive a car—but it has no relevance to whether we treat her exclusively as a resource and disregard her fundamental interests, including her interest in not suffering and in her continued existence, if it benefits us to do so.

The same analysis applies to every human characteristic beyond sentience that is offered to justify treating animals as resources. There will be some humans who also lack this characteristic, or possess it to a lesser degree than do normal humans. This "defect" may be relevant for some purposes, but not for whether we treat humans exclusively as resources. We do not treat as things those humans who lack characteristics beyond sentience simply out of some sense of charity. We realize that to do so would violate the principle of equal consideration by using an arbitrary reason to deny similar treatment to similar interests in not being treated exclusively as a means to the ends of others.[97] "[T]he question is not, Can they *reason*? nor, Can they *talk*? but, Can they *suffer*?"

---

97. In this sense, the equality of all humans is predicated on factual similarities shared by all humans irrespective of their particular characteristics beyond sentience. All humans have an

In sum, there is no characteristic that serves to distinguish humans from all other animals for purposes of denying to animals the one right that we extend to all humans. Whatever attribute we may think makes all humans special and thereby deserving of the right not to be the property of others is shared by nonhumans. More important, even if there are uniquely human characteristics, some humans will not possess those characteristics, but we would never think of using such humans as resources. In the end, the only difference between humans and animals is species, and species is not a justification for treating animals as property any more than is race a justification for human slavery.

ANIMALS AS PERSONS

If we extend the right not to be property to animals, then animals will become moral persons. To say that a being is a person is merely to say that the being has morally significant interests, that the principle of equal consideration applies to that being, that the being is not a thing. In a sense, we already accept that animals are persons; we claim to reject the view that animals are things and to recognize that, at the very least, animals have a morally significant interest in not suffering. Their status as property, however, has prevented their personhood from being realized.

The same was true of human slavery. Slaves were regarded as chattel property. Laws that provided for the "humane" treatment of slaves did not make slaves persons because, as we have seen, the principle of equal consideration could not apply to slaves. We tried, through slave welfare laws, to have a three-tiered system: things, or inanimate property; persons, who were free; and in the middle, depending on your choice of locution, "quasi-persons" or "things plus"(the slaves). That system could not work. We eventually recognized that if slaves were going to have morally significant interests, they could not be slaves any more, for the moral universe is limited to only two kinds of beings: persons and things. "Quasi-persons" or "things plus" will necessarily risk being

---

interest in not being treated exclusively as means to the ends of others. All humans value themselves even if no one else values them. *See* Francione, *supra* note 6, at 128, 135, n.18. Moreover, justice (not charity) may require that we be especially conscientious about protecting humans who lack certain characteristics precisely because of their vulnerability.

treated as things because the principle of equal consideration cannot apply to them.

Nor can we use animal welfare laws to render animals "quasi-persons" or "things plus." They are either persons, beings to whom the principle of equal consideration applies and who possess morally significant interests in not suffering, or things, beings to whom the principle of equal consideration does not apply and whose interests may be ignored if it benefits us. There is no third choice. We could, of course, treat animals better than we do; there are, however, powerful economic forces that militate against better treatment in light of the status of animals as property. But simply according better treatment to animals would not mean that they were no longer things. It may have been better to beat slaves three rather than five times a week, but this better treatment would not have removed slaves from the category of things. The similar interests of slave owners and slaves were not accorded similar treatment because the former had a right not to suffer at all from being used exclusively as a resource, and the latter did not possess such a right. Animals, like humans, have an interest in not suffering at all from the ways in which we use them, however "humane" that use may be. To the extent that we protect humans from suffering from these uses and we do not extend the same protection to animals, we fail to accord equal consideration to animal interests in not suffering.

If animals are persons, that does not mean that they are human persons; it does not mean that we must treat animals in the same way that we treat humans or that we must extend to animals any of the legal rights that we reserve to competent humans. Nor does this mean that animals have any sort of guarantee of a life free from suffering, or that we must protect animals from harm from other animals in the wild or from accidental injury by humans. As I argue below, it does not necessarily preclude our choosing human interests over animal interests in situations of genuine conflict. But it does require that we accept that we have a moral obligation to stop using animals for food, biomedical experiments, entertainment, or clothing, or any other uses that assume that animals are merely resources, and that we prohibit the ownership of animals. The abolition of animal slavery is required by any moral theory that purports to treat animal interests as morally significant, even if the particular theory otherwise rejects rights, just as the abolition of human slavery is required by any theory that purports to treat human interests as morally significant.[98]

FALSE CONFLICTS

The question of the moral status of animals addresses the matter of how we ought to treat animals in situations of conflict between human and animal interests. For the most part, our conflicts with animals are those that we create. We bring billions of sentient animals into existence for the sole purpose of killing them. We then seek to understand the nature of our moral obligations to these animals. Yet by bringing animals into existence for uses that we would never consider appropriate for any humans, we have already placed nonhuman animals outside the scope of our moral community altogether. Despite what we say about taking animals seriously, we have already decided that the principle of equal consideration does not apply to animals and that animals are things that have no morally significant interests.

Because animals are property, we treat every issue concerning their use or treatment as though it presented a genuine conflict of interests, and invariably we choose the human interest over the animal interest even when animal suffering can be justified only by human convenience, amusement, or pleasure. In the overwhelming number of instances in which we evaluate our moral obligations to animals, however, there is no true conflict. When we contemplate whether to eat a hamburger, buy a

---

98. *See supra* notes 73, 78 and accompanying text; Francione, *supra* note 6, at 148. The theory presented in this essay is different in significant respects from that of Tom Regan. *See* Tom Regan, *The Case for Animal Rights* (1983). Regan argues that animals have rights and that animal exploitation ought to be abolished and not merely regulated, but he limits protection to those animals who have preference autonomy, and he thereby omits from the class of rights holders those animals who are sentient but who do not have preference autonomy. The theory discussed in this essay applies to any sentient being. Regan uses the concept of basic rights and although he does not discuss the status of animals as property or the basic right not to be property, he maintains that some animals should be accorded the right not to be treated exclusively as means to human ends. Moreover, Regan does not acknowledge that this basic right can be derived solely from applying the principle of equal consideration to animal interests in not suffering, nor that the right must be part of any theory that purports to accord moral significance to animal interests even if that theory otherwise rejects rights. For a further discussion of the differences between my theory and that of Regan, see Francione, *supra* note 6, at xxxii–xxxiv, 94 n.25, 127–28 n.61, 148 n.36, 174 n.1.

fur coat, or attend a rodeo, we do not confront any sort of conflict worthy of serious moral consideration. If we take animal interests seriously, we must desist from manufacturing such conflicts, which can only be constructed in the first place by ignoring the principle of equal consideration and by making an arbitrary decision to use animals in ways in which we rightly decline to use any human.

Does the use of animals in experiments involve a genuine conflict between human and animal interests? Even if a need for animals in research exists, the conflict between humans and animals in this context is no more genuine than a conflict between humans suffering from a disease and other humans we might use in experiments to find a cure for that disease. Data gained from experiments with animals require extrapolation to humans in order to be useful at all, and extrapolation is an inexact science under the best of circumstances. If we want data that will be useful in finding cures for human diseases, we would be better advised to use humans. We do not allow humans to be used as we do laboratory animals, and we do not think that there is any sort of conflict between those who are afflicted or who may become afflicted with a disease and those humans whose use might help find a cure for that disease. We regard all humans as part of the moral community, and although we may not treat all humans in the same way, we recognize that membership in the moral community precludes such use of humans. Animals have no characteristic that justifies our use of them in experiments that is not shared by some group of humans; because we regard some animals as laboratory tools yet think it inappropriate to treat any humans in this way, we manufacture a conflict, ignoring the principle of equal consideration and treating similar cases in a dissimilar way.

There may, of course, be situations in which we are confronted with a true emergency, such as the burning house that contains an animal and a human, where we have time to save only one. Such emergency situations require what are, in the end, decisions that are arbitrary and not amenable to satisfying general principles of conduct. Yet even if we would always choose to save the human over the animal in such situations, it does not follow that animals are merely resources that we may use for our purposes.[99] We would draw no such conclusion when mak-

---

99. A common argument made against the animal rights position is that it is acceptable to treat animals as things because we are justified in choosing humans over animals in situations of

ing a choice between two humans. Imagine that two humans are in the burning house. One is a young child; the other is an old adult, who, barring the present conflagration, will soon die of natural causes anyway. If we decide to save the child for the simple reason that she has not yet lived her life, we would not conclude that it is morally acceptable to enslave old people, or to use them for target practice. Similarly, assume that a wild animal is just about to attack a friend. Our choice to kill the animal in order to save the friend's life does not mean that it is morally acceptable to kill animals for food, any more than our moral justification in killing a deranged human about to kill our friend would serve to justify our using deranged humans as forced organ donors.

In sum, if we take animal interests seriously, we are not obliged to regard animals as the same as humans for all purposes any more than we regard all humans as being the same for all purposes; nor do we have to accord to animals all or most of the rights that we accord to humans. We may still choose the human over the animal in cases of genuine conflict—when it is truly necessary to do so—but that does not mean that we are justified in treating animals as resources for human use.[100] And if the treatment of animals as resources cannot be justified, then we should abolish the institutionalized exploitation of animals. We should care for domestic animals presently alive, but we should bring no more into existence. The abolition of animal exploitation could not, as a realistic matter, be imposed legally unless and until a significant portion of us took animal interests seriously. Our moral compass will not find animals while they are lying on our plates. In other words, we have to put our vegetables where our mouths are and start acting on the moral principles that we profess to accept.

If we stopped treating animals as resources, the only remaining human-animal conflicts would involve animals in the wild. Deer may nibble our ornamental shrubs; rabbits may eat the vegetables we grow. The occasional wild animal may attack us. In such situations, we should, despite the difficulty inherent in making interspecies comparisons, try our best to apply the principle of equal consideration and to treat similar

conflict. *See, e.g.,* Richard A. Posner, "Animal Rights," Slate, June 12, 2001, http://slate.msn.com/id/110101/entry/110129/ (last visited Dec. 1, 2003).

100. The choice of humans over animals in situations of genuine emergency or conflict does not necessarily represent speciesism because there are many reasons other than species bias that can account for the choice. *See* Francione, *supra* note 6, at 159–62.

interests in a similar way. This will generally require at the very least a good-faith effort to avoid the intentional killing of animals to resolve these conflicts, where lethal means would be prohibited if the conflicts involved only humans. I am, however, not suggesting that the recognition that animal interests have moral significance requires that a motorist who unintentionally strikes an animal be prosecuted for an animal equivalent of manslaughter. Nor do I suggest that we should recognize a cause of action allowing a cow to sue the farmer. The interesting question is why we have the cow here in the first instance.

CHAPTER 2 / REFLECTIONS ON
ANIMALS, PROPERTY, AND THE LAW
AND *RAIN WITHOUT THUNDER*

I

INTRODUCTION

In my 1995 book, *Animals, Property, and the Law*, I argue that animal-welfare laws do not provide any significant protection to nonhuman animals because nonhumans are the property of humans.[1] Animals are *things* that we own and that have only extrinsic or conditional value as means to our ends. We may as a matter of personal choice attach a higher value to our companion animals, such as dogs and cats, but as far as the law is concerned, even these animals are nothing more than commodities. As a general matter, we do not regard animals as having any intrinsic value and we protect animal interests only to the extent that it benefits us to do so.

We claim to take animal interests seriously from both a moral and legal perspective, which is why we have anticruelty and other animal-welfare

The essay was published originally in *Law and Contemporary Problems,* vol. 7, pp. 9–57 (Winter 2007).

Copyright © 2007 by Gary L. Francione. I would like to thank Anna E. Charlton not only for her comments on this article but for her assistance over the years helping me to develop my thoughts on the human–nonhuman relationship. I am also grateful to Professor William Reppy, who served as the editor for this essay, and to Darian Ibrahim and the other participants at the Animal Law Conference at Duke University School of Law, April 7, 2006, for comments. Many thanks to Kelly Smith, Sr. Production Assistant at Duke Law School, for her assistance with the preparation of the manuscript. I acknowledge research assistance from Suzanna Polhamus and support from the Dean's Research Fund of the Rutgers University School of Law—Newark.
1. GARY L. FRANCIONE, ANIMALS, PROPERTY, AND THE LAW (1995). Throughout this article, I use "nonhuman" and "animal" interchangeably, but it should not be forgotten that humans are

laws in the first place. We purport to balance human and animal interests, but because animals are property, there can be no meaningful balance. Animal interests will almost always be regarded as less important than human interests, even when the human interest at stake is relatively trivial and the animal interest at stake is significant. The result of any supposed balancing of human and nonhuman interests required by animal-welfare laws is predetermined from the outset by the property status of the nonhuman as a "food animal," "experimental animal," "game animal," et cetera.

Although we supposedly prohibit the infliction on animals of "unnecessary" suffering, we do not ask whether particular animal uses are necessary even though most of the suffering that we impose on animals cannot be characterized as necessary in any meaningful sense.[2] Rather, we ask only whether particular treatment is necessary given uses that are per se not necessary. We look to the customs and practices of the various institutions of exploitation and we assume that those involved in the activity would not inflict more pain and suffering than required for the particular purpose because it would be irrational to do so, just as it would be for the owner of a car to dent her vehicle for no reason.

For example, although it is not necessary for humans to eat meat or dairy products and these foods may well be detrimental to human health and the environment, we do not ask about the necessity per se of using animals for food. We ask only whether the pain and suffering imposed on animals used for food go beyond what is regarded as acceptable according to the customs and practices of animal agriculture. To the extent

---

animals as well. In addition, I use "animal who" rather than "animal that" to emphasize that nonhumans are not objects, as implied by our reference to them as "it."

2. For a discussion of the necessity of animal use, see GARY L. FRANCIONE, INTRODUCTION TO ANIMAL RIGHTS: YOUR CHILD OR THE DOG? 1–49 (2000). Courts have explicitly recognized that prohibitions against "unnecessary" suffering or "needless" killing must be interpreted by reference to institutional uses that are per se not necessary:

> The flesh of animals is not necessary for the subsistence of man, at least in this country, and by some people it is not so used. Yet it would not be denied that the killing of oxen for food is lawful. Fish are not necessary to any one, nor are various wild animals which are killed, and sold in market; yet their capture and killing are regulated by law. The words "needlessly" and "unnecessarily" must have a reasonable, not an absolute and literal, meaning attached to them.

State v. Bogardus, 4 Mo. App. 215, 216–17 (1877). Courts have also recognized that practices that are regarded as "cruel" as we normally use that term in ordinary discourse are permitted within the meaning of anticruelty laws. See FRANCIONE, *supra* note 1, at 146; FRANCIONE, *supra* note 2, at 58–63; *see also infra* notes 174–78 and accompanying text (discussing anticruelty laws).

it is customary for farmers to castrate or brand farm animals, both very painful activities, we regard such actions as "necessary" because we assume that farmers would not mutilate animals for no reason.

The result of this framework is that the level of care required by animal-welfare laws rarely rises above that which a rational property owner would provide in order to exploit the animal in an economically efficient way. Because animals are property, we consider as "humane" treatment that we would regard as torture if it were inflicted on humans.

In my 1996 book, *Rain Without Thunder: The Ideology of the Animal Rights Movement,*[3] I argue that there are important theoretical and practical differences between the animal-rights and animal-welfare positions and that welfarist regulation intended to make animal treatment more "humane" will, for the most part, do nothing but make animal exploitation more efficient. Welfarist regulation, I maintain, does not recognize or protect the inherent value of animals and will not lead in some incremental way to the abolition of animal exploitation. For example, the federal Humane Slaughter Act,[4] which supposedly requires the "humane" slaughter of nonhumans for food purposes, prohibits suffering only to the extent that it ensures worker safety, reduces carcass damage, and provides other economic benefits for humans.[5] It would, however, be an absurd use of the word to characterize any slaughterhouse as "humane."

To the extent that animal advocates seek protection for animals that exceeds what is necessary to exploit them for a particular purpose, the

---

3. *See* GARY L. FRANCIONE, RAIN WITHOUT THUNDER: THE IDEOLOGY OF THE ANIMAL RIGHTS MOVEMENT (1996).

4. Humane Methods of Slaughter Act of 1958, Pub. L. No. 85-765, 72 Stat. 862 (codified at 7 U.S.C. §§ 1901-1907 (2000)). Usually referred to as the "Humane Slaughter Act," the Act originally applied to animals slaughtered for sale to the federal government, but was reauthorized in 1978 and covers animals slaughtered in federally inspected plants. For a discussion of the considerations that motivated the Humane Slaughter Act, *see* FRANCIONE, *supra* note 3, at 95-102. *See also infra* notes 107-09 and accompanying text (discussing failure to enforce the Humane Slaughter Act).

5. *See* FRANCIONE, *supra* note 3, at 95-102. The "[f]indings and declarations of policy" of the Humane Slaughter Act make clear the importance of economic considerations in assessing matters of animal welfare:

> The Congress finds that the use of humane methods in the slaughter of livestock prevents needless suffering; results in safer and better working conditions for persons engaged in the slaughtering industry; brings about improvement of products and economies in slaughtering operations; and produces other benefits for producers, processors, and consumers which tend to expedite an orderly flow of livestock and livestock products in interstate and foreign commerce.

7 U.S.C. § 1901 (2000).

property status of nonhumans and the political compromise that is re-quired invariably result in regulations that do little—if anything—to affect adversely the interests of human property owners or to improve the treatment of nonhumans. The primary effect of these measures is to make the public feel better about animal exploitation, which actu-ally may result in a net increase of animal suffering through increased use. A central thesis of *Rain Without Thunder,* as well as my later work,[6] is that, if animal interests are to be morally significant, we must accord to nonhumans the basic right not to be treated as property, and this re-quires that we seek to abolish, and not merely to regulate, institutional-ized animal exploitation.

A number of my critics have argued that, although we do treat ani-mals badly, there is nothing inherent in the property status of animals that would prevent us from changing the law to require that animals be accorded better treatment and so animal advocates ought to pursue in-cremental improvements in animal welfare.[7] Although I maintain that we cannot justify the property status of nonhumans irrespective of how "humanely" we may treat them—just as we cannot justify human slavery even if it is "humane"—I certainly agree that we could treat animals bet-ter than we do and stated so explicitly in *Animals, Property, and the Law.*[8] The status of nonhumans as property, however, militates strongly against

---

6. *See generally* FRANCIONE, *supra* note 2; Gary L. Francione, *Animals—Property or Persons?*, *in* AN-IMAL RIGHTS: CURRENT DEBATES AND NEW DIRECTIONS 108 (Cass R. Sunstein & Martha C. Nussbaum eds., 2004).

7. *See, e.g.,* ROBERT GARNER, ANIMALS, POLITICS AND MORALITY (2d ed. 2004); MIKE RADFORD, ANIMAL WELFARE LAW IN BRITAIN: REGULATION AND RESPONSIBILITY 102–04, 394–95 (2001); David Favre, *Integrating Animal Interests into Our Legal System,* 10 ANIMAL L. 87 (2004); Robert Garner, *Political Ideology and the Legal Status of Animals,* 8 ANIMAL L. 77 (2002); Jerrold Tannen-baum, *Animals and the Law: Property, Cruelty, Rights,* 62 SOC. RES. 539 (1995); Cass R. Sunstein, *Slaughterhouse Jive,* NEW REPUBLIC, Jan. 29, 2001, at 40 (reviewing GARY L. FRANCIONE, INTRO-DUCTION TO ANIMAL RIGHTS: YOUR CHILD OR THE DOG? (2000)); Steven M. Wise, *Thunder Without Rain: A Review/Commentary of Gary L. Francione's Rain Without Thunder: The Ideology of the Animal Rights Movement,* 3 ANIMAL L. 45 (1997).

8. In the Introduction to *Animals, Property, and the Law,* I state:

I do not maintain that characterizing sentient beings as property *necessarily* means that those beings will be treated exactly the same as inanimate objects or that property can never have rights as a matter of formal jurisprudential theory. For example, although slaves were, for some purposes, considered "persons" who technically held certain rights, those rights were not particularly effective in providing any real protection for slaves. We *could* decide to grant certain rights to animals while continuing to regard them as property. The problem is that as long as property is, as a matter of legal theory, regarded as that which cannot have interests or

significant improvement in our treatment of animals, and animal welfare will do little more than make animal exploitation more economically efficient and socially acceptable.

There can be no doubt that the animal-protection community in the United States—and, indeed, throughout the world—has in the years since I wrote these books achieved a greater degree of economic power and social prominence than at any point in history. Therefore, if my critics are correct, and the property status of nonhumans is not as significant an obstacle as I have claimed, it would seem that there should be some evidence of progress that does not fit the model that I have described. That is, there should be evidence of animal protection that goes beyond what is required for efficient exploitation, reflecting at least a nascent recognition of the inherent value of animals as opposed to their exclusively extrinsic value as property. Instead, the events of the past decade or so reinforce the view that the property status of nonhumans is a greater obstacle than my critics and the animal-protection movement have recognized or appreciated.

Part II of this article examines whether animal welfare in the United States has moved us closer to recognizing the inherent value of nonhumans and concludes that it has not. This is not a complete survey of federal and state law or of changes that have occurred through the voluntary action of animal users; rather, it focuses on those developments that animal advocates appear to regard as most significant. Part III discusses some general reasons why the property paradigm militates against better treatment of nonhumans. These remarks are made primarily in the context of responding to criticisms of my views made by Cass Sunstein.[9] Part IV discusses the false dichotomy promoted by my critics that we must either pursue traditional welfarist regulation or sacrifice nonhumans to the "utopian" goal of abolition that will not be achieved for many years, if ever. Part V offers some observations on the field of "animal law" as it has emerged in the past decade. Part VI addresses the view advanced by some in the legal community that we

---

cannot have interests that transcend the rights of property owners to use their property, then there will probably always be a gap between what the law permits people to do with animals and what any acceptable moral theory and basic decency tell us is appropriate.

FRANCIONE, *supra* note 1, at 14.

9. *See* Sunstein, *supra* note 7.

ought to treat certain animals, such as great apes, in a different manner based on their cognitive similarities to humans.

II

THE FAILURE OF ANIMAL WELFARE

In the years since I first proposed the thesis about the property status of animals, and despite claims by my critics that the property paradigm is consistent with recognizing the inherent value of animal interests, there have been no significant improvements in animal welfare or animal-welfare laws in the United States,[10] and almost all changes have

---

10. Peter Singer claims as one of the general "successes" of the animal-rights movement that the numbers of animals used in experiments in Britain has fallen to less than half of what it was in 1970. Peter Singer, *Animal Liberation at 30,* N.Y. REV. BOOKS, May 15, 2003, at 25. Singer does not mention, however, that the number of animals used in Britain has increased in recent years. For example, in 2003, there were 2.8 million experiments involving animals in Britain, which was the largest number since 1994 and followed an increase of four percent from the previous year. Moreover, there have been significant increases in experiments involving physical trauma, psychological trauma, thermal injury, and aversive training. *See* BRITISH UNION FOR THE ABO-LITION OF VIVISECTION, UK ANIMAL EXPERIMENTS STATISTICS 2003, *available at* http://www .buav.org/pdf/Stats2003.pdf (discussing report by the Home Office of the United Kingdom).

Robert Garner states that "[i]n many European countries . . . factory farming is much nearer to being phased out by state action" than it is in the United States. Garner, *supra* note 7, at 90. Garner's statement is certainly not accurate in that intensive agriculture is still very much the norm in Europe. In any event, there cannot be any real doubt that nonhumans in Europe are, despite any differences, still treated very badly. Moreover, there have been difficulties with domestic legislation to implement certain E.U. animal-welfare measures and the effect of free-trade agreements and other globalization efforts on domestic animal-welfare measures, many of which do not take effect until after 2010, remains to be seen. As a general matter, whenever human interests are implicated, nonhuman interests are ignored. For example, fear over the H5N1 virus, which is commonly called the "bird flu," has resulted in producers of free-range chickens returning to more intensive methods. *See, e.g.,* Brian Brady and Richard Gray, *Jabs for Poultry Workers as Bird Flu Fears Grow,* SCOTLAND ON SUNDAY, Feb. 26, 2006, at 11. Finally, European animal-welfare measures are often based on consideration of economic efficiency and have nothing to do with recognizing the inherent value of nonhumans.

Another comparative example offered frequently involves the fact that some nations, such as Britain, Sweden, and New Zealand, have laws or policies that afford more protection to great apes based on their similarity to humans. For the most part, there had been very little use of great apes in those countries, and restrictions were both easier to enact and less meaningful. Differential treatment of great apes also serves to reinforce speciesist hierarchies rather than to erode them. *See infra* notes 181–86 and accompanying text (discussing "similar-minds" theory).

been linked explicitly to making animal use more efficient. That is, welfare changes are based on such considerations as increasing productivity or reducing labor costs and do not recognize that animals have inherent value requiring that we respect their interests even when there is no benefit to us. These developments serve to confirm my views about animals as property and of the generally ineffective and often counterproductive nature of alleged advances in animal welfare. This part discusses several examples of the "victories" proclaimed by animal advocates during this time.

A. Farm Animals and Industry Self-Regulation: A "[R]ay of [H]ope"?

Peter Singer, author of *Animal Liberation*[11] and a defender of animal-welfare regulation, cites as an example of a "successful American campaign[ ]" efforts by animal advocates and organizations, such as People for the Ethical Treatment of Animals (PETA), that led to agreement by McDonald's to "set and enforce higher standards for the slaughterhouses that supply it with meat" and to provide increased space to hens confined in egg batteries.[12] Singer claims that these actions by McDonald's, which were followed by Wendy's and Burger King, are a "ray of hope" and "the first hopeful signs for American farm animals since the modern animal movement began."[13] PETA claims that "'[t]here's been a real change in consciousness'"[14] concerning the treatment of animals used for food and praises McDonald's as "'leading the way' in reforming the practices of fast-food suppliers, in the treatment and the killing of its beef and poultry."[15]

To the contrary, however, this supposed "change in consciousness" is, for the most part, no different from the concerns for increasing the efficiency of animal exploitation that motivated the passage in 1958 of the Humane Slaughter Act and does not reflect any recognition that animals have interests that should be protected even if there are no economic ad-

---

11. PETER SINGER, ANIMAL LIBERATION (2d ed. 1990).

12. Singer, *supra* note 10, at 26.

13. *Id.*

14. Stephanie Simon, *Killing Them Softly; Voluntary Reforms in the Livestock Industry Have Changed the Way Animals Are Slaughtered*, L.A. TIMES, Apr. 29, 2003, at A1 (quoting Bruce Friedrich of PETA).

15. David Shaw, *Matters of Taste; Animal Rights and Wrongs; When It Comes to Defending Livestock, Some Activists Are Going to Extremes*, L.A. TIMES, Feb. 23, 2005, at F2 (quoting Lisa Lange of PETA).

vantages to humans.[16] The slaughterhouse standards praised by Singer and PETA were developed by Temple Grandin, who designs "humane" slaughter and handling systems and who is discussed at length in *Rain Without Thunder.*[17] Grandin's guidelines, which involve techniques for moving animals through the slaughtering process and stunning them, are based explicitly on economic concerns. According to Grandin:

> Once livestock—cattle, pigs and sheep—arrive at packing plants, proper handling procedures are not only important for the animal's well-being, they can also mean the difference between profit and loss. Research clearly demonstrates that many meat quality benefits can be obtained with careful, quiet animal handling. . . . Properly handled animals are not only an important ethical goal, they also keep the meat industry running safely, efficiently and profitably.[18]

In talking about stunning animals before slaughter, Grandin states:

> Stunning an animal correctly will provide better meat quality. Improper electric stunning will cause bloodspots in the meat and bone fractures. Good stunning practices are also required so that a plant will be in compliance with the Humane Slaughter Act and for animal welfare. When stunning is done correctly, the animal feels no pain and it becomes instantly unconscious. An animal that is stunned properly will produce a still carcass that is safe for plant workers to work on.[19]

---

16. *See supra* notes 4–5 and accompanying text; *see also infra* notes 107–09 and accompanying text (discussing enforcement of the Humane Slaughter Act).

17. *See* FRANCIONE, *supra* note 3, at 99–100, 199–202. Grandin, who claims that her autism enables her to understand the emotions of cows and other nonhumans, was the subject of a 1998 documentary, *Stairway to Heaven,* by filmmaker Errol Morris. The title of the film is based on a ramp designed by Grandin that is supposed to lead cows more calmly from the holding pen to their slaughter. Grandin maintains that "[p]roperly performed, 'slaughter is more humane than nature.'" OLIVER SACKS, AN ANTHROPOLOGIST ON MARS 268 (1995) (quoting Temple Grandin). Grandin ignores that cows would not die in "nature" as they would not exist if we did not cause them to come into being for the purpose of eating them. *See also* TEMPLE GRANDIN & CATHERINE JOHNSON, ANIMALS IN TRANSLATION: USING THE MYSTERIES OF AUTISM TO DECODE ANIMAL BEHAVIOR (2005) (discussing the ways in which Grandin's autism supposedly provides her with insight about animal cognition).

18. TEMPLE GRANDIN, RECOMMENDED ANIMAL HANDLING GUIDELINES AND AUDIT GUIDE 6 (2007), *available at* http://www.animalhandling.org/ht/a/GetDocumentAction/i/1774.

19. Temple Grandin, Humane Slaughter: Recommended Stunning Practices, http://www.grandin.com/humane/rec.slaughter.html (last visited Mar. 19, 2007).

She maintains that "[g]entle handling in well-designed facilities will minimize stress levels, improve efficiency and maintain good meat quality. Rough handling or poorly designed equipment is detrimental to both animal welfare and meat quality."[20]

In discussing as a general matter the slaughter and battery-cage improvements to which Singer refers, McDonald's states:

Animal welfare is also an important part of quality assurance. For high-quality food products at the counter, you need high quality coming from the farm. Animals that are well cared for are less prone to illness, injury, and stress, which all have the same negative impact on the condition of livestock as they do on people. Proper animal welfare practices also benefit producers. Complying with our animal welfare guidelines helps ensure efficient production and reduces waste and loss. This enables our suppliers to be highly competitive.[21]

Wendy's also emphasizes the efficiency of its animal-welfare program: "Studies have shown that humane animal handling methods not only prevent needless suffering, but can result in a safer working environment for workers involved in the farm and livestock industry."[22] In a report about voluntary reforms in the livestock industry, the *Los Angeles Times* stated that "[i]n part, the reforms are driven by self-interest. When an animal is bruised, its flesh turns mushy and must be discarded. Even stress, especially right before slaughter, can affect the quality of meat."[23]

In short, the producers of animal products—working with prominent animal advocates—are becoming better at exploiting animals in an economically efficient manner by adopting measures that improve meat quality and worker safety. But this has absolutely nothing to do with any recognition that animals have inherent value or that they have interests that should be respected even when it is not economically beneficial for humans to do so. Any supposed improvements in animal welfare are

---

20. Temple Grandin, Stress and Meat Quality: Lowering Stress to Improve Meat Quality and Animal Welfare, http://www.grandin.com/meat/meat.html (last visited Mar. 19, 2007).
21. Bruce Feinberg & Terry Williams, Animal Welfare Update: North America, http://www.mcdonalds.com/content/corp/values/report/archive/progress_report/north_america.html (last visited Mar. 19, 2007).
22. Wendy's, Wendy's Animal Welfare Program, http://www.wendys.com/community/animal_welfare.jsp (last visited Mar. 19, 2007).
23. Simon, *supra* note 14.

limited to and justified by economic benefits for institutional exploiters. Moreover, there is serious doubt whether these changes actually provide any significant improvement in animal treatment. A slaughterhouse that follows Grandin's guidelines for stunning, prod use, and other aspects of the killing process is still an unspeakably horrible place and it is misleading for Singer, PETA, or anyone else to suggest otherwise. Battery hens that supply some of the major fast-food chains may now live in an area equivalent to a square of approximately 8.5 inches rather than the average industry standard—a square of approximately 7.8 inches—but it would be nonsense to claim that the existence of a battery hen in the larger cage is anything but miserable. Indeed, "cage-free" hens are often packed together so tightly in sheds that they are crushed and have very limited movement.

To the extent that McDonald's and others are incurring any costs whatsoever in making these changes, they are surely outweighed significantly by the fact that these corporations can now point to the praise of animal advocates such as Singer and PETA for their supposedly "humane" treatment of nonhuman animals. PETA presented its 2004 Visionary of the Year Award to Grandin, who is a consultant to McDonald's and other fast-food chains, for her "innovative improvements" in slaughtering processes.[24] Some welfarists, such as Paul Waldau, director of the Center for Animals and Public Policy at Tufts University, proclaim that these supposed improvements in animal agriculture indicate that "'[a] certain segment of the population is beginning to consume with conscience.'"[25] This is precisely the sort of comment that encourages the public to believe that it is now more acceptable to eat animal products because animals are being treated more "humanely," and that demonstrates the generally counterproductive nature of animal welfare.

B. Legislation

A cursory review of federal and state animal-welfare legislation in the past dozen years provides several notable examples of the sort of legis-

---

24. PETA, http://www.peta.org/MC/NewsItem.asp?id=5667&pf=true (last visited Mar. 19, 2007).
25. Patricia Leigh Brown, *Is Luxury Cruel? The Foie Gras Divide,* N.Y. TIMES, Oct. 6, 2004, at F10 (quoting Paul Waldau). *See also infra* notes 137–41 (discussing the idea that we can be "conscientious omnivores").

lation described in *Rain Without Thunder* as providing a greater benefit to animal-advocacy organizations, which need legislative "victories" to raise funds, than to nonhuman animals.

1. **FEDERAL LEGISLATION: THE CHIMPANZEE HEALTH IMPROVEMENT, MAINTE-NANCE, AND PROTECTION (CHIMP) ACT**[26] The CHIMP Act of 2000 was enthusiastically supported by many national animal-advocacy organizations and by primatologist Jane Goodall, and many animal advocates regard the CHIMP Act as the most significant piece of federal legislation since the 1985 amendments to the federal Animal Welfare Act,[27] itself an extremely modest law. The stated purpose of the CHIMP Act is to establish a national sanctuary system for chimpanzees that are designated by the Secretary of Health and Human Services (the Secretary) as no longer needed for research conducted or supported by federal agencies.[28] Chimpanzees not owned by the federal government may also be accepted into the sanctuary program if the owner transfers title and other conditions are met.[29] The sanctuary system is to be operated by a nonprofit private entity chosen by the Secretary, and costs are to be shared, with the nonprofit entity paying not less than ten percent of costs to establish the sanctuary and twenty-five percent of the costs of operation.[30]

Although the Act purports to express a moral concern about chimpanzees used in research, it is clear from the legislative history that Congress was at least equally as concerned about the high costs of warehousing these nonhumans in laboratories and regarded the sanctuary system as being a cost-effective solution that would be financed in part through private funds.[31] The CHIMP Act was described as "fiscally sound legisla-

---

26. 42 U.S.C. § 287a-3a (2000) (establishing a sanctuary system for surplus chimpanzees).

27. 7 U.S.C. §§ 2131-2159 (2000). For a discussion of the Animal Welfare Act, *see* FRANCIONE, *supra* note 1, at 185-249. *See also infra* notes 104-06 and accompanying text (discussing exclusion of animals from coverage under the Act).

28. 42 U.S.C. § 287a-3a(a), (b).

29. *Id.* § 287a-3a(c), (d)(4).

30. *Id.* § 287a-3a(e)(4)(A), (B).

31. *See* 146 CONG. REC. S11654-55 (daily ed. Dec. 6, 2000). Senator Smith stated: "It costs $8-$15 per day per animal to care for chimpanzees in a sanctuary, where they live in groups in a naturalized setting. That is compared to the $20-$30 per day per animal that the federal government is now spending to maintain the chimpanzees in laboratory cages." *Id.* at 11654. Senator Durbin added: "And this legislation creates a public-private partnership, to generate non-federal dollars that will help pay for the care of these chimpanzees. Right now, their care is financed strictly

tion that will better serve the taxpayers as well as the animals."[32] Animal advocates also promoted the legislation as cost-efficient.[33]

Moreover, the CHIMP Act was explicitly proposed as a way of ensuring that research involving chimpanzees can continue. Senate sponsor Robert Smith (R-NH) stated that the CHIMP Act was "basically a cost of doing business. If the federal government wants to keep using chimpanzees for medical research, it has to assume the responsibility for their care after the research is done."[34] Euthanizing the animals was not an option:

> "Some of the best and most caring members of the support staff, such as veterinarians and technicians would, for personal and emotional reasons, find it impossible to function effectively in an atmosphere in which euthanasia is a general policy, and might resign. A facility that adopted such a policy could expect to lose some of its best employees."[35]

According to Senator Smith, "because chimpanzees and humans are so similar, those who work directly in chimpanzee research would find it untenable to continue using these animals if they were to be killed at the conclusion of the research."[36] Senate co-sponsor Richard Durbin (D-Ill) stated that "if the Federal government is to keep using chimpanzees to advance human health research goals, long-term care of the animals is a pre-requisite."[37] Like the supposed improvements in farm-animal welfare

---

through taxpayer dollars. Under the bill, the private sector will cover 10 percent of the start-up costs and 25 percent of the operating costs of the sanctuary system." *Id.* For further discussion on the legislative rationale for the CHIMP Act, see S. REP. NO. 106–494, at 3 (2000) ("The CHIMP Act provides a cost-effective solution to the long term care needs of these chimpanzees. Sanctuary care for animals requires less intensive management than animals in research facilities, and therefore entails lower daily costs.")

32. 146 CONG. REC. S11655 (daily ed. Dec. 6, 2000) (statement of Senator Durbin).

33. *See, e.g., Chimpanzee Health Improvement, Maintenance, and Protection Act: Hearing on H.R. 3514 Before the Subcomm. on Health and Environment of the H. Comm. on Commerce,* 106th Cong. 34 (2000). Tina Nelson, Executive Director of the American Anti-Vivisection Society, stated: "I wish to emphasize the cost effectiveness of this solution. Sanctuaries offer considerable savings compared to the cost of housing chimpanzees in laboratories." Nelson's statement was offered on behalf of her own organization as well as the American Society for the Prevention of Cruelty to Animals, the National Anti-Vivisection Society, Society for Animal Protective Legislation, and The Humane Society of the United States.

34. 146 CONG. REC. S11655 (daily ed. Dec. 6, 2000) (statement of Senator Smith).

35. *Id.* (quoting NATIONAL RESEARCH COUNCIL, CHIMPANZEES IN RESEARCH: STRATEGIES FOR THEIR ETHICAL CARE, MANAGEMENT, AND USE 39 (1997)).

36. *Id.* (statement of Senator Smith).

37. *Id.* (statement of Senator Durbin).

discussed in the previous section, the CHIMP Act provides yet another, and a particularly relevant, illustration of a point made continually in my work: Animal-welfare measures, which are regarded as a "cost of doing business," may very well facilitate continued animal exploitation by making it more acceptable.[38]

Although the CHIMP Act purports to prohibit further invasive research on "retired" chimpanzees in the sanctuary system, the Act has two important exceptions. First, sanctuary chimpanzees can be used for

noninvasive behavioral studies or medical studies based on information collected during the course of normal veterinary care that is provided for the benefit of the chimpanzee, provided that any such study involves minimal physical and mental harm, pain, distress, and disturbance to the chimpanzee and the social group in which the chimpanzee lives.[39]

Second, the Act permits invasive research on a "retired" chimpanzee if the Secretary finds that the research "is essential to address an important public health need";[40] a sanctuary chimpanzee is needed because there is no other chimpanzee "reasonably available" outside the sanctuary system with a similar medical history and prior research protocol;[41] and that there are "technological or medical advancements that were not available at the time the chimpanzee entered the sanctuary system, and that such advancements can and will be used in the research."[42] The exception for invasive research also requires that "the design of the research involves minimal pain and physical harm to the chimpanzee, and otherwise minimizes mental harm, distress, and disturbance to the chimpanzee and the social group in which the chimpanzee lives (including with respect to removal of the chimpanzee from the sanctuary facility involved)."[43]

---

38. *See generally* FRANCIONE, *supra* note 3 (arguing that animal-welfare regulations do not lead to the abolition of animal exploitation and, indeed, make exploitation more acceptable as a general matter).

39. 42 U.S.C. § 287a-3a(d)(3)(A)(i) (2000).

40. *Id.* § 287a-3a(d)(3)(A)(ii)(III).

41. *Id.* § 287a-3a(d)(3)(A)(ii)(I).

42. *Id.* § 287a-3a(d)(3)(A)(ii)(II).

43. *Id.* § 287a-3a(d)(3)(A)(ii)(IV).

The exception for noninvasive behavioral studies or medical studies is not qualified, and it appears as though this research may be done without limitation. Although the exception for invasive research appears to be carefully qualified, it is easy to satisfy. If the government and researchers want to do research, it is, by definition, to address an "important public health need." No two chimpanzees will have the exact same medical history even if they were involved in the same research protocol, so this exception leaves the door wide open for researchers to claim that a sanctuary chimpanzee is in some way or other unique. Technological and medical advances occur every day and there is no qualification as to what is required. The requirement that the design of any invasive research involve "minimal" pain and harm is, in my view, as meaningless as a requirement that we not impose "unnecessary" suffering on animals.

Furthermore, whether the proposed design for invasive research satisfies the exception is to be evaluated by the board of directors of the entity operating the sanctuary system, and the Secretary must accept those findings unless he or she finds them to be arbitrary or capricious.[44] There is a notice-and-comment requirement for research on sanctuary chimpanzees,[45] and no one who has been previously "fined for, or signed a consent decree for, any violation of the Animal Welfare Act" can use a sanctuary chimpanzee for any research.[46] There is no review or approval mechanism specified in the Act for noninvasive behavioral studies or medical studies.

Animal advocates who supported the CHIMP Act either failed to appreciate that such a sanctuary system controlled by the government would facilitate, and not inhibit, research on "retired" chimpanzees, or they ignored that fact.[47] Before the CHIMP Act, many chimps were be-

---

44. *Id.* § 287a-3a(d)(3)(B)(ii). The requirements for invasive research do not apply to noninvasive behavioral studies or medical studies. *Id.* § 287a-3a(d)(3)(A)(i).

45. *Id.* § 287a-3a(d)(3)(B)(iii).

46. *Id.* § 287a-3a(d)(3)(C). This provision appears to apply to both noninvasive and invasive research.

47. Some organizations that initially supported the CHIMP Act claimed to withdraw support when the bill was amended to allow continued invasive research on sanctuary chimpanzees. This withdrawal of support was often done quietly. For example, the American Anti-Vivisection Society, which actively supported the bill, see *supra* note 33, claimed to withdraw support after the bill was amended, but this withdrawal consisted only of a withdrawal of active support and not any public opposition to the bill. *See* Letter from Tina Nelson, Executive Director of the American Anti-Vivisection Society, to Hon. James Greenwood (Oct. 23, 2000) (on file with the author). I was unable to find any indication that organizations that supported the Act objected at

ing warehoused in laboratories, and record keeping was spotty at best. A vivisector trying to find chimpanzees for particular experiments faced considerable opportunity costs in locating suitable animals. The creation of a national sanctuary system under the effective control of the Department of Health and Human Services (HHS) considerably reduces those opportunity costs through a centralized information bank that makes the location and medical histories accessible to the research community. This system allows vivisectors to locate supposedly unique chimpanzees whose use in experiments will arguably satisfy the "public health need" requirement.

Supporters of the CHIMP Act claimed that the exception for invasive research was needed to get support for the bill by the National Institutes of Health (NIH)—and that is precisely the problem. NIH was not willing to drop its opposition unless sanctuary chimpanzees continued to be available for research, which suggests that NIH regards these supposedly retired chimpanzees as being more on a leave of absence. Many advocates pointed to statements by legislators that invasive research on these chimpanzees "would rarely, if ever, take place."[48] It must be remembered, however, that in the matter of the "Silver Spring monkeys," who were removed from a federally funded laboratory after authorities determined that the animals were being treated in a cruel manner, NIH made an explicit written representation to Congress that the primates would never be used in experiments once they were transferred to the Delta Regional Primate Center.[49] Despite its commitment to Congress, NIH allowed further experiments because the monkeys were claimed to be unique in light of their previous medical histories. Congress com-

---

any point to the exception for noninvasive behavioral research or medical studies, even though these may involve some level of harm, pain, distress, and disturbance.

The National Institutes of Health proposed regulations to implement the CHIMP Act. *See* Standards of Care for Chimpanzees Held in the Federally Supported Chimpanzee Sanctuary System, 70 Fed. Reg. 1843 (Jan. 11, 2005) (to be codified at 42 C.F.R. pt. 9). A coalition of animal-protection organizations commented on the proposed regulations and argued that there should be no further research on animals in the "sanctuary" system. *See* Center for Great Apes, et al., Comment on Proposed Rules for Chimpanzees Held in the Federally Supported Chimpanzee Sanctuary System, (Mar. 14, 2005), http://www.neavs.org/downloads/programs/campaigns/Comments_on_Proposed_Rules.pdf. As of the time that this essay went to press, the regulations were not available.

48. 146 Cong. Rec. S11654 (daily ed. Dec. 6, 2000) (statement of Senator Smith).

49. For a discussion of the Silver Spring monkey case, including NIH representations to Congress, *see* Francione, *supra* note 1, at 72–78, 86–89.

plained strenuously but NIH ignored the protest, claiming scientific need. It is unclear why any animal advocate believes that the CHIMP Act sanctuary situation will not involve a repeat of what occurred with the Silver Spring monkeys.

In the face of concerns expressed by myself and others about the CHIMP Act before its enactment, animal advocates who supported the Act argued that the solution to the problem presented by the exception allowing invasive research was to support the Act and then to challenge in court any determination to use sanctuary chimpanzees in further research.[50] The problem is that, for all intents and purposes, it is virtually impossible to challenge the discretionary decisions of an administrative agency.

First, it is not even clear that animal advocates would have legal standing to bring a judicial challenge to a decision by the Secretary to allow use of a "retired" chimpanzee in further research. That is, the court may very well dismiss the challenge without considering the merits of the Secretary's decision.

Second, and more important, even if animal advocates were found to have standing, the applicable standard of judicial review would effectively insulate these decisions from challenge. The CHIMP Act provides two levels of protection to administrative decisions to perform experiments on sanctuary chimpanzees. Under the Act, the sanctuary system is to be operated by a non-profit organization that is awarded a contract by the Department of Health and Human Services (HHS), or that is established by HHS.[51] The board of directors of the sanctuary is given the power to determine whether the design of invasive research complies with the requirement to minimize pain and harm, and, assuming that the Secretary determines that the other conditions are satisfied (that is, that an exemption should be granted), the Secretary is bound by the board's determination unless it is arbitrary or capricious. In addition, the Secretary's determination about the board's determination, as well as the Secretary's

---

50. *See, e.g.*, Statement of GAP [The Great Ape Project], Nov. 29, 2000 (on file with author): "Some major supporters of GAP choose to support the amended bill (Jane Goodall, Marc Bekoff, Steve Wise), arguing that the sanctuary should be created and then we should fight with all our might if someone attempts to remove a 'retired' chimpanzee." I was unable to find any discussion of concern about noninvasive behavioral research or medical studies.

51. 42 U.S.C. § 287a-3a(e).

own determination about whether an exemption should be granted, will be insulated from challenge unless it is can be demonstrated to be arbitrary or capricious. Finally, the "retired" chimpanzees can be used without limit for noninvasive behavioral studies or certain medical studies as long as only "minimal physical and mental harm, pain, distress, and disturbance" are involved, and there is no mechanism in the Act for review of this research.

In September 2002, the National Center for Research Resources of NIH awarded the contract for the sanctuary to Chimp Haven, Inc., the board of which includes several members who either are presently or who have been involved with the use of nonhumans, including nonhuman primates, in experiments.[52] The board of Chimp Haven will determine whether the design of a proposed experiment on a "retired" chimpanzee minimizes physical and mental harm, and that decision must be accorded deference by the Secretary whose own decision about whether the board has acted properly, and whether the research should be done at all, must also be accorded deference. In short, decisions by the Secretary to allow invasive research on sanctuary chimpanzees will be immune from any meaningful legal challenge, even if animal advocates have standing to bring such a challenge. Although the Act contains a notice-and-comment provision so the public can comment about proposed experiments on chimpanzees in the sanctuary system, federal agencies are notorious for ignoring the often considerable public objection to animal use in experiments.

In sum, the CHIMP Act recognized that a "sanctuary" system—particularly one financed in part by and effectively approved by animal advocates—is a much cheaper way to house these animals and makes continued use of chimpanzees in research more acceptable to the public. The system lowers the cost for researchers of identifying the existence of animals with particular medical histories, and "retired" animals can still be used for certain noninvasive behavioral or medical studies, and for inva-

---

52. For the announcement by the National Center on Research Resources of the award of the contract to Chimp Haven, Inc., see http://www.ncrr.nih.gov/compmed/cm_chimp.asp (last visited Mar. 19, 2007). For information about Chimp Haven, Inc., including its board of directors, see http://www.chimphaven.org/about-board.cfm (last visited Mar. 19, 2007). Chimp Haven is apparently facing financial difficulties. Melody Brumble, *Chimp Haven Faces Money Problems,* THE TIMES (Shreveport, La.), Feb. 23, 2006, at 1A.

sive research if there is a "public health need." The Act fits perfectly the model of welfarist legislation that I have described in that it has nothing to do with recognizing the inherent value of nonhumans and everything to do with economics and perpetuating animal use. The Act did not move any distance at all from the property paradigm; indeed, it reinforced the notion that chimpanzees are commodities and that animal-welfare standards should be linked to the economically efficient exploitation of those commodities.

2. STATE LEGISLATION: FLORIDA'S "BAN" ON GESTATION CRATES Many animal advocates see state law as a more fertile ground for welfarist change than federal, but the results over the past years do not support that view. Peter Singer characterizes the amendment in 2002 of the Florida Constitution to "ban the keeping of pregnant sows in crates so narrow that they cannot even turn around" as "[a]n even greater triumph" than the voluntary changes in the handling and slaughter of animals used for food.[53] Animal advocates, led by The Humane Society of the United States (HSUS), Farm Sanctuary, and others, succeeded in getting nearly 700,000 signatures to put on the ballot a proposal to ban what are known as "gestation crates." Florida voters approved the proposal, and the Florida Constitution now makes it a misdemeanor to confine a pregnant pig in "an enclosure," or to tether a pregnant pig "in such a way that she is prevented from turning around freely."[54]

For a number of reasons, characterization of the Florida amendment as a "triumph" demonstrates that the bar of progress is ridiculously low where animal welfare measures are concerned. First, the campaign against gestation crates, which began in Florida but is now being conducted

---

53. Singer, *supra* note 10, at 26. In response to the question, "In your opinion, what has been the most important victory for the animal movement?," Singer responded that in addition to a campaign against vivisection by the late animal-welfare advocate Henry Spira, he would:

    also put the recent referendum victory on sow crates [gestation crates] in Florida very near the top, because that was the first time that a major form of factory farming has been banned in any state in America, and it showed that the public is on our side, when they have a chance to vote on the kind of confinement that is standard in factory farms.

    COK Talks with Peter Singer, COMPASSION OVER KILLING, http://www.cok.net/abol/15/06.php (last visited Mar. 19, 2007).

54. FLA. CONST. art. X, § 21(a). The amendment takes effect in 2008. *See id.* § 21(g) (effective six years after approval by voters).

in other states, is based explicitly on economic considerations. Animal advocates promoted the amendment as a way to keep larger, intensive hog operations out of Florida, and thereby protect property values and tourism.[55] These advocates maintain, as a general matter, that alternatives to the gestation crate, such as group housing, will reduce production costs and increase productivity.[56] Second, there were only two hog farmers in the state of Florida who were affected by the amendment, and there was almost no opposition to the amendment.[57] On the other hand, large animal-advocacy organizations spent well more than $1 million on the campaign.[58] Third, the amendment defines "enclosure" as "any cage, crate or other enclosure in which a pig is kept for all or the majority of any day,"[59] and this would presumably mean that the use of a gestation crate for less than the majority of a day would not be prohibited. Fourth, the amendment explicitly allows the use of the gestation crate

---

55. According to Floridians for Humane Farms, the Amendment "will prevent mega hog factories from moving into Florida as they have in North Carolina. We don't want Florida to follow North Carolina's experience where the environment has been damaged, property values have gone down, and the tourist industry has suffered." Floridians for Humane Farms, http://www.bancruelfarms.org/ faq_print.htm (last visited Mar. 19, 2007).

56. The Humane Society of the United States, which, with Farm Sanctuary, is promoting the prohibition of gestation crates in other states, focuses heavily on the economic argument, and maintains that European studies demonstrate that sows raised in group housing with electronic sow feeding are generally more healthy, sow productivity is higher, and production costs are lower. THE HUMANE SOCIETY OF THE UNITED STATES, AN HSUS REPORT: THE ECONOMICS OF ADOPTING ALTERNATIVE PRODUCTION SYSTEMS TO GESTATION CRATES (2006) [hereinafter HSUS REPORT: GESTATION CRATES], *available at* http://www.hsus.org/web-files/PDF/farm/econ_gestation.pdf. A similar proposal on crates for sows, also applicable to calves, was passed in Arizona in November 2006, and Smithfield Foods stated in January 2007 that it would phase out gestation crates over a ten-year period. *See The Humane Society of the United States Praises Smithfield Move to End Confinement of Pigs in Gestation Crates,* U.S. NEWSWIRE, Jan. 25, 2007, http://news.corporate.findlaw.com/prnewswire/ 20070125/25jan20071000.html. Time constraints and editorial deadlines made it impossible to discuss these developments in this article, but they do not in any way affect my view that welfare reforms are generally linked to the efficient exploitation of animals.

57. The only two Florida hog farms that used gestation crates sent their animals to slaughter and closed their hog operations. Both could be eligible for state grants of up to $275,000. Allison North Jones, *State Hog Farmers Receive a Bailout from Lawmakers,* TAMPA TRIB., May 14, 2005, at Metro 1.

58. Curtis Krueger, *1.2-Million Greases Path of Pig Proposal,* ST. PETERSBURG TIMES, Oct. 13, 2002, at 1B. The Florida Elections Commission charged Farm Sanctuary and its president, Gene Bauston, with 210 violations of Florida law for collecting "thousands of dollars in donations and funnel[ing] them to the amendment campaign, violating a law that requires that the names of all contributors be disclosed." *See* Lucy Morgan, *Panel Says Pig Proposal Backers Broke Election Law,* ST. PETERSBURG TIMES, Oct. 30, 2002, at 5B.

59. FLA. CONST. art. X, § 21(c)(1). This is significant because some producers are moving toward a modified system in which pregnant sows will be confined for part of the day.

for "prebirthing period," which is defined as "the seven day period prior to a pig's expected date of giving birth,"[60] and allows for the use of crates for "veterinary purposes" for a period "not longer than reasonably necessary."[61] Like the "unnecessary suffering" language discussed earlier, any legal standard concerning nonhumans that allows an action to be done if, or as long as, "reasonably necessary" is an invitation to ignore relevant animal interests. Fifth, although advocates suggested that the amendment would likely result in any affected pigs being raised in group housing systems,[62] the amendment provides only that the pig must be able to turn around "without having to touch any side of the pig's enclosure"[63] and not that the pig must be kept in group housing. Sixth, the amendment served as the "poster child" for a successful campaign to require a supermajority to amend the Florida Constitution and thereby restrict such initiatives in the future.[64]

The Florida amendment may have been a fund-raising "triumph" for animal organizations that claim it as a victory. But the amendment and similar efforts do little to help animals and, indeed, are counterproductive. HSUS claims that farmers who adopt alternatives to the gestation crates can not only increase productivity and decrease production costs, but can "increase demand for their products or earn a market premium."[65] Making exploitation more efficient and increasing demand for meat have nothing to do with recognizing the inherent value of animals or doing anything other than treating animals strictly as economic commodities.

---

60. *Id.* § 21(b)(2), (c)(6).

61. *Id.* § 21(b)(1).

62. *See, e.g.*, Ban Cruel Farms, Frequently Asked Questions, http://www.bancruelfarms.org/faq_print.htm (last visited Mar. 19, 2007) ("In European countries where similar legislation has been enacted, pig farmers have generally gone to a group housing system where the sows are kept together in more spacious conditions.").

63. FLA. CONST. art. X, § 21(c)(5).

64. Etan Horowitz, *Amending Constitution Polarizes Sides*, ORLANDO SENTINEL, Nov. 4, 2006, at B1. Supporters of the amendment offered as "[t]heir poster child a $1.6 million campaign by animal-rights groups in 2002 that won passage of an amendment preventing the caging of pregnant pigs, an amendment that affected only two farmers in the state." *Id.* The supermajority amendment was approved by voters on November 7, 2006. Howard Troxler, *Stop Us Before We Amend Again!*, ST. PETERSBURG TIMES, Nov. 8, 2006, at 8A. The first line of the article reads: "It must have been the pregnant pigs that did it." *Id.*

65. HSUS REPORT: GESTATION CRATES, *supra* note 56, at 2.

3. STATE LEGISLATION: CALIFORNIA'S FOIE GRAS "BAN" The state law that has elicited the most enthusiastic response from animal advocates, however, was passed in California. In 2004, Governor Schwarzenegger signed into law Senate Bill 1520, which nominally prohibits the force feeding of birds to produce foie gras[66] and the sale of products that are the "result of force feeding a bird for the purpose of enlarging the bird's liver beyond normal size."[67] Senate Bill 1520, characterized as "an 'unprecedented victory for animals,'"[68] was supported by most of the large animal-advocacy groups and by numerous celebrities.[69]

The California law is one of the few instances in which animal welfare is not linked explicitly to economic concerns. That is, the law does not seek to make exploitation more "humane" incidental to making it more beneficial economically through lowering costs or increasing productivity. Although foie gras certainly involves the barbarous treatment of animals, so does most of our other animal food. Foie gras is unusual because it is not part of domestic food culture; indeed, it is associated with France, toward which many Americans are hostile as the result of various political differences. It is produced in the United States by only two companies, and is consumed by the relatively few people who can afford it and regard it as a desirable luxury. Foie gras is analogous in certain respects to bullfighting, which is no more barbaric than rodeos or some other, more traditionally American, forms of animal "entertainment," but, because fois gras is a "foreign" form of exploitation, can inspire passionate opposition.[70]

---

66. CAL. HEALTH & SAFETY CODE §§ 25980–84. (Deering 2005).

67. *Id.* § 25982. Some animal advocates have claimed that consumption of foie gras in California will be prohibited after July 1, 2012. This claim is unwarranted. Californians will still be able to purchase foie gras from sellers outside of California for personal use but may not resell it within the state. Restaurants may be able to continue to serve foie gras if it is served as a "chef's gift" with a meal and is not sold. The legislation has no effect on the production, marketing, or consumption of liver from birds who have not been force fed.

68. *2004 Legislative Review*, 11 ANIMAL L. 325, 360 (2005) (quoting HSUS sources).

69. Andrew Gumbel & John Lichfield, *An Ending Made in Hollywood for an Epic Fight Over Foie Gras; The Headlines Proclaim That Arnold Schwarzenegger Has Saved the Geese,* THE INDEPENDENT (LONDON), Oct. 1, 2004, at 12.

70. *See, e.g.,* Justin Berton, *When All Else Fails, Throw Your Muleta at the Bull and Run,* S.F. CHRON., June 18, 2006, at A1 (describing the experience of Americans at a bullfighting school in California). Another example of this phenomenon involves animal sacrifices. Practitioners of a Caribbean religion known as Santeria—usually immigrants and people of color—have been prosecuted for conducting ritual animal sacrifice as part of their religion. Animal sacrifice, although

Although Senate Bill 1520 may arguably be said to recognize that at least some animals have more than extrinsic or conditional value, there are a number of reasons why the law is more properly characterized as a victory for California's only foie gras producer, Sonoma Foie Gras. First, the law does not take effect until July 1, 2012, and it explicitly provides that this date reflects "the express intention of the Legislature . . . to allow a seven and one-half year period for persons or entities engaged in agricultural practices that include raising and selling force fed birds to modify their business practices."[71] In transmitting the signed bill to the Senate, Governor Schwarzenegger stated:

> This bill provides [seven] and one half years for agricultural husbandry practices to evolve and perfect a humane way for a duck to consume grain to increase the size of its liver through natural processes. If agricultural producers are successful in this endeavor, the ban on foie gras sales and production in California will not occur.[72]

Second, the law explicitly provides that Sonoma Foie Gras is immunized until July 1, 2012, from civil or criminal lawsuits concerning the practice of force feeding or sale of products resulting from that practice, and that any pending civil action against Sonoma concerning the practice of force feeding shall not proceed.[73] This immunity has the practical

---

quite horrific, is really no different from what goes on at a federally regulated slaughterhouse. *See* FRANCIONE, *supra* note 2, at 163–64 (discussing prohibitions of particular practices associated with other cultures or certain socioeconomic groups).

71. CAL. HEALTH & SAFETY CODE § 25984(a), (c) (Deering 2005).

72. Governor's Message to the California State Senate on Signing Cal. S.B. 1520 (Sept. 29, 2004), *available at* LEXIS, 2003 Legis. Bill Hist. CA S.B. 1520.

73. CAL. HEALTH & SAFETY CODE § 25984(b)(1), provides that "[n]o civil or criminal cause of action shall arise on or after January 1, 2005, nor shall a pending action commenced prior to January 1, 2005, be pursued under any provision of law against a person or entity for engaging, prior to July 1, 2012, in any act prohibited by this chapter." Section 25984(b)(3) provides that this immunity applies only "to persons or entities who were engaged in, or controlled by persons or entities who were engaged in, agricultural practices that involved force feeding birds at the time of the enactment of this chapter." Sonoma Foie Gras was the only producer of foie gras involved in the force feeding of birds at the time that the law was enacted. *See* Gumbel & Lichfield, *supra* note 69. "Until 2012, meanwhile, Sonoma Foie Gras will be immune from all lawsuits—two of which had been pending before the courts but will now be dropped." *Id.*

When Governor Schwarzenegger signed Senate Bill 1520 into law, a number of animal advocacy groups announced the signing as a victory for animals, and not one that I saw mentioned that any pending civil action against Sonoma would be dismissed and that Sonoma

effect of legalizing force feeding until 2012, although the status of that practice was in question at the time the law was passed.

Third, the owner of Sonoma Foie Gras, Guillermo Gonzalez, actually supported the law and lobbied for its passage. He stated that "'[w]e will go on with our business'" and "'[w]e supported this bill and thank the governor and the legislature for their very serious consideration and deliberation.'"[74] Gonzalez "professed to welcome the measure, which grants him immunity from lawsuits, and gives him seven and a half years, in the governor's words, 'for animal husbandry practices to evolve' and to 'perfect a humane way for a duck to consume grain to increase the size of its liver through natural processes.'"[75] But Gonzalez also "hopes to use the reprieve to prove the ducks do not suffer"[76] and he will "work with scientists and scholars to find 'clear, unbiased answers on the question of the welfare of the ducks,' including stress tests."[77] Mr. Gonzalez claims to have already identified animal scientists who maintain that force feeding does not cause animals to suffer.[78] Further,

> [t]he University of California-Davis has been working behind the scenes with the governor's office to put a plan into place that would allow the university's animal science department and the veterinary medicine school to conduct research to determine whether foie gras production is humane. If the research indicates that the process is humane, it could be used as ammunition to challenge the law.[79]

Moreover, the California legislature may well repeal the law or modify it to allow force feeding with specially designed equipment or accompanied

---

was immunized from civil and criminal action until 2012. For example, Farm Sanctuary, an organization that sponsored the legislation, omitted any reference to these crucial facts. *See* NoFoieGras.org, Schwarzenegger Terminates Form of Animal Cruelty, http://nofoiegras.org/ FS_cabill_PR2.htm (last visited Apr. 1, 2007).

74. Gumbel & Lichfield, *supra* note 69 (quoting Guillermo Gonzalez).

75. Brown, *supra* note 25.

76. Gabrielle Banks, *Duck Farm Is on Capitol Agenda; The Owner's Production of Foie Gras is the Focus of Legislation That Would Ban Force-Feeding of the Birds, Decried as Cruel*, L.A. TIMES, July 7, 2004, at B1.

77. Brown, *supra* note 25.

78. *Id.*

79. Carolyn Jung, *Study Could Disrupt Planned Foie Gras Ban*, SAN JOSE MERCURY NEWS, Oct. 27, 2004, at 1F.

by the use of drugs that supposedly mitigate any suffering if the legislature determines that such changes make the practice "humane." Given that the legislature expressed its intention to delay the effective date of the law precisely to allow those involved in force feeding birds "to modify their business practices," such an outcome seems more likely than not.

Senate Bill 1520 provides an excellent example of why animal-welfare legislation is so problematic. This law requires the dismissal of pending litigation and effectively insulates the industry completely at least until 2012 although the prohibition is unlikely ever to come into effect in any event. In the meantime, researchers will use animals in painful experiments in order to determine whether force feeding is "humane" or to develop a way to get enlarged liver through "natural processes." If by some miracle the law does come into effect in 2012, these birds will still be able to be raised intensively and slaughtered. Although they may not have tubes shoved down their throats, their livers will be enlarged in some way determined to be "natural," or about which there will be litigation for years, and the birds will continue to live bleak lives. Moreover, this sort of law deludes people into thinking that animal welfare works, that things are getting significantly better for nonhumans whom we exploit for food, and that we can "consume with conscience."[80]

The California foie gras law was such a victory for Sonoma Foie Gras that the only other domestic producer of foie gras, Hudson Valley Foie Gras, in upstate New York, is seeking to have a similar law passed in New York that would provide complete immunity from any criminal prosecution or civil action through 2016 for force feeding birds.[81]

C. Legal Standing: *Animal Legal Defense Fund, Inc. v. Glickman*[82]

As far as judicial decisions are concerned, animal advocates have stated that *Animal Legal Defense Fund, Inc. v. Glickman* provides broad standing

---

80. *See* Brown, *supra* note 25.

81. Lawrence Downes, *Face to Face With the Foie Gras Problem*, N.Y. TIMES, June 26, 2005, at 11: "One Senate sponsor, John Bonacic, is an upstate Republican who says he has no special sympathy for ducks or geese, despite what his bill says. He says he wants only to help a Sullivan County constituent—Hudson Valley Foie Gras, the nation's leading producer of fresh foie gras, which has not only lobbied for the bill, but also helped to write it."

82. 154 F.3d 426 (D.C. Cir. 1998) (en banc).

to sue to "enforce the Animal Welfare Act."[83] It is, however, more accurate to characterize the case as providing a "small window for standing"[84] in certain limited situations.

In *Glickman,* an animal advocate claimed that he suffered aesthetic injury when he visited a game farm and saw nonhuman primates in what he regarded as inhumane conditions. He argued that if the United States Department of Agriculture (USDA), which enforces the Animal Welfare Act, had promulgated appropriate regulations as required under the 1985 Amendments to the Act,[85] the animals would not have been in these conditions. An en banc D.C. Circuit held that the advocate had standing to challenge the failure of USDA to promulgate regulations to establish minimum requirements for a physical environment that would promote the psychological well-being of primates.

The plaintiff did not appeal the portion of the lower-court ruling which held that agency decisions to enforce the Animal Welfare Act were generally not reviewable by courts as such decisions were committed to the discretion of the agency.[86] The appellate court holding was limited only to whether the advocate was standing to challenge the failure of the agency to promulgate regulations as required under the Act. Therefore, assertions that *Glickman* established standing to enforce the Act are not correct.

Moreover, the appellate court explicitly distinguished the situation of the game farm from the use of primates or other animals in experiments because, in the latter situation, Congress had explicitly provided for oversight in the form of an animal-care committee with "private citizen members."[87] Therefore, claims by animal advocates that *Glickman* provided for standing to challenge the use of animals in experiments are unfounded.

Finally, en banc consideration was limited to the question of the standing of the individual advocate, and the court left for a future panel of the

---

83. *The Legal Status of Nonhuman Animals,* 8 ANIMAL L. 1, 3–4 (2002) (comment by David Favre). *See also* Favre, *supra* note 7, at 95 (claiming that *Glickman* held that there was standing "to question the decisions of a federal agency" concerning animals). Favre is a national officer of the Animal Legal Defense Fund.

84. Rebecca J. Huss, *Valuing Man's and Woman's Best Friend: The Moral and Legal Status of Companion Animals,* 86 MARQ. L. REV. 47, 81 (2002).

85. 7 U.S.C. § 2143(a)(2)(B) (2000).

86. *Glickman,* 154 F.3d at 431 n.3.

87. *Id.* at 445.

court review of the trial court's finding that the agency did violate the Act by failing to promulgate adequate regulations. A subsequent panel of the Court of Appeals considered the claim on the merits and held that the standards that were promulgated by USDA, which in essence delegated the development of standards to on-site veterinarians employed by the dealers, research facilities, and exhibitors covered by the Act, were sufficient.[88]

In sum, it is inaccurate to characterize *Glickman* as anything more than a narrow decision based only on the aesthetic interests of the plaintiff and not the interests of nonhumans, in a situation in which Congress had not provided other oversight mechanisms. Moreover, the subsequent litigation made clear that regulations that provide no meaningful protection for animal interests will suffice.

D. Additional Failures of the Welfarist Approach

The foregoing is not intended to be a complete survey of all developments that have occurred in the past dozen years. Rather, it focuses on what most animal advocates regard as the most significant advances during that period. There certainly have been some minor successes, particularly at the state level. For example, many states have now made felonies of at least some violations of state anticruelty laws,[89] and a number of states have increased penalties and closed loopholes concerning animal fighting.[90] But given the amount of time, energy, and money that has been expended by the animal-protection movement, a complete lack of success would be as shocking as what animal advocates appear to regard as major victories. Moreover, anticruelty laws

---

88. Animal Legal Defense Fund, Inc. v. Glickman, 204 F.3d 229 (D.C. Cir. 2000). The appellate court reversed a trial court decision, Animal Legal Defense Fund, Inc. v. Glickman, 943 F. Supp. 44 (D.D.C. 1996), which held that the USDA had not promulgated the regulations required by the Animal Welfare Act.

89. Stephan K. Otto, *State Animal Protection Laws—The Next Generation,* 11 ANIMAL L. 131, 134–38 (2005). *See also* FRANCIONE, *supra* note 2, at 68 (discussing whether this change will make any difference given the scope of application of anticruelty laws, the mens rea requirement, and the general reluctance to prosecute anticruelty cases); *infra* notes 174–78 and accompanying text (discussing anticruelty laws generally).

90. *2004 Legislative Review, supra* note 68, at 351–54 (2005).

affect a relatively small number of nonhumans, and animal fighting is one of the very few activities that we have historically been willing to prohibit. The brutal Hegins Pigeon Shoot, where thousands of pigeons were killed and wounded in a carnival-like setting every Labor Day in Hegins, Pennsylvania, which had for many years been the target of protests by animal advocates, was stopped by its organizers, but live bird shoots continue throughout Pennsylvania.[91]

There have been, however, no major success stories. Fur was a major target of animal organizations throughout the 1990s. Peter Singer claims that, as the result of efforts of animal advocates, the fur industry has been damaged and has not recovered.[92] Singer's claim is unfounded. Although fur sales in the United States in the 1990s to a reported $1 billion, "[s]ince 1999, sales have climbed steadily, reaching a record $1.8 billion in 2003."[93] The sale of furs "jumped to $11.3 billion worldwide in 2002, from $8.1 billion in 1998."[94] There has been a dramatic increase in the number of stores carrying fur and the number of designers using fur combined with a significant drop in the average age of fur buyers.[95] "In 2004, a Gallup poll found that 63 percent of respondents pronounced the buying and wearing of clothing made with animal fur 'morally acceptable.'"[96]

The failure of the anti-fur campaign presents a case study in the failure of welfarist strategy. Even advocacy organizations that purport to oppose all fur garments, including those made from "ranch-raised" animals, have routinely focused on the fur of certain animals, such as dogs and cats, or seals, as somehow morally distinguishable from the fur of other nonhumans.[97] This nonsensical distinction, combined with the general

---

91. Ian Urbina, *Animal Lovers See an Interstate Trade in Moving Targets,* N.Y. TIMES, June 10, 2004, at B1. For a description of the Hegins event, see FRANCIONE, *supra* note 1, at xiii–xv.

92. Singer, *supra* note 10, at 25.

93. Julie Scelfo, *Real Fur Is Fun Again,* NEWSWEEK, Oct. 11, 2004, at 48.

94. Lizette Alvarez, *'New Fur' Doesn't Look as if It Ever Kept a Mink Warm,* N.Y. TIMES, Oct. 15, 2004, at A4.

95. Wendy Navratil, *Fur's Hot Again; The Animal-Rights Message Has Skipped a Generation,* CHI. TRIB. Jan. 18, 2004, at Q1.

96. Rob Walker, *The Way We Live Now: Consumed; Pelt Appeal,* N.Y. TIMES, Feb. 12, 2006, at 30.

97. For example, both PETA, FurIsDead.com, China's Shocking Dog and Cat Fur Trade, http://www.furisdead.com/feat-dogcatfur.asp (last visited Mar. 19, 2007), and HSUS, Dog and Cat Victims of the Fur Trade, http://www.hsus.org/furfree/dogs_cats/dog_and_cat_victims.html (last visited Mar. 19, 2007), recommend that consumers purchase no fur products, but have campaigns that focus on dog and cat fur. *See infra* note 102 on the seal campaign.

failure of the movement to confront squarely that clothing made from other animal parts, such as leather and wool, is no less morally problematic than fur, has understandably made many people conclude that the campaign against fur is arbitrary. Finally, PETA's continued use of sexist campaigns to oppose fur (and other animal uses) has alienated many progressives and has trivialized the issue of fur in particular and animal exploitation in general.[98]

There have been a considerable number of instances in which animal advocates have failed to get even modest and ostensibly uncontroversial legislative changes. For example, attempts starting in 1975 to get a federal ban on leghold traps, which are prohibited or seriously restricted in only a handful of states, have been unsuccessful even though these traps are illegal in approximately ninety countries.[99] Attempts to pass a federal law to provide for the immediate and "humane" euthanasia of non-ambulatory, or "downed" animals, have been unsuccessful.[100] Efforts by legislators to ban shooting animals in enclosed areas, or "canned hunts," have been unsuccessful on the federal level, and only about half the states have laws that prohibit or regulate this activity even though many hunting groups regard these captive "hunts" as unsporting.[101] Despite decades of protests and boycotts by animal advocates, the Canadian seal cull continues, and the Canadian "government announced in 2003 a three-year total allowable catch of 975,000 animals."[102]

This article does not discuss the myriad instances in which there were new laws that actually have moved the animal-welfare agenda backward and have sought to strengthen or expand animal exploitation in various

---

98. I have often discussed PETA's use of sexism in campaigns. *See, e.g.,* FRANCIONE, *supra* note 3, at 74–76.

99. *2003 Legislative Review,* 10 ANIMAL L. 363, 364–67 (2004).

100. *Id.* at 367–70.

101. *2002 Legislative Review,* 9 ANIMAL L. 331, 338–40 (2003).

102. Canadian Press, *Eyes of World on Seal Hunt That Starts Tomorrow,* GUELPH MERCURY, Mar. 24, 2006, at A6. A number of animal-advocacy organizations, including HSUS, have formed a coalition, the ProtectSeals Network, to end the seal slaughter through a boycott of Canadian seafood. The Network urges those opposed to the seal slaughter to sign a pledge "not to buy Canadian seafood products such as snow crab, cod, scallops, and shrimp until Canada ends its commercial seal hunt for good." The petition may be found at https://community.hsus .org/campaign/protectseals (last visited Mar. 19, 2007). This suggests, of course, that sea animals have a different moral status than do seals, and implies that it is acceptable to eat Canadian seafood as soon as the commercial seal hunt ends.

respects. For example, a number of states are strengthening protections for hunters and preempting restrictions on hunting through amendments to make hunting a constitutional right.[103] There are, however, two examples involving the primary federal animal-welfare laws—the federal Animal Welfare Act and the federal Humane Slaughter Act—that demonstrate just how ineffective animal-welfare legislation is and thus deserve special mention.

The first example involves the application of the federal Animal Welfare Act[104] to rats, mice, and birds—approximately ninety percent of the animals used in laboratories. In 1970, Congress amended the Act to define "animal" to include "any live or dead dog, cat, monkey (nonhuman primate mammal), guinea pig, hamster, rabbit, or such other warm-blooded animal, as the Secretary [of Agriculture] may determine is being used, or is intended for use, for research, testing, experimentation, or exhibition purposes, or as a pet."[105] The Secretary consistently refused to determine that rats, mice, and birds were used for research or were pets, and for thirty years, animal advocates tried in a variety of ways to challenge this exclusion by the Secretary. In 2002, after the Secretary agreed to a regulation that would include rats, mice, and birds, Congress amended the Act to explicitly exclude rats, mice, and birds bred for use in research,[106] thus ending one of the longest campaigns in the history

---

103. *2003 Legislative Review, supra* note 99, at 378–82 (2004).

104. *See supra* note 27. Singer acknowledges that it is not possible to know the number of animals used in experiments in the United States, but he claims that estimates "suggest a similar story" of significant decline as in Britain. Singer, *supra* note 10, at 25. Putting aside the validity of this claim as applied to Britain, *see* note 10 *supra,* it is unclear how Singer can make such a claim about the United States since rats, mice, and birds, which account for over ninety percent of the nonhumans used in the United States, are not covered by the Animal Welfare Act and their numbers are not reported. Therefore, no one knows the number of animals used. Government statistics on the relatively small numbers of animals covered by the Act indicate that animal use has decreased somewhat but not in the dramatic way Singer suggests. *See, e.g.,* USDA, ANIMAL WELFARE REP. FISCAL YEAR 2004, at 10 (2004), *available* at http://www.aphis.usda.gov/ac/awreports/awreport2004.pdf.

105. Animal Welfare Act of 1970, Pub. L. No. 91-579, 84 Stat. 1560, 1561 (codified as amended at 7 U.S.C. § 2132(g) (2000)).

106. The exclusion of rats, mice, and birds from the definition of "animal" in the Animal Welfare Act was included as title X, subtitle D, section 10301, of the Farm Security and Rural Investment Act of 2002, Pub. L. No. 107-171, 116 Stat. 134 (2002). The exclusion is now codified at 7 U.S.C. § 2132(g) (2002). All vertebrate animals used in activities conducted or supported by the Public Health Service (PHS) are regulated in accordance with PHS policy. *See* OFFICE OF LABORATORY

of the animal-protection movement and establishing that the minimal provisions of the Act do not apply to the overwhelming percentage of nonhumans used in biomedical research in the United States.

The second example involves the other major centerpiece of animal welfare, the federal Humane Slaughter Act.[107] In 2001, *The Washington Post* published a story exposing widespread serious violations of the Act in slaughterhouses across the country.[108] This report, which discussed incidents such as the skinning and dismemberment of animals who were still alive, made clear that the Act was doing little to alleviate the suffering of nonhumans being slaughtered and that the USDA was not enforcing the Act. The response was a resolution stating that it is the sense of Congress that the Secretary of Agriculture should enforce the Act and "prevent needless suffering."[109] It is unclear which is more disturbing—the meaningless congressional response, or the reaction of the animal-protection community that the resolution is meaningful coupled with the persistent belief of many animal advocates that the Humane Slaughter Act is a significant piece of legislation in the first place.

ANIMAL WELFARE, NATIONAL INSTITUTES OF HEALTH, PUBLIC HEALTH SERVICE POLICY ON HUMANE CARE AND USE OF LABORATORY ANIMALS 8 (2002).

107. *See supra* note 4. The United States Department of Agriculture, which enforces the Humane Slaughter Act, interprets the Act to exclude poultry, which account for the largest number of animals slaughtered for food. *See* 9 C.F.R. §§ 313.1–.90 (2006). The exclusion of poultry under the Humane Slaughter Act parallels the exclusion of rats and mice under the Animal Welfare Act (although rats and mice are covered under other federal laws). *See supra* notes 104–06 and accompanying text. Animal advocates, led by HSUS, filed a lawsuit over the USDA's exclusion of poultry. *See* Elizabeth Williamson, *Humane Society to Sue Over Poultry Slaughtering; Suit Demands That Birds Be Killed or Rendered Unconscious Before Butchering,* WASH. POST, Nov. 21, 2005, at B02. HSUS argues that the present system of stunning poultry in an electrified water bath causes illness in humans through fecal contamination and increases injuries to slaughterhouse workers. The alternative proposed by HSUS is "controlled atmosphere killing," or gassing, of poultry. According to HSUS, this alternative "results in cost savings and increased revenues by decreasing carcass downgrades, contamination, and refrigeration costs; increasing meat yields, quality, and shelf life; and improving worker conditions" and "can improve worker conditions and safety, decreasing labor costs due to production line inefficiencies, injuries, and turnover from handling conscious birds." THE HUMANE SOCIETY OF THE UNITED STATES, AN HSUS REPORT: THE ECONOMICS OF ADOPTING ALTERNATIVE PRODUCTION PRACTICES TO ELECTRICAL STUNNING SLAUGHTER OF POULTRY 2 (2006), *available at* http://www.hsus.org/web-files/PDF/farm/econ_elecstun.pdf.

108. Joby Warrick, *'They Die Piece by Piece'; In Overtaxed Plants, Humane Treatment of Cattle Is Often a Battle Lost,* WASH. POST, Apr. 10, 2001, at A01.

109. The resolution on "humane" slaughter was included as title X, subtitle D, section 10305 of the Farm Security and Rural Investment Act of 2002, Pub. L. No. 107-171, 116 Stat. 134 (2002).

III

PROPERTY: STRUCTURAL LIMITS ON THE PROTECTION OF THE INTERESTS OF NONHUMANS

We could, of course, treat animals better than we do even if they retained their status as our property. For instance, the treatment of animals in certain European countries may be marginally better than it is in the United States, although animals have property status in those countries as well.[110] But it is important to understand that the property paradigm presents important structural and practical limitations on the human–animal relationship. Moreover, if we do accord protection to animal interests beyond what is required to be protected in order to facilitate their exploitation in a cost-effective manner, that may in a formal sense represent a diminution of the property status of the nonhuman, but it would not necessarily represent a recognition of the inherent value of nonhumans or be a step in the direction of recognizing the right of a nonhuman not to be treated as the property of humans.[111] Also, such additional protection, like animal-welfare measures generally, may perpetuate and even increase animal exploitation by making people feel better about supposedly more "humane" animal exploitation.

In discussing my views on animals as property, Professor Cass Sunstein claims that there is nothing inherent in property status that limits the protections that we can provide to animals and that property ownership is limited in all sorts of ways. He notes:

> You own your house, but you are probably not allowed to burn it down or blow it up, or to use it as a concert hall. You own your stereo, but if you have nearby neighbors you cannot play music as loud as you want. In most domains, the rights of "owners" are severely qualified.[112]

---

110. *See supra* note 10.

111. *See* FRANCIONE, *supra* note 3, at 190–219 (discussing welfarist changes that may represent incremental eradication of the property status of nonhumans); *see also infra* notes 132–55 and accompanying text (discussing new welfarism and incremental change, including whether changes result in change in property status).

112. Sunstein, *supra* note 7, at 44.

Sunstein argues that "the status of 'owner' is not incompatible, in principle, with a firm commitment to preventing the unnecessary suffering of animals or even with treating animals as beings with both legal rights and intrinsic value."[113] He claims that "[t]he fact of ownership even protects animals in important ways" through the duties imposed by animal-welfare laws.[114] He argues that we should seek to ban and to restrict "the most indefensible practices" concerning nonhumans.[115] Sunstein's position is problematic in several respects.[116]

A. Animal Property and Animal Interests

Sunstein is, of course, correct to say that property ownership is qualified and limited, but he ignores certain aspects of property theory and the distinction between property and persons, which make his comments inapplicable to animal property. Although there are limitations on how we use our property, those limits are imposed to benefit other persons (natural or corporate); they are not imposed for the benefit of the property

---

113. *Id.* Similarly, David Favre argues that "[i]t is an incorrect legal analysis that the interests of animals cannot be accommodated within the legal system if they remain legal property." Favre, *supra* note 7, at 91. He states that we can accord animals "the legal respect that they deserve," *id.*, "by dividing the concept of title into legal and equitable categories and then awarding the equitable title to the animal." *Id.* at n.11. Putting aside the lack of clarity of the expression "the legal respect that they deserve," there are at least three responses to Favre's proposal. First, however Favre wants to characterize it, what he is doing is proposing limits on property ownership. It is not clear why he thinks that going about this limitation in the rather peculiar way that he proposes will be any more socially or legally acceptable than would the conceptually more simple prohibitions on the use of animals that are presently available and largely rejected. Second, to the extent that the rights of "equitably self-owned" nonhumans will be shaped by anticruelty laws, as Favre proposes, nonhumans will receive little protection because anticruelty laws provide almost no protection to animals. Third, Favre also suggests that the human–nonhuman relationship be modeled on the parent–child relationship, which does not address anything more than the relationship that humans have with companion animals and would have no application to nonhumans used in other contexts.
114. Sunstein, *supra* note 7, at 44. Sunstein once again finds an ally in David Favre. *See* David Favre, *Equitable Self-Ownership for Animals,* 50 DUKE L.J. 473, 495 (2000) ("Under our present system, full responsibility comes with ownership."). *See infra* note 196 and accompanying text (discussing the "benefit" that nonhumans receive from property status).
115. Sunstein, *supra* note 7, at 43.
116. For a further discussion of Sunstein's views, *see* Gary L. Francione, *Equal Consideration and the Interest of Nonhuman Animals in Continued Existence: A Response to Professor Sunstein,* 2006 U. CHI. LEGAL F. 231.

itself. It is true that I cannot burn my house down or blast my stereo so that it disturbs my neighbors. But that is because we are concerned about the effect of my actions on other persons—others who may be in or near my house when I set it ablaze or my neighbors, who might be trying to sleep. Prohibitions on the destruction of landmarks are not imposed for the benefit of the property involved but to protect human interests in the enjoyment of that property.

Sunstein is also correct to note that "current law forbids people from treating animals however they wish to treat them."[117] But he overemphasizes the extent to which the law regulates our treatment of animals. Although the law requires that I provide food and shelter to my dog, there is nothing to stop me from beating her on a regular basis to train her as a guard dog or to discipline her, or from keeping her on a chain in the back yard and never having contact with her, or from taking her to a veterinarian and having her "put to sleep" for no reason other than that I no longer want her. Indeed, I can as a general matter kill her myself as long as I do so in a "humane" way and as long as I do not violate other laws and regulations that are not in any way concerned with the welfare of the dog, such as local prohibitions on slaughtering animals in multi-family dwellings or discharging firearms in particular places. I have an obligation to provide food and water to the animals whom I keep on my farm, but I may keep them in confined conditions and perform a number of procedures on them that are very painful.

Sunstein also fails to appreciate the limiting principle that animates the legal regulations that do exist. To the extent that the law applies (and many animal uses are exempt from regulation) and recognizes that certain animal interests must be protected, that protection is, for the most part, limited to ensuring that the animal can be exploited for a particular purpose. In order for us to exploit animals, we must provide some minimal protection for their interests so that they can serve the purposes for which we are using them. The law allows me to treat a dog that I use as a guard animal very badly, but I cannot (at least in theory) starve her to death. I am legally obligated to provide a minimal level of care to her, but not much more than is required to keep her alive so that she can serve that purpose. If I do not provide minimal sustenance and veterinary care

---

117. Sunstein, *supra* note 7, at 44.

to my cows and pigs, they will die prematurely and their corpses will not be suited to be sold as meat. If I do not provide adequate food or water to a laboratory animal, and the experiment does not call for starvation or dehydration (as some do), then I have introduced a variable that may result in invalid scientific data. Given that we allow researchers to conduct starvation and dehydration experiments on nonhumans, a requirement that animals exploited in laboratories receive food and water has nothing to do with recognizing that animals have inherent value or that their interests have moral significance. The standards of animal welfare are more concerned with recognizing that if we want to exploit animals in particular ways we have no choice but to provide at least some protection for their interests.

B. Animal Property and "Unnecessary" Suffering

Sunstein argues that the status of animals as property is not inconsistent with a commitment to prevent "unnecessary" suffering and that we ought to prohibit or ban "the most indefensible practices." The problem is that Sunstein does not—and, indeed, cannot—provide a coherent theory of what constitutes "unnecessary" suffering and what is an "indefensible" practice. A central point of my argument that Sunstein and other critics fail to address is that *most* of our uses of animals cannot plausibly be described as "necessary" and that these uses per se are, indeed, morally indefensible irrespective of whether we treat animals "humanely."[118] We do not need to eat animals, wear animals, or use animals for entertainment purposes, and our only defense of these uses is our pleasure,

---

118. Robert Garner argues that the welfarist approach is

> not trying to show that the use of animals is morally wrong regardless of the benefits to humans. Rather, the movement is trying to show that most, if not all, of the cruel and harmful techniques currently employed on animals are unnecessary in the sense that they do not produce human benefits or that such benefits can be achieved in other ways.

Robert Garner, *Animal Welfare: A Political Defense,* 1 J. ANIMAL L. & ETHICS 161, 167 (2006). Garner claims that I accept this analysis, *id.,* and that it is "somewhat ironic" that I do so given my criticism of Garner's defense of welfarism. GARNER, *supra* note 7, at 41 n.2. Garner fails to understand that my discussion of necessity concerns animal use per se and not the treatment of animals, which, as Garner correctly notes, is the focus of the welfarist approach. *See* FRANCIONE, *supra* note 2, at 1–49.

amusement, and convenience.[119] *Any* suffering that we impose on animals incidental to these uses is "unnecessary" and "indefensible."

Sunstein does not agree with my position that we should all adopt a vegan lifestyle and stop eating or using all animal products. Rather, he argues that we should not inflict more suffering than is necessary given the unnecessary uses of animals. It is difficult to understand how this can mean anything more than that we ought not to inflict *gratuitous* suffering on animals. But no one would disagree with that position; indeed, generally this is all that is required under animal-welfare laws. Sunstein appears to believe that the law presently gives animals "rights" because it prohibits the infliction of "unnecessary" suffering and requires "humane" treatment.[120] A right to "humane" treatment and to be free from "unnecessary" suffering is no "right" at all in that it prohibits only those actions that do not benefit humans and would, in any event, not be committed by rational property owners.[121]

---

119. It may be argued that the use of nonhumans in experiments to find cures for serious human illnesses is not trivial in the same way as our other uses of animals. Necessity claims are suspect in this context as well, and I maintain that animal use cannot be justified morally even if it is necessary in some sense. *See* Gary L. Francione, *The Use of Nonhuman Animals in Biomedical Research: Necessity and Justification,* 35 J.L. MED. & ETHICS 241 (2007).

120. *See* Cass R. Sunstein, *The Rights of Animals,* 70 U. CHI. L. REV. 387, 389–90 (2003). Sunstein argues that the primary problem is a lack of standing to enforce these "rights." *Id.* at 391–92.

121. British lawyer Mike Radford maintains that, at least as far as English and Scottish law are concerned, I am wrong to maintain that when human and nonhuman interests are balanced, the animal loses whenever the human has a commercial interest. *See* RADFORD, *supra* note 7, at 249. According to Radford, *Ford v. Wiley,* 23 Q.B.D. 203 (1889), a case in which a British court held that dehorning older cattle with saws violated the anticruelty law because it caused unnecessary suffering, establishes the application of a two-stage process to determine necessity. "First, it must be shown that the animal's treatment was to effect an 'adequate and reasonable object'; secondly, 'There must be proportion between the object and the means'." RADFORD, *supra* note 7, at 248 (quoting 23 Q.B.D. at 210, 215). A closer examination of *Ford v. Wiley,* including other painful procedures discussed approvingly by the court, such as castration of animals and the severity used in the breaking of horses, provides a context for the meaning of the test that Radford regards as refuting my notion about the general interpretation of necessity. Moreover, *Ford v. Wiley* actually reinforces my view that suffering for economic reasons is generally considered as necessary as long as the practice in question is commonly accepted by those involved in animal agriculture. The opinions of both Lord Chief Justice Coleridge and Justice Hawkins noted that the practice of the dehorning older cattle had been discontinued in England, Wales, and most of Scotland, and was no longer an accepted agricultural practice. For a further discussion of *Ford v. Wiley* and subsequent British case law holding that if an agricultural practice is commonly accepted there is no violation of the anticruelty law even if there are less painful alternatives, *see* FRANCIONE, *supra* note 2, at 61–62.

To the extent that Sunstein wants to go beyond prohibiting gratuitous suffering, which no one defends, it is difficult to understand how he can regard suffering incidental to efficient exploitation as "unnecessary" or "indefensible." Indeed, animal exploiters routinely argue that the practices identified as objectionable by welfarists actually do provide a sufficient level of animal welfare. For example, the National Pork Producers Council maintains that although a number of different production systems are used in the pork industry, intensive confinement systems, such as gestation crates, are actually beneficial to the pigs and that producers would not use them if they were not consistent with the welfare of the animals: "Producers' livelihoods depend on the well being and performance of their livestock. To do anything short of providing the best, humane care possible would be self-defeating."[122] Those involved in the ranch-raising of animals used to make fur coats claim that if the animals were not properly cared for they would not produce top-quality fur.[123] Indeed, animal exploiters claim that these sorts of performance measures are the only, or at least the primary, way of measuring welfare in an objective and non-anthropomorphic manner. If all that Sunstein is saying is that forms of exploitation that are not efficient should be replaced by more efficient forms of exploitation, then he is merely promoting the traditional welfarist position that treats animals as nothing more than commodities with only extrinsic value, and again, no animal exploiter would disagree with him.

Sunstein may be claiming that certain practices are unnecessary for the production of animal products under a different system. He may, for instance, be saying that intensive confinement would not be necessary if we were to raise animals on family farms, which, of course, would cause the price of animal products to rise dramatically. Such an alternative form of animal agriculture may very well improve animal welfare, but animals would still suffer a great deal and that suffering would be no more defensible or necessary given that it is not necessary to eat animal

---

122. National Pork Producers Council, Gestation Stalls: The Facts, http://www.nppc.org/public _policy/gestation_stalls.html (last visited Mar. 19, 2007). Some welfarists argue that gestation crates are not as economically beneficial as alternative production systems. *See supra* notes 56 and 65 and accompanying text.

123. *See, e.g.*, FUR COMMISSION USA, FUR FACTS 5 (2005), *available at* http://www.furcommission .com/resource/Resources/FAF.pdf.

products at all. Once we acknowledge that most of our uses of nonhumans—however "humane" we may treat those involved—are not necessary in any meaningful sense of that term, then the notion that we ought to prohibit "unnecessary" suffering becomes unprincipled and reflective only of subjective and often elitist preferences.

C. Animal Property and Inherent Value

Sunstein agrees that "sentient animals have intrinsic value, and that animal well-being is a good in itself,"[124] but he maintains that it is possible to recognize that intrinsic value even if animals remain the property of humans. Although we certainly could treat animals better even if they remain our property, Sunstein fails to recognize the limitations that exist as the result of our regarding them as our property, as things that we own. Property has only extrinsic or conditional value. When we say that a person has inherent or intrinsic value, what we mean is that she has value that is not solely extrinsic and conditional. We recognize that she has value because she values herself, even if no one else values her. We may use other humans as means to our ends, but we cannot use them exclusively as means to our ends.[125]

---

124. Sunstein, *supra* note 7, at 45. Owners of companion animals may regard those animals as having more than market value, and one might say that the owner regards the animal as having "intrinsic" or "inherent" value. That sense of intrinsic value, which concerns sentimental or idiosyncratic valuation by particular animal owners, is, however, different from the notion of moral value that Sunstein uses when he talks about intrinsic value.

125. *See* FRANCIONE, *supra* note 2, at 90–98. Sunstein maintains that "[i]n many domains human beings seem to be 'used,' and the relevant practices are not objectionable for that reason." Sunstein, *supra* note 7, at 45. He argues that "[w]hen you hire a plumber, a lawyer, an architect, or someone to clean your house, you are treating them as means, not as ends." *Id.* Although it is true that we use others as means to our ends, we are not allowed to treat them exclusively as means to ends. We can, for instance, value our plumber as a means to the end of repairing a leak. But if we do not think that the plumber is competent, we are not allowed to treat her solely as an economic commodity all of whose interests may be ignored if it benefits us to do so. We cannot enslave the incompetent plumber in a forced-labor camp; we cannot use her as a nonconsenting subject in a biomedical experiment or as an unwilling organ donor. Even if we do not value the plumber as a plumber, she still has residual value that prevents us from valuing her fundamental interests at zero. In the book that Sunstein was reviewing in the context of making these comments, I use the plumber example and distinguish between treating the plumber as a means to an end and treating her exclusively as a means to an end. *See* FRANCIONE, *supra* note 2, at 90–91.

As a legal matter, we do not regard animals as having any value apart from the value we accord them. For the most part, that valuation is tied to their status as property. We treat animals exclusively as means to our ends. Sunstein may be correct that we can do a better job of taking animal interests seriously, but that is much easier said than done. Consider the situation of human slavery in North America.[126] This institution was structurally identical to the institution of animal ownership. The slave was regarded as property, and the slave owner was able to disregard almost all of the slave's interests if it was economically beneficial to do so. The law generally deferred to the slave owner's judgment as to the value of the slave. There was no meaningful balancing of interests, as the owner's property interest in the slave almost always trumped any interest of the slave who was ostensibly protected under the law. Slave-welfare laws failed to establish any meaningful limit on the use of slaves, just as animal-welfare laws fail to establish any meaningful limit on our use of nonhumans. There are powerful economic, legal, political, and social forces that militate against treating property as anything other than property. We should, of course, provide as much animal welfare as can be economically justified; for instance, we ought to substitute group housing for the gestation crate if that, in fact, reduces production costs and increases productivity. But this use of "ought" is related to economic rationality and not to any recognition of the inherent value of animals.

Sunstein claims that "the language of property does not necessarily signify that animals will be treated as means."[127] It is not clear what Sunstein means by distinguishing between the language of property discourse and the fact of property status. In any event, we talk about animals as property because animals *are* property. To the extent that Sunstein is suggesting that animal welfare is consistent with recognizing that animals have inherent value, I do not think that Sunstein appreciates that welfarist measures rarely, if ever, require that we protect animal interests in the absence of an identifiable—usually economic—human benefit, and even when they do, they are not related to inherent value. Sunstein frequently uses the example of dogs and cats—the nonhumans who most often serve as companions of humans—as beings to whom we

---

126. *See* ALAN WATSON, SLAVE LAW IN THE AMERICAS (1989); FRANCIONE, *supra* note 2, at 86–90.
127. Sunstein, *supra* note 7, at 44.

can and do accord inherent value despite their property status. Certainly, many of us regard our nonhuman companions as having inherent value. But those of us who do so do not really regard our nonhumans primarily as our property or as anything remotely similar to our televisions, cars or the like. Indeed, we regard those nonhumans as members of our families. As far as the law is concerned, however, companion animals have no inherent value except in an idiosyncratic sense.[128] The law protects the ability of property owners to treat property *as if* it had inherent value.

D. Animal Property and Equal Consideration

Finally, the property status of animals effectively and as a very practical matter precludes our giving *serious* consideration to their interests, even though it certainly is possible, at least in theory, to do better than we presently do. It is, however, not possible to accord nonhuman animals *equal* consideration if they are the property of humans.[129] Although we do not and cannot protect humans from all suffering, the laws of virtually every nation and customary international law recognize that all humans have the right not to be chattel and not to suffer at all from their use exclusively as resources of others—however "humane" that use may be. It is not possible to accord equal consideration to animal interests if animals are property because their very status as property means that they will be used in ways that we would regard as inappropriate to use any humans.

I have argued elsewhere that there is a compelling argument that utilitarian philosopher Jeremy Bentham (1748–1832) rejected human slavery not only because he thought that slavery had social disutility, but because he recognized that the interests of slaves would never count for as much as the similar interests of slave owners.[130] Therefore, even though Bentham rejected moral rights as a general matter, it is certainly arguable

---

128. *See supra* note 124 and accompanying text.
129. *See* FRANCIONE, *supra* note 2, at 81–102; *see also* Francione, *supra* note 116, at 239–45 (discussing equal consideration, property status, and the interests of animals in continued existence).
130. *See* FRANCIONE, *supra* note 2, at 130–50. Bentham, who is regarded as an act-utilitarian (one for whom the right act is that which maximizes net welfare in the particular situation) was, at the very least, a rule-utilitarian (one for whom the right act is that which, when followed as a general matter, will maximize net welfare even if it does not do so in the particular situation) when it came to slavery in that he rejected the morality of slavery as an institution.

that he recognized that every human had to have at least a right not to be the property of others in order to be a member of the moral community in the first place. Bentham and others who have sought to apply the principle of equal consideration to nonhuman property have erred in not recognizing that the same analysis applies to animals. The principle of equal consideration cannot be applied meaningfully to animals who are property any more than it can be applied to humans who are property.[131] In short, the equal consideration of animal interests necessarily requires the recognition that nonhumans have a right not to be treated as the property of humans.

IV

NEW WELFARISM: A FALSE DILEMMA AND AN INCORRECT ASSUMPTION

Many animal advocates recognize that the property status of animals is problematic, and they claim to seek, as a long-term objective at least, the modification of the legal status of animals and perhaps even the eradication of property status and the abolition of animal exploitation. Nevertheless, these advocates, to whom I refer as "new welfarists,"[132] maintain that at this time we do not really have a choice. We must pursue welfarist change or do nothing. They maintain that the abolition of exploitation is "idealistic" or "utopian" because it cannot be achieved immediately

---

131. *See id.* Both Bentham and Peter Singer seek to apply the principle of equal consideration to animal interests. Although both reject human slavery, neither rejects the property status of animals, in part because both believe that animals do not have an interest in their lives and only have an interest in not suffering. As a result, neither sees a problem per se with using animals for human purposes. I argue that sentience implies an interest in continued life and that Bentham and Singer err by linking an interest in life with reflective self-awareness or human-like self-consciousness. The view that animals do not have an interest in continued existence also appears to be the basis of Sunstein's position that animal use per se does not raise a serious moral issue. *See* Francione, *supra* note 116.

132. *See generally* FRANCIONE, *supra* note 3 (discussing the phenomenon of "new welfarism" or the view that animal rights offers no normative guidance in the short term and animal-welfare regulation will lead to the abolition of exploitation, or to some significant recognition of the inherent value of nonhumans, in the long term). All of my critics promote a version of new welfarism. *See supra* note 7. Modern "animal law" is also based on new welfarism and assumes that the alternative to traditional welfare is to forsake the welfare of animals now and that welfare regulation will lead to the recognition of the inherent value of nonhumans. *See infra* note 160 and accompanying text.

and that animal-welfare reform is the only way to reduce the suffering of animals now. Moreover, many claim that incremental welfarist change will eventually bring about the abolition of animal exploitation. Both tenets of new welfarism are wrong.

A. The Rights Position Provides Normative Guidance

First, new welfarism establishes a false dilemma: pursue traditional animal welfare or do nothing to help nonhumans who are suffering now. The dilemma is false because, in addition to the general failure of traditional animal welfare to alleviate animal suffering, the rights position does provide meaningful normative guidance and is not "idealistic" or "utopian." Although the rights position is often misrepresented,[133] it does not maintain that there is any possibility of the immediate abolition of all institutionalized exploitation or reject incremental change as a means of achieving abolition.[134] Rather, the rights position seeks change that incrementally eradicates the property status of nonhumans and recognizes that nonhumans have inherent value.

The rights position provides definite normative guidance for incremental change on an individual level, as well as on the level of social and legal change.[135] On the individual level, rights theory prescribes incremental change in the form of veganism.[136] Veganism is not merely a

---

133. For example, Robert Garner incorrectly states that my position is "that reforms to the treatment of animals short of abolition are not worth having." GARNER, *supra* note 7, at 221.

134. *See, e.g.*, Favre, *supra* note 7, at 90. Favre, commenting on what he understands to be my position, states that those who criticize welfarist incremental change "possess an incorrect understanding of property law" and that "[i]t is highly unlikely that the elimination of property status will occur in the foreseeable future." Favre misses the point on a number of levels. No one maintains that property status is going to be eliminated anytime soon. The point is whether we should pursue its elimination incrementally through regulations that diminish property rights in nonhumans rather than pursue welfarist regulations that, for the most part, merely reinforce the property paradigm. For a discussion of this issue, see FRANCIONE, *supra* note 3, at 160–62. For a discussion about how incremental change as steps toward an identifiable goal has worked in another context (the victims' rights movement), and why the incremental approach that I propose is preferable to the approach urged by others to seek change in the status of nonhumans through common-law adjudication, *see* Douglas E. Beloof, *Crime Victims' Rights: Critical Concepts for Animal Rights*, 7 ANIMAL L. 19, 25–29 (2001).

135. *See* FRANCIONE, *supra* note 3, at 147–219. Indeed, it is the welfarist position, which maintains that we ought to pursue any measure that reduces suffering, that fails to provide normative guidance because almost any measure can be said to reduce suffering. *See id.* at 156–62.

136. *See, e.g., id.* at 152.

matter of diet; it is a moral and political commitment to abolition on the individual level and extends not only to matters of food, but to clothing and other products. Many animal advocates claim to favor animal rights and to want to abolish animal exploitation but continue to eat animal products. That is no different from someone who claims to be in favor of the abolition of slavery but who continues to own slaves. Moreover, there is no meaningful distinction between eating meat and eating dairy or other animal products. Nonhumans exploited in the dairy industry live longer than those used for meat, but they are treated worse during that life, and they end up in the same slaughterhouse after which we consume their flesh anyway. There is probably more suffering in a glass of milk or an ice cream cone than there is in a steak.

Some animal advocates claim that veganism is a matter of personal philosophy and should not be identified as a baseline principle of the rights movement. But that claim is incoherent. It is not necessary in any sense to eat meat or dairy products. If the animal-rights movement cannot take a principled position on an activity that results in the suffering and death of billions of animals for no reason other than that we enjoy the taste of meat and dairy, then the movement can take no principled stand on any institutional exploitation.

Rather than embrace veganism as a clear moral baseline, the animal-advocacy movement has instead adopted the notion that we can "consume with conscience." For example, Peter Singer maintains that we can be "conscientious omnivores" and exploit animals ethically if, for example, we choose to eat only animals who have been well-cared-for and then killed without pain or distress.[137] Singer praises purveyors of "humanely" exploited animal products, such as Whole Foods Markets, Inc. and its CEO, John Mackey, as "ethically responsible."[138] Animal advocate Tom Regan featured Mackey as a keynote speaker for a 2005 conference entitled "The Power of One,"[139] which focused on the ability of individuals to make meaningful changes for nonhumans. PETA gave Whole

---

137. PETER SINGER & JIM MASON, THE WAY WE EAT: WHY OUR FOOD CHOICES MATTER 81–183 (2006).

138. *See id.* at 177–83.

139. *See* Promotional Brochure from The Culture and Animals Foundation and The Institute for Animals and Society, The Power of One: The Twentieth Annual International Compassionate Living Festival, *available at* http://www.animalsandsociety.org/documents/PowerofOnebrochure .pdf (last visited Mar. 19, 2007). Regan is the author of THE CASE FOR ANIMAL RIGHTS (1983).

Foods an award in 2004, claiming that the company "has consistently done more for animal welfare than any retailer in the industry, requiring that its producers adhere to strict standards."[140]

Putting aside whether these supposedly "strict standards" make any real difference to the nonhumans involved,[141] it is, as a general matter, always better to do less harm than more once we have decided to inflict harm. But the notion that the animal movement actively promotes doing less harm as a morally acceptable solution to the problem of animal exploitation is troubling. That is, if X is going to rape Y, it is "better" that X not beat Y as well. It would, however, be morally repugnant to maintain that we can be "conscientious rapists" by ensuring that we not beat rape victims. Similarly, it is disturbing that animal advocates are promoting the notion that we can be morally "conscientious omnivores" if we eat the supposedly "humanely" produced products of Whole Foods and other purveyors. Not only is such a position in conflict with the notion that animal lives have moral significance, but it strongly encourages those concerned about nonhumans to see continued consumption as a morally acceptable alternative to adopting a vegan lifestyle.

In any event, any claim to embrace the rights or abolitionist position without accepting that veganism is the only morally consistent way to take immediate action to make that happen at least in one's own life makes no sense. Veganism represents a rejection of the commodity status of nonhumans and a recognition of their inherent value.

On the social and legal level, there needs to be a paradigm shift as a social matter before the legal system will respond in a meaningful way. I disagree with those who maintain that the legal system will lead in the struggle for animal rights or that significant legal change will occur in the absence of the development of a political and social movement in support of animal rights and the abolition of animal exploitation.[142]

The most important form of incremental change on a social level is education about veganism and the need to abolish, not merely to regulate,

---

140. PETA, 2004 PETA Progress Awards, http://www.peta.org/feat/proggy/2004/winners.html #retailer (last visited Mar. 19, 2007).

141. Professor Ibrahim maintains that the "strict standards" of Whole Foods do not provide much protection for animals. *See* Darian M. Ibrahim, *A Return to Descartes: Property, Profit, and the Corporate Ownership of Animals*, 70 LAW & CONTEMP. PROBS. 89, 109–11 (Winter 2007).

142. *See, e.g.*, STEVEN M. WISE, RATTLING THE CAGE: TOWARD LEGAL RIGHTS FOR ANIMALS (2000).

the institutionalized exploitation of animals.[143] The animal-advocacy movement in the United States has seriously failed to educate the public about the need for the abolition of animal exploitation. Although there are many reasons for this failure, a primary one is that animal-advocacy groups find it easier to promote welfarist campaigns aimed at reducing "unnecessary" suffering that have little practical effect and are often endorsed by the industry involved. Such campaigns are easy for advocates to package and sell and they do not offend anyone. It is easier to tell people that they can be morally "conscientious omnivores" than it is to take the position that veganism is a moral baseline. That, however, is precisely the problem. No one disagrees with the principle that it is wrong to inflict "unnecessary" suffering and that we ought to treat animals "humanely." But, as 200 years of animal welfare have made plain, these are merely platitudes in light of the property status of animals.

To the extent that national organizations promote abolition, they do so simultaneously with promoting welfarist campaigns, and the result is a confusing message that provides no clear direction for social change. For example, PETA claims to promote the abolition of animal exploitation while giving awards to various animal exploiters, such as Temple Grandin and Whole Foods, Inc. On one hand, PETA claims to support veganism; on the other hand, it encourages the notion that "humane" animal exploitation is morally acceptable and praiseworthy.

Veganism and abolitionist education provide practical and incremental strategies both in terms of reducing animal suffering now and in terms of building a movement in the future that will be able to obtain legislation more meaningful than regulations (mischaracterized as "bans") on the use of gestation crates in states that do not even have producers who use gestation crates, or the establishment of "sanctuaries"

---

143. *See, e.g.,* FRANCIONE, *supra* note 3, at 177–89. I am bewildered by those critics who claim that I emphasize the importance of legislation over non-legal social changes, such as education and the activities of grassroots activists. *See, e.g.,* Matthew Pamental, *Pragmatism and Pets: Best Friends Animal Sanctuary, Maddie's Fund^{sm}, and No More Homeless Pets in Utah, in* ANIMAL PRAGMATISM: RETHINKING HUMAN-NONHUMAN RELATIONSHIPS 210, 211 (Erin McKenna & Andrew Light eds., 2004) ("[B]y focusing solely on animal rights legislation Francione overlooks two crucial components in any reconstruction of social conditions: community support and education. He therefore ignores the successes of local, grassroots, volunteer activities in improving the treatment of animals."). In addition to being critical of legislation and emphasizing education as the primary means of social change, I have also emphasized the importance of grassroots activities. *See, e.g.,* FRANCIONE, *supra* note 3, at 71–74.

where "retired" animals can be used for experiments if there is a "public health need." If, in the late 1980s—when the animal-advocacy community in the United States decided very deliberately to pursue a welfarist agenda—a substantial portion of movement resources had been invested in vegan and abolitionist education, there would likely be hundreds of thousands more vegans than there are today. This is a very conservative estimate given the hundreds of millions of dollars that have been expended by animal-advocacy groups to promote welfarist legislation and initiatives. I maintain that having the increased number of vegans would reduce suffering more by decreasing demand for animal products than all of the welfarist "successes" put together and multiplied ten-fold.[144] Increasing the number of vegans would also help to build a political and economic base required for the social change that is a necessary predicate for significant legal change.[145] Given limited time and limited financial resources, it is not clear how anyone who seeks abolition as a long-term goal, or who at least accepts that the property status of animals is a most serious impediment to any significant change and must at least be radically modified, could believe that expansion of traditional animal welfare is a rational and efficient choice, putting aside any considerations about inconsistencies in moral theory.

There are "compelling reasons for animal rights advocates to spend their limited time and resources on incremental changes achieved through various forms of education, protest, and boycotts," rather than legislative or administrative regulation.[146] The primary reason is that regulation cannot succeed unless it has at least the tacit support of in-

---

144. An average omnivore in the United States is responsible for at least thirty-two nonhuman deaths per year. This number is based on an estimate of 9.5 billion animals killed in the United States and consumed by a population of 300 million. The number of animals killed does not include fish or other sea animals, and only reflects animal use for food and not for other purposes.

145. Robert Garner defends the welfarist strategy because he views it as earning the respect of decisionmakers and making possible short-term improvements, although he admits they often do not amount to much. GARNER, *supra* note 7, at 220–30. Garner apparently believes that minimal change is all we can expect given the lack of public support for more. But he concedes defeat on the root cause of the problem—the lack of public support for more significant change—and instead focuses on masking its symptoms. Garner discusses the importance of unification of the movement but fails to consider that if animal advocates were to unify behind the abolitionist position, and not the welfarist position, this might lead to the formation of a political movement that would be able to obtain more significant change.

146. *See* FRANCIONE, *supra* note 3, at 163.

stitutional animal exploiters. The price of this support is compromise that generally eviscerates the regulation and limits it to measures that make exploitation more economically beneficial to exploiters.[147] This is why education and social change are so important and must precede legal change. There is simply no political base to support any radical legal change at this time. Although many people have vague sympathies toward animals, most eat animals and there is no abolitionist movement to support measures that would challenge the property status of animals in any serious way. Indeed, the leaders of the animal-advocacy movement actively encourage the public to believe that being a "conscientious omnivore" is morally acceptable.

If, despite these cautions, which have become more pronounced in my mind in the past dozen years, animal advocates nevertheless want to pursue change through legislation, administrative regulation, or litigation, those campaigns ought to be explicitly targeted at eradicating the property status of animals in an incremental way. On the one hand, no single incremental measure will succeed in achieving equal consideration for nonhumans because equal consideration is not possible as long as animals are property. On the other hand, most welfarist measures do nothing but require that animal exploiters act in a more rational way and do a more efficient job exploiting their animal property.

The problem is that it is tempting for animal advocates who need successful campaigns for fundraising purposes to portray any measure that protects an animal interest and that is arguably not required to be protected for economic reasons as a meaningful step away from property status. For example, a proposal not based on meat quality or similar concerns to give battery hens additional cage space may be regarded as not treating the hen exclusively as property. But such a measure obviously does little, if anything, to relieve suffering and any good that such a measure does is probably more than offset by the public perception that animal use has been made more "humane" and is, therefore, more acceptable. Moreover, such a measure does nothing to eradicate property status in the long term in any meaningful sense and may even reinforce that status.

---

147. *See* William A. Reppy, Jr., *Broad Exemptions in Animal-Cruelty Statutes Unconstitutionally Deny Equal Protection of the Law*, 70 LAW & CONTEMP. PROBS. 255, 256–60 (Winter 2007).

In order for incremental change to be a step in the direction of abolition rather than marching in place within the property paradigm, it is
necessary to identify measures that explicitly and progressively recognize
that nonhumans have more than extrinsic or conditional value alone.
Since no one incremental step will achieve abolition, identifying criteria
for incremental steps in diminishing the property status of nonhumans
will necessarily be imprecise. In *Rain Without Thunder*, I recognized this
necessary lack of precision and I presented my preliminary thoughts on
five conjunctive criteria that might be used to identify incremental measures that would necessarily fall short of abolishing the property status
of nonhumans but that would nevertheless represent significant steps
away from property status.[148] The idea was to identify regulations that, although not abolishing property status altogether, went well beyond the
efficient exploitation of traditional welfare and rejected the status of animals as commodities through the explicit recognition that nonhumans
have inherent value and interests that must be protected irrespective of
economic consequences. Given that these incremental measures do not
abolish property status, their primary value is as stepping stones on the
path toward abolition. Incremental measures cannot lead to more incremental measures without reflecting a progressive recognition of the inherent value of animals.

Briefly summarized, these criteria involve prohibitions[149] of significant institutional activities,[150] as opposed to traditional welfarist regulation requiring "humane" treatment or relatively minor prohibitions. For
example, a prohibition on the use of any leghold trap is to be preferred
over a requirement that any trapping be done "humanely," or with the
use of a "padded" leghold trap. A prohibition on the use of any animals
in a particular type of experiment is to be preferred over a requirement
of an animal-care committee to monitor the treatment of animals used

---

148. *See* FRANCIONE, *supra* note 3, at 190–219. Critics who claim that I propose no incremental le-
gal change have apparently overlooked this aspect of my work. *See, e.g.,* Andrew Light & Erin
McKenna, *Introduction: Pragmatism and the Future of Human-Nonhuman Relationships, in* ANI-
MAL PRAGMATISM, *supra* note 143, at 7–8. I accept, however, that this portion of *Rain Without
Thunder,* which I presented explicitly as a preliminary analysis, was not as clear as it could
have been and I plan to clarify my views on incremental regulatory change in future writing.

149. *See* FRANCIONE, *supra* note 3, at 192–96 ("Criterion 1: An Incremental Change Must Constitute
a Prohibition").

150. *See id.* at 196–98 ("Criterion 2: The Prohibited Activity Must Be Constitutive of the Exploitative Institution").

in experiments. A prohibition on the production of any veal is to be preferred to promoting non-crated veal.

Moreover, the incremental change must protect interests beyond those necessary in order to exploit the animal in an efficient way (the limiting principle of most animal welfare)[151] and should be explicitly promoted as recognizing that nonhumans have interests that are not tradable or able to be ignored merely because humans will benefit from doing so.[152] These criteria together involve the recognition that animals have interests apart from those necessary to protect in order to exploit them, and value that is not exclusively extrinsic or conditional. Finally, animal advocates should never be in a position of promoting an alternative, more "humane" or "better" form of exploitation, or substituting one species for another. Any incremental legislative or regulatory measure ought to be accompanied by an unrelenting and clear call for the abolition of all institutionalized exploitation.[153]

An example of a measure satisfying these conjunctive criteria would be a prohibition on the use of animals for a particular sort of experiment, such as a ban on the use of all animals in psychological experiments, based on the recognition that animals have morally significant interests in not being used for such experiments irrespective of human benefits. A ban on the use of one species of animal might be acceptable if it were not based on any supposed moral superiority of that particular species and if no other species were proposed as an alternative. Any ban should be presented explicitly as part of an agenda that rejects all vivisection.

A prohibition that satisfied all these criteria would not have any significant chance of succeeding at the present time, but the process of promoting such a prohibition would at least have the effect of educating the legal and political system, as well as society in general, about the need for radical change.[154] In any event, advocates are better advised to put their time and resources into incremental change through vegan and abolitionist

---

151. *See id.* at 199–203 ("Criterion 3: The Prohibition Must Recognize and Respect a Noninstitutional Animal Interest").

152. *See id.* at 203–07 ("Criterion 4: Animal Interests Cannot Be Tradable").

153. *See id.* at 207–11 ("Criterion 5: The Prohibition Shall Not Substitute an Alternative, and Supposedly More 'Humane,' Form of Exploitation").

154. *See, e.g., id.* at 187. Given that traditional welfarist regulation does little if anything to help animals and merely reinforces the property paradigm, such regulation does not even provide a useful educational vehicle for more sustained change.

education and to engage in hands-on work involving the care of individual animals. Advocates should avoid campaigns that seek incremental change through legislation or regulation, for any measure that might help to eradicate the property status of animals cannot succeed as a practical matter and any campaign that can succeed will, in all likelihood, merely reinforce the property status of animals. Advocates should also avoid campaigns that seek to get industry to make voluntary changes as these efforts are usually futile at best and are often counterproductive.

B. Welfare and Abolition

Second, new welfarism maintains that traditional incremental changes in animal welfare will eventually lead to abolition or to a significant change in the property status of animals, and it is neither necessary nor desirable to have a strategy focused explicitly on veganism and eradication of that property status. There is, however, absolutely no historical evidence for the position that welfarist regulation today will lead to abolition or to greater protection tomorrow. Indeed, the empirical evidence shows that the opposite is true. Animal welfare seems to lead only to continued and increased use.

The CHIMP Act is a good example of how animal welfare facilitates animal exploitation.[155] Those sponsoring the legislation recognized the view shared by many that research involving chimpanzees was morally problematic and that, if the public were to be expected to continue to support such research, it would be necessary to create a more "humane" environment for the chimpanzees. It must be remembered that the most significant form of animal exploitation in history—intensive agriculture—developed during the latter part of the twentieth century, when concern about animal welfare was at a high point. Moreover, recent

---

155. *See supra* notes 26–52 and accompanying text. An interesting example of the false dilemma of welfarist change or no change is illustrated in this context by one animal advocate who criticizes those who did not support the CHIMP Act. *See* Favre, *supra* note 7, at 90. Favre claims that the CHIMP Act "provided positive alternatives for many chimpanzees" and animal advocates should support such laws as a "next step . . . because otherwise next steps will not happen." *Id.* Favre assumes not only that the choice is between the CHIMP Act or nothing but also that the CHIMP Act is itself a desirable piece of legislation.

supposed reform of some aspects of intensive agriculture is not leading toward veganism. If anything, it is encouraging the notion that animal consumption can be morally acceptable if we are "conscientious omnivores" and eat animals who have been raised more "humanely."

In any event, we have had animal welfare in most western nations for the better part of 200 years, and we are inflicting pain, suffering, and death on more nonhumans today than at any time in human history. There is no empirical reason to believe that animal welfare will lead to abolition or to any significant change in the property status of nonhumans.

V

THE EMERGENCE OF "ANIMAL LAW"

In the past decade, a significant number of American law schools have begun to offer courses on "animal law."[156] There is also a growing body of legal scholarship focused on animals.[157] These developments, together with an increase in the number of practicing attorneys concerned with issues involving animals, have led the media to conclude that "[a]nimal law is a specialty whose time has come"[158] and that "animal rights law has begun to blossom into a viable career path for a new generation of attorneys."[159]

Although there can be no doubt that animal issues have become more prominent both in the legal academy and in law practice, it is important

---

156. For the most part, these courses are taught by adjunct instructors, not full-time faculty members.

157. Much of the increase in scholarship is as the result of *Animal Law,* a journal that was begun by the Animal Legal Defense Fund (ALDF) and existed as an independent journal housed at the Lewis and Clark Law School. The journal is now an official publication of Lewis and Clark. Given the origin of *Animal Law,* many of the authors of articles in *Animal Law* have been officers, directors, or employees of ALDF. It remains to be seen whether *Animal Law* will continue to focus on ALDF authors and practitioner-oriented articles. There are, however, other publications starting to appear. For example, students at the University of Pennsylvania Law School launched an annual publication in 2006, the *Journal of Animal Law and Ethics,* which purports to be a more traditional law review with an interdisciplinary focus. In addition, there is the *Journal of Animal Law,* produced by David Favre.

158. Zay N. Smith, *She's Raising Bar in Fight for Animal Rights,* CHI. SUN-TIMES, Mar. 18, 2004, at 24.

159. Douglas Belkin, *Animal Rights Gains Foothold as Law Career: Harvard Hosts Court Competition for 50 Students,* BOSTON GLOBE, Mar. 6, 2005, at 6.

to understand that, for the most part, what is meant by "animal law" has little to do with animal rights and abolition and very much embraces the false dichotomy that we can choose either to pursue traditional animal-welfare measures or we can "sacrifice the welfare of existing animals."[160] Modern animal law, for the most part, promotes traditional welfarist change as a way of modifying the property status of animals. "Pet custody, wrongful death cases, veterinary malpractice suits, pet cruelty cases, and even pet trusts in which people set aside money in their wills to care for their companion animals are slowly reaching a critical mass in lower courts."[161] Animal advocates claim that these cases are "laying the legal foundation establishing that pets have intrinsic worth" that will serve eventually to "support a ruling that animals are not property but have rights of their own and thus legal standing."[162]

These sorts of cases and legal issues may, indeed, provide career opportunities for lawyers, but they will also reinforce the property paradigm rather than challenge it. For example, because nonhumans are property, the fair market value of an animal or the actual economic value of the animal to the owner are the predominant measures of damages used when one person tortiously injures or kills an animal belonging to another.[163] This has effectively prevented owners from obtaining redress for injury to their animals because many companion animals do not have a significant market or actual economic value.

The traditional approach is being changed by case law and statute in some states in favor of recognizing the emotional bond between humans and their animal property, and this is claimed by some animal advocates to be a significant step in the direction of eroding the property status of animals.[164] Such a claim, however, is not justified. Courts have long recognized that there can be instances in which fair-market value is an inadequate measure of damages for property that does not have a market value, such as photographs and heirlooms, and they have

---

160. Favre, *supra* note 7, at 90.

161. Belkin, *supra* note 159. These traditional welfarist topics are the primary focus of the casebook used in a number of courses. *See* SONIA S. WAISMAN, BRUCE A. WAGMAN, & PAMELA D. FRASCH, ANIMAL LAW (3d ed. 2006).

162. Belkin, *supra* note 159.

163. *See, e.g.*, Petco Animal Supplies, Inc. v. Schuster, 144 S.W.3d 554, 560 (Tex. Ct. App. 2004) (limiting recovery to economic value of the animal).

164. *See* Belkin, *supra* note 159.

allowed alternative measures.[165] That some courts are analogizing dogs to heirlooms and photographs that lack market value is, of course, a good thing for the owners of animals just as it is a good thing for owners of otherwise worthless heirlooms and photographs. It does not, however, amount to change—or a step toward a change—in the legal status of the animal any more than it means that heirlooms and photographs are regarded less as property because courts have recognized that fair-market value may not be an adequate measure of damages in a particular case.

Even if animal advocates persuade courts or legislatures to accept that nonhuman companions injured or killed by another are "special property" and similar to heirlooms, or permit damages for loss of companionship or emotional distress, that is not going to change the legal status of the nonhumans as property or represent a recognition that the animal has inherent or intrinsic worth. It will recognize only that some people value their animal property more than do others and that, in certain instances, the law will respect that valuation and not limit the property owner to a measure of damages that does not compensate the loss suffered.

Moreover, looking to the emotional reaction of an owner to determine the value of a nonhuman may have anomalous results. In *Fredeen v. Stride,* the owner took her injured dog, who had been shot in the right hind leg, to a veterinarian and decided to have the dog euthanized because she could not afford the cost of treatment.[166] The veterinarian agreed to do so but instead nursed the animal back to health, and the dog was ultimately placed in another home. The owner saw the dog six months later and claimed to suffer mental anguish because she feared that her children would encounter the dog and attempt to reunite with him. She sued the veterinarian and was awarded $500 for conversion, $4000 for mental anguish, and $700 in punitive damages, and the Oregon Supreme Court affirmed. *Fredeen* involves one of the largest awards for the emotional distress suffered by a human in connection with

---

165. *See, e.g.,* Jankoski v. Preiser Animal Hosp., Ltd., 510 N.E.2d 1084 (Ill. App. Ct. 1987). For a discussion of the inadequacy of the fair-market measure of damages, see FRANCIONE, *supra* note 1, at 57–63.

166. 525 P.2d 166 (Or. 1974).

the treatment of her nonhuman companion, and the damages were awarded because the human was deprived of the death of her dog.[167]

Similarly, that some states now permit trusts for pets[168] is not likely to lead to a change in the legal status of animals or to the recognition that nonhumans have inherent value as a general matter. It is certainly desirable to allow the owners of animals to provide for their animals after their deaths, but again, all this amounts to as a legal matter is a recognition that property owners should be able to decide how to devise and bequeath their property as they see fit, including to benefit other property that they own. In many respects, allowing pet owners to establish trusts for their pets is no different from allowing them to establish trusts to maintain a historical building that they own. Pet trusts cannot credibly be characterized as "a conceptual breakthrough for the United States legal system" on the theory that "[a]nimals have been granted legal personhood for purposes of trust enforcement" and that for probate and trust purposes "animals are juristic persons with equal rights before the court."[169]

Some animal advocates claim that cases involving the custody of animals indicate that "[c]ourts across the country have begun to adopt the more enlightened view that companion animals are more than mere chattels"[170] or that these cases represent "'one way of taking down the wall'"[171] between humans and nonhumans. Again, such a claim is unfounded, although it is clear that at least some animal lawyers are developing lucrative practices with these sorts of cases.[172] When couples separate, they often have disputes about all sorts of property, including

---

167. An increase in litigation against veterinarians will most likely cause malpractice insurance to become more expensive and this will result in higher costs being charged for veterinary services. Although health insurance is available for companion animals, it is limited, often does not apply to older animals, and is costly. In any event, increased veterinary costs will invariably result in less veterinary care for some nonhumans.

168. *See, e.g.*, ARIZ. REV. STAT. § 14–2907(B) (2006).

169. Favre, *supra* note 7, at 94.

170. Barbara Newell, *Animal Custody Disputes: A Growing Crack in the "Legal Thinghood" of Nonhuman Animals*, 6 ANIMAL L. 179, 180 (2000).

171. Sanjiv Bhattacharya, *To Love, Honor and Belly-Scratch; Marriages Come and Go. Judging by the Rising Number of Pet-Custody Disputes, Though, Some Passions Endure*, L.A. TIMES MAG., Jan. 9, 2005, at 20 (quoting Bruce Wagman).

172. *See id.* (discussing attorney Sandra Toye, who has earned "fees in excess of $100,000" doing pet-custody cases).

nonhuman animals. That a court enforces a custody agreement involving a nonhuman is no different from the court enforcing an agreement about the shared use of a car. Although some courts may have focused on the "best interest" of the nonhuman involved in a custody matter, this is not an indication of any shift—even an attenuated or indirect one—in the property status of nonhumans. The animals involved are still chattels.[173] Moreover, the law has through anticruelty laws explicitly recognized for the better part of 200 years that animals have interests in the way that inanimate property does not. The problem is that this recognition has had no significant impact on the property status of animals, and it is unclear why anyone believes that it will have a different effect as the result of custody cases involving animals.

Finally, many animal advocates maintain that anticruelty statutes and prosecutions brought under those statutes will improve our treatment of nonhuman animals and help to erode the property status of animals.[174] As I have argued, anticruelty laws were originally at least in part a response to changing social attitudes and a recognition that humans had moral and legal obligations that they owed to nonhumans.[175] However, the notion of having direct moral and legal obligations is inconsistent with the property status of nonhumans, and, as a result, anticruelty statutes have been largely ineffective in providing significant protection to nonhumans.[176] Many anticruelty laws contain explicit exemptions for most forms of institutionalized exploitation. In those situations in which they do apply, courts have interpreted the concept to prohibit only those activities that are not customary or usual given the particu-

---

173. For example, Barbara Newell cites *Raymond v. Lachmann,* 695 N.Y.S.2d 308 (N.Y. App. Div. 1999) as an example of a custody case in which the court recognizes a nonhuman as being more than a chattel. Newell, *supra* note 170, at 180 n.6. In *Raymond,* the trial court awarded ownership and possession of a cat to the plaintiff conditioned on plaintiff's payment of certain veterinary costs. The appellate court reversed and awarded ownership and possession to defendant claiming that was "best for all concerned." 695 N.Y.S.2d at 309. Although Newell supplies facts about this case from the unpublished lower court decision, the published opinion, which is very brief, did not discuss the nature of the dispute over the cat or any competing property interests. But most significantly, the decision did not affect the cat's status as property.

174. *See* Belkin, *supra* note 159.

175. *See* FRANCIONE, *supra* note 2, at 7–9.

176. For a discussion of the inadequacies of anticruelty laws, see FRANCIONE, *supra* note 1, at 121–60; FRANCIONE, *supra* note 2, at 54–73; *see also* Reppy, *supra* note 147; Darian M. Ibrahim, *The Anticruelty Statute: A Study in Animal Welfare,* 1 J. ANIMAL L. & ETHICS 175 (2006).

lar use.[177] Moreover, anticruelty laws are criminal laws and require proof
of intent. Intent is difficult to show as a general matter, and it becomes
even more difficult in anticruelty cases, in which the alleged crime oc-
curs in a societal context in which the killing of billions of animals is routine. Finally, violation of an anticruelty statute has generally been a misdemeanor or summary offense and has carried an insignificant penalty,
although in recent years a considerable number of states have made felonies of at least some violations.[178]

In any event, state anticruelty laws do not even apply to the overwhelming number of instances in which we impose suffering or death
on nonhumans either because the laws include explicit exemptions or
because courts effectively read exemptions into them. It is not accurate
to say that these laws apply to "cruel" behavior because much of what
is regarded as legal animal use is "cruel" as that term is normally used
in moral discourse. It is not even accurate to say that these laws are limited to situations in which humans inflict suffering or death on animals
merely for "fun" as many forms of animal-based "entertainment," such
as rodeos, circuses, and pigeon shoots, are legal. Rather, anticruelty laws
apply only to the miniscule portion of animal uses that fall completely
outside the considerably broad scope of permissible institutionalized animal exploitation. And, given that animals are property, virtually any use
that generates some sort of economic benefit is permissible.

There is, however, an alternative to the dominant paradigm of "animal law," and it is the one that guided our work in the Rutgers Animal

---

177. For a discussion of the difficulties involved in applying anticruelty laws to conduct that con-
forms to the customs and norms of various animal uses, see Ibrahim, *supra* note 176. A review
of the *McDonald's Corp. v. Steel* case in Great Britain indicates that when judgments about what
constitutes "cruel" treatment or "necessary" suffering are not connected to what is customary,
they become very arbitrary and idiosyncratic and could never be used in a context involving
criminal liability. *See* McDonald's Corp. v. Steel, No. 1990-M-NO. 5724 (Q.B. 1997) (summary
of the judgment), *available at* http://www.hmcourts-service.gov.uk/judgmentsfiles/j379/
mcdonalds_190697.htm. This case, commonly referred to as *"McLibel,"* is to date the most
lengthy case in the history of the English legal system. McDonald's sued two defendants for,
inter alia, allegations that McDonald's was culpably responsible for farming practices that
the defendants characterized as cruel and inhumane. Justice Bell refused to apply the standard of the industry to determine whether the statements were defamatory and held that he
must judge for himself, based on expert testimony, whether particular farming practices were
cruel. Justice Bell's ad hoc analysis makes clear that such a standard could never suffice to support a criminal conviction.

178. *See supra* note 89 and accompanying text.

Rights Clinic[179] over the decade of its existence and that we owed in part to wise advice from a mentor, the late civil rights attorney, William M. Kunstler.[180] Kunstler believed that the primary role of a progressive lawyer was to protect the rights of those in society who were trying to cause a paradigm shift in thinking. That is, he did not see the lawyer as the primary engine for social change; rather, it was the social activist, the person who sought to educate, persuade, and change fundamental thinking about particular issues. Such activists would invariably be vulnerable to attack by a political and legal system that was not amenable to the change, and it was the job of the attorney to use every tool available to her to protect that activist. Kunstler's advice fit in with our general view that the first task of the animal-rights movement was to educate society about why such a movement was necessary in the first place and to shift the paradigm away from the commodity status of nonhumans.

As a result, we concentrated our efforts on assisting animal advocates in their efforts to educate about the need to abolish and not merely to regulate particular instances of animal exploitation. They included students in high schools, universities, medical schools, and veterinary schools who did not want to vivisect or dissect any animals in their courses; those who wanted to engage in peaceful demonstration to try to educate others about animal rights, veganism, and abolition; prisoners who wanted vegan food; those who were trying to develop "no kill" options to the problem of the companion animal population; those who sought to stop the round-up and removal of wild horses from federal lands and to prohibit the killing of deer in suburban areas; and those who wanted to organize lawful boycotts to stop particular forms of animal exploitation.

We advised animal advocates how to design legislation and regulations that were abolitionist rather than regulationist. We sued to get information about experiments at federally funded institutions, not because we wanted to achieve better regulation of vivisection, but because

---

179. I began to teach animal rights and the law in 1985 as part of my jurisprudence course at the University of Pennsylvania Law School. In 1989, I moved to Rutgers University School of Law—Newark and, with Anna E. Charlton, started the Rutgers Animal Rights Law Clinic in 1990. Students enrolled in the Clinic received six academic credits per semester for working with us on actual animal-rights cases while also learning animal-rights theory in a weekly seminar. We closed the Clinic in 2000, but we continue to teach regular courses on animal rights and the law.

180. Kunstler wrote the Foreword to *Animals, Property, and the Law. See* FRANCIONE, *supra* note 1, at ix–xii.

we wanted to help to provide the information that advocates could use to build a consensus against vivisection and to make clear that the public was watching what went on behind the laboratory doors. When we represented the owners of Taro, a dog that was scheduled to be killed under New Jersey's "dangerous dog" law, we used the opportunity to focus attention on the irony of the worldwide response to Taro's plight at the same time that most of us were eating animals who were in no morally relevant way different from Taro. And, most importantly, we spent a good deal of our time trying to empower animal advocates by teaching them about how they could use the law to become more effective educators about the need for abolition. Not a single pet trust was ever drafted in our offices. But that may have been because no client was ever charged for our services, and because we were free of business considerations.

Modern animal law as it has developed in the past decade or so is not focused on the efforts of the animal advocate to effect fundamental changes in the political and social system; it is more focused on the lawyer as the primary force for social change within the existing legal system. The past 200 years of animal welfare are compelling proof that this latter approach will not advance things further in the next decade than it has in the past one.

VI

SIMILAR-MINDS THEORY

Rain Without Thunder expressed concern that the animal-rights movement was moving toward welfarism and away from rights. In the past decade, the animal-advocacy movement in the United States has, for the most part, gone further in the welfarist direction than even I had contemplated when I wrote that book. The one area in which animal advocates still talk about rights is in the context of great apes and other animals, such as dolphins, who are thought to have human-like intelligence.[181] According to this view, if animals are cognitively like us—if they have

---

181. *See, e.g.,The Evolving Legal Status of Chimpanzees,* 9 ANIMAL L. 1 (2003) (remarks at a symposium linking moral status with humanlike cognitive characteristics).

similar minds—then we must rethink the human–nonhuman relationship and, perhaps, even grant certain rights to those animals.

What I have called "similar-minds theory"[182] became popular among animal advocates as the result of *The Great Ape Project: Equality Beyond Humanity* in 1993.[183] Although I certainly support prohibiting any exploitation of the great apes, dolphins, and any other nonhuman, the similar-minds theory reinforces the very paradigm that has resulted in excluding nonhumans from the moral community.[184] We have historically justified our exploitation of nonhumans on the ground that there is a qualitative distinction between humans and other animals. The latter may be sentient, but they are not intelligent, or rational, or emotional, or self-conscious. The similar-minds approach claims that, as an empirical matter, we may have been wrong in the past and at least some nonhumans may have some of these cognitive characteristics. But this approach does not question the underlying—and fundamental—moral question: Why is anything more than sentience necessary?[185] The similar-minds approach threatens to perpetuate a speciesist hierarchy in which we treat some animals as "special" and continue to exploit the rest. There are at least two reasons to reject the similar-minds theory.[186]

First, the similar-minds theory is a prescription to engage in more research, which will ironically involve a good deal of vivisection, so that

182. *See* Gary L. Francione, *Our Hypocrisy*, NEW SCIENTIST, June 4–10, 2005, at 51; *see also* Gary L. Francione, *Taking Sentience Seriously*, 1 J. ANIMAL L. & ETHICS 1 (2006).

183. THE GREAT APE PROJECT: EQUALITY BEYOND HUMANITY (Paola Cavalieri & Peter Singer eds., 1993).

184. I was a contributor to *The Great Ape Project* and was one of the original signers of A Declaration on Great Apes. *See* Gary L. Francione, *Personhood, Property and Legal Competence, in id.* at 248. In my chapter in *The Great Ape Project,* I argued that sentience was the only characteristic necessary for full membership in the moral community. *See id.* at 253. Nevertheless, I regard *The Great Ape Project* as ill-conceived and I regret my participation.

185. Although Professor Taimie Bryant rejects the similar-minds approach and does not believe that particular humanlike cognitive characteristics are necessary for moral status or legal protection, she also argues that arguments based on sentience alone are similarly misguided. *See generally* Taimie L. Bryant, *Similarity or Difference as a Basis for Justice: Must Animals Be Like Humans to Be Legally Protected from Humans?*, 70 LAW & CONTEMP. PROBS. 207 (Winter 2007). I disagree in part with Bryant's analysis because I do not accept that a being that is not sentient can have interests.

186. For a further discussion of the difficulties involved in relying on similarities beyond sentience between humans and nonhumans to justify the moral significance of nonhumans, *see* FRANCIONE, *supra* note 2, at 116–27. For an excellent general discussion of the moral status of nonhumans, including the significance of their cognitive characteristics, *see* GARY STEINER, ANTHROPOCENTRISM AND ITS DISCONTENTS: THE MORAL STATUS OF ANIMALS IN THE HISTORY OF WESTERN PHILOSOPHY (2005).

we can determine how much like humans nonhumans really are. And at the end of the day, no matter how similar human minds are to those of nonhumans, there will always be differences that will allow us to justify exploitation if personhood is based on possession of these cognitive characteristics. After all, we have known about the cognitive and genetic similarities between human and nonhuman great apes for a long while, yet we continue to use the latter in biomedical experiments and to imprison them in zoos.

Second, the similar-minds theory is arbitrary. We identify some characteristic, such as humanlike self-awareness or rationality, and we maintain that any nonhuman without the characteristic is not a member of the moral community. There is, however, no reason to conclude that being able to do calculus is better than being able to fly with only your wings, or to breathe underwater with only your gills. These characteristics may be relevant for some purposes, but they are not relevant to whether we make a being suffer or kill that being.

This notion is clear where humans are involved. Consider two humans, one of whom is a gifted mathematician and one who is severely mentally disabled. Their relative cognitive capacities may be relevant for purposes of determining how to allocate a particular resource, such as a university scholarship. But for the purposes of determining whether it is permissible to subject either or both to painful experiments or to kill them to harvest their organs for the benefit of others, nearly all of us would regard these two humans as similarly situated and as having an equal interest in not being treated as a resource for others. Indeed, we may regard our moral obligation to the disabled human as even greater precisely because of her vulnerability.

VII

CONCLUSION

The property status of nonhumans remains a substantial impediment to the meaningful protection of nonhuman interests. Although animal advocates claim that traditional welfarist strategies can protect animal interests without any significant modification of the property status of nonhumans, or that welfarist strategies will lead to modification of the property status of nonhumans, the past dozen years offers no proof of either of these claims. There have been no notable improvements in animal welfare and most changes that have occurred have been linked explicitly to making animal exploitation more beneficial for humans. Making exploitation more efficient may reduce suffering in minimal ways, but it is clear that the welfarist approach is rooted in the property paradigm and perpetuates the view that nonhumans are commodities with only extrinsic value.

Moreover, animal advocates have lost ground in a number of areas. Discourse about animal welfare as connected to economic efficiency is no less prevalent than it was a decade ago and, indeed, is arguably more prevalent. The animal movement has drifted in a more traditional welfarist direction in that most of the animal organizations have openly embraced a program of efficient exploitation. PETA and Peter Singer praise McDonald's, Wendy's, and Burger King for adopting slaughter standards that keep the meat industry operating "safely, efficiently and profitably."[187] HSUS and Farm Sanctuary campaign against gestation crates, arguing that alternative production systems will reduce production costs, increase productivity, and increase demand for pork.[188] HSUS urges that gassing poultry is preferable to electrical stunning because it will mean less carcass damage, better meat quality, and reduced labor costs.[189]

Humane Farm Animal Care,[190] with its partners HSUS, American Society for the Prevention of Cruelty to Animals, Animal People, World Society for the Protection of Animals, and others,[191] promotes the "Certified Humane Raised & Handled Label," which it describes as "a consumer certification and labeling program" to give consumers assurance that a

---

187. *Supra* note 18; *see also supra* notes 11–25 and accompanying text.

188. *See supra* notes 56 and 65 and accompanying text.

189. *See supra* note 107.

190. The Executive Director of Humane Farm Animal Care, Adele Douglass, "serves as an invited participant on numerous industry animal welfare committees including for the Food Marketing Institute, National Council of Chain Restaurants, and Burger King," and in 2003, "was a keynote speaker at the Animal Welfare Conference of the American Meat Institute." Humane Farm Animal Care, The Staff, http://www.certifiedhumane.com/people.html (last visited Mar. 19, 2007). Temple Grandin is a member of the Scientific Committee of Humane Farm Animal Care. *Id.*

191. The partners of Humane Farm Animal Care are listed on the homepage of the organization's website. *See* Humane Farm Animal Care, http://www.certifiedhumane.com/default.html (see pull-down menu "Other Organizations") (last visited Mar. 19, 2007).

labeled "egg, dairy, meat or poultry product has been produced with the welfare of the farm animal in mind."[192] Humane Farm Animal Care emphasizes that "[i]n 'food animals, stress can affect meat quality . . . and general [animal] health,'"[193] and that the label "creates a win-win-win situation for retailers and restaurants, producers, and consumers. For farmers, the win means they can achieve differentiation, increase market share and increase profitability for choosing more sustainable practices."[194] These approaches merely reinforce the notion that animals are commodities and that animal interests should be protected if and only if there is an economic benefit for humans in doing so. Linking animal welfare with efficient exploitation is inconsistent with the recognition of the inherent value of nonhumans. Moreover, the animal movement has explicitly embraced the notion that being a "conscientious omnivore" is a morally acceptable solution to the problem of animal exploitation.[195]

The emerging field of "animal law" has collapsed into nothing more than an attempt to apply traditional property doctrines to nonhumans. There is no attempt to challenge the property paradigm through laws or regulations that recognize that animals have fundamental interests that cannot be disregarded irrespective of human benefit.

A movement's ends should define its means. If the goal is abolition, animal welfare is a means not fitted to that goal either as a matter of moral theory or of practical strategy. As a moral matter, animal welfare assumes and reinforces the notion that animals are commodities with only extrinsic or conditional value. As a practical matter, animal welfare provides almost no benefit to animals and only makes exploitation more efficient for producers at the same time that it makes animal users more comfortable about exploiting nonhumans.

The choice is not between doing nothing or pursuing traditional welfare. The choice is between reinforcing the property paradigm or challenging it. We can pursue the incremental eradication of the property status—and we can do so now—in a variety of ways starting with our own veganism and with our educational efforts directed toward building

---

192. *Id.* at http://www.certifiedhumane.com/whatis.html.
193. *Id.* (quoting unspecified article in *Agricultural Research*).
194. *Id. at* http://www.certifiedhumane.com/whyproduce.html.
195. *See supra* notes 137–41 and accompanying text.

an abolitionist movement with veganism as its moral baseline. To the extent that we choose to pursue laws, administrative regulations, or litigation, those efforts should be consistent with the abolitionist goal of the progressive recognition of the inherent value of nonhumans.

Property status and the animal-welfare laws based upon it "benefit" nonhumans[196] in the same way that property status and slave-welfare laws "benefited" human slaves. Any use of "benefit" in either context is perverse. There is, of course, at least one very significant difference between the abolition of human slavery and the abolition of the property status of nonhumans. Our accepting that we have no moral justification to continue to treat nonhumans as commodities would not entail letting domesticated nonhumans run free in the streets. It would, however, entail that we stop bringing animals into existence for the purpose of human exploitation.[197] We should care for those who are here now, but we should stop causing more to come into existence. We would still have to work through what equal consideration would mean in our dealings with non-domesticated animals. But even that would be much easier to do if we accepted that the property status of nonhumans has no justification other than as a result of a speciesist hierarchy that we created and that we perpetuate.

❖ ❖ ❖

Postscript (2008): In December 2007, the CHIMP act (*see supra* notes 26–52 and accompanying text) was amended to prevent further invasive research on chimpanzees in the sanctuary. Chimp Haven is Home Act, Pub. L. No. 110-170, 121 Stat. 2465 (2007). The chimpanzees may be used for noninvasive research and, of course, the federal government may refuse to retire any chimpanzee who may potentially be useful for research purposes.

---

196. This position is presented by a number of welfare advocates. *See supra* note 114 and accompanying text.

197. For a further discussion of the consequences of accepting that nonhumans have a right not to be treated as property, see FRANCIONE, *supra* note 2, at 153–60.

CHAPTER 3 / TAKING SENTIENCE SERIOUSLY

INTRODUCTION

In 1993, a number of scholars collaborated on a book of essays entitled *The Great Ape Project (GAP).*[1] The book was accompanied by a document, *A Declaration on Great Apes,* to which the editors and contributors subscribed. The *Declaration* stated that the great apes "are the closest relatives of our species" and that these nonhumans "have mental capacities and an emotional life sufficient to justify inclusion within the community of equals."[2] In recent years, reflecting the inquiry and concerns of *GAP* and the organization of the same name that evolved from it,[3] a considerable

The essay was published originally in the *Journal for Animal Law and Ethics,* vol. 1, pp. 1–18. (2006).

© 2006 by Gary L. Francione. I appreciate helpful comments from Anna E. Charlton, Taimie Bryant, Darian Ibrahim, Rupert Read, and Gary Steiner. I acknowledge research assistance from Suzanna Polhamus and support from the Dean's Research Fund at the Rutgers University School of Law—Newark.

I am delighted to contribute this Article to the inaugural issue of the *Journal of Animal Law and Ethics.* I began my teaching career at the University of Pennsylvania Law School in 1984, and I first taught about animal rights and the law in my course on jurisprudence during the 1985–86 academic year. As far as I am aware, this was the first time that animal rights theory was taught at an American law school. Moreover, I was deeply involved in efforts to close the Head Injury Clinical Research Laboratory, a facility that used nonhuman primates in brain-injury experiments, which was located at the Penn Medical School. *See* GARY L. FRANCIONE, ANIMALS, PROPERTY, AND THE LAW 179–83 (1995). My experiences at Penn—both inside and outside the classroom—were crucial in forming my views on the practical and theoretical problems presented by the property status of animals.

1. THE GREAT APE PROJECT: EQUALITY BEYOND HUMANITY (Paola Cavalieri & Peter Singer eds., 1993).

2. *Id.* at 5.

3. *See* www.greatapeproject.org.

literature has developed that discusses the extent to which the great apes, dolphins, parrots, and perhaps other animals have certain cognitive characteristics thought to be uniquely human.[4] These characteristics include self-awareness, emotions, and the ability to communicate with a symbolic language. This literature poses the question whether we must, therefore, rethink our relationship with nonhumans and accord those who possess these characteristics greater moral consideration and legal protection. *GAP* popularized what I call the "similar-minds theory" of the human/nonhuman relationship.[5]

The similar-minds approach has spawned an industry of cognitive ethologists eager to investigate—ironically often through animal experiments—the extent to which nonhumans have human-like cognitive characteristics. The flipside of the similar-minds theory is that those nonhumans who are merely sentient—capable of experiencing pain and suffering but who lack these other cognitive capacities—are still *things,* entitled to "humane" treatment but not the preferential treatment that we are obligated to accord nonhumans with minds like ours.

I was a contributor to *GAP*[6] and an original signatory to *A Declaration on Great Apes.* Nevertheless, in my 1993 essay in *GAP*[7] and at greater length in my subsequent writing, particularly in *Introduction to Animal Rights: Your Child or the Dog?,*[8] I have expressed the view that sentience alone is sufficient for full membership in the moral community and that no other cognitive characteristic is required.

The similar-minds theory is presented by its proponents as progressive because it appears to allow the inclusion of at least some nonhumans in the community of equals. This characterization is inaccurate in that the

---

4. *See, e.g.,* MARC D. HAUSER, THE EVOLUTION OF COMMUNICATION (1996); MARC D. HAUSER, WILD MINDS: WHAT ANIMALS REALLY THINK (2001); WILLIAM A. HILLIX & DUANE RUMBAUGH, ANIMAL BODIES, HUMAN MINDS: APE, DOLPHIN, AND PARROT LANGUAGE SKILLS (2004); READINGS IN ANIMAL COGNITION (Marc Bekoff & Dale Jamieson eds., 1996); SUE SAVAGE-RUMBAUGH & ROGER LEWIN, KANZI: THE APE AT THE BRINK OF THE HUMAN MIND (1994); STEVEN M. WISE, DRAWING THE LINE: SCIENCE AND THE CASE FOR ANIMAL RIGHTS (2002); STEVEN M. WISE, RATTLING THE CAGE: TOWARD LEGAL RIGHTS FOR ANIMALS (2000).

5. *See* Gary L. Francione, *Our Hypocrisy,* NEW SCIENTIST, June 4-10, 2005, at 51-52.

6. *See* Gary L. Francione, *Personhood, Property and Legal Competence,* in THE GREAT APE PROJECT, *supra* note 1, at 248.

7. *See id.* at 253.

8. GARY L. FRANCIONE, INTRODUCTION TO ANIMAL RIGHTS: YOUR CHILD OR THE DOG? 116-27 (2000). *See also* Gary L. Francione, *Animals—Property or Persons?, in* ANIMAL RIGHTS: CURRENT DEBATES AND NEW DIRECTIONS 108 (Cass R. Sunstein & Martha C. Nussbaum eds., 2004).

opposite is true: similar-minds theory will only facilitate our continuing to exclude virtually all nonhumans from the moral community. The problem lies in the attempt to link cognitive characteristics with moral significance. Although similar-minds theory is ostensibly a recent phenomenon, linking the moral status of nonhumans to cognitive characteristics beyond sentience is not new. Indeed, this idea has, in one form or another, characterized our thinking about the moral status of nonhumans for a long time, and it is responsible for a good deal of mischief.

In this Article, I very briefly discuss the history of this idea. I then present several reasons why we should abandon the theory in favor of requiring only sentience for full membership in the moral community.

I. BENTHAM, SENTIENCE, AND ANIMAL USE

Until the nineteenth century, nonhumans were for the most part regarded as things and not as moral persons because we believed that they lacked some supposedly uniquely human characteristic that made us qualitatively different from them and deprived them of any moral significance. From the pre-Socratics through Plato and Aristotle, to the Middle Ages and St. Thomas Aquinas, and through the Enlightenment and Descartes, Locke, and Kant, theorists maintained that animals, unlike humans, were not rational, self-aware, or capable of abstract thought, language use, or reciprocal moral concern for humans.[9]

As a result of these supposed differences, humans could not have any moral obligations that they owed directly to nonhumans and the latter could not be members of the moral community.[10] To the extent

---

9. There were, of course, some exceptions to this view. For an excellent discussion of the treatment of nonhumans in Western philosophy, see GARY STEINER, ANTHROPOCENTRICISM AND ITS DISCONTENTS: THE MORAL STATUS OF ANIMALS IN THE HISTORY OF WESTERN PHILOSOPHY (2005).

10. *See* FRANCIONE, INTRODUCTION TO ANIMAL RIGHTS, *supra* note 8, at 1–3, 103–06, 111–13. There is a sense in which Descartes should be considered separately in that he arguably maintained that animals are not sentient whereas the others acknowledged that animals are sentient and have interests but that we may ignore those interests because animals lack other cognitive characteristics. If animals are not sentient, then they can have no interests and it would make no sense to talk about having any obligations to them. *See id.* at 2–3, 104. *See also infra* note 46 (discussing sentience as a necessary and sufficient condition for possessing interests). In addition to having minds that are dissimilar, animals are regarded by some as lacking souls and as being spiritually inferior to humans. *See* FRANCIONE, INTRODUCTION TO ANIMAL RIGHTS, *supra* note 8, at 106–11.

that humans had any obligations that concerned animals, these obligations were actually owed to other humans. A moral obligation not to inflict gratuitous harm on animals was really one owed to other humans to avoid conduct that would lead to the unkind treatment of humans. Similarly, there were virtually no laws before the nineteenth century that established legal obligations that were owed to animals as distinguished from those that concerned animals but that were really owed to humans in their capacity as owners of animals.[11]

Progressive social movements developed that demanded greater rights for women and the abolition of human slavery and proposed that we have moral obligations to other animals not connected to whether our treatment of them affects other humans. Although there were many theorists and advocates concerned about our treatment of nonhumans, a particularly important and influential one was British lawyer and philosopher Jeremy Bentham (1748–1832). Bentham rejected the view that we could exclude nonhumans from the moral community and treat them as things because they lack certain characteristics that we regard as necessary for moral personhood. According to Bentham,

> a full-grown horse or dog, is beyond comparison a more rational, as well as a more conversible animal, than an infant of a day, or a week, or even a month, old. But suppose the case were otherwise, what would it avail? the question is not, Can they *reason?* nor, Can they *talk?* but, Can they *suffer?*[12]

Bentham thereby rejected the link between cognitive characteristics and moral status that had dominated Western thinking about nonhumans for the past several thousand years in favor of the position that only sentience is required for animals to be members of the moral community. Or did he?

Bentham did not conclude from the view that only sentience mattered that we should stop using and killing animals for human purposes. Although he ostensibly argued that rationality or language ability is not required for moral significance, he certainly did not regard cognitive

---

11. *See* FRANCIONE, INTRODUCTION TO ANIMAL RIGHTS, *supra* note 8, at 3.

12. JEREMY BENTHAM, AN INTRODUCTION TO THE PRINCIPLES OF MORALS AND LEGISLATION, ch. XVII, para. 4, at 282–83 n.b. (J. H. Burns & H. L. A. Hart eds., Athlone Press 1970) (1781).

differences between humans and nonhumans as irrelevant. He believed that nonhumans, unlike humans, are not self-aware and do not have a sense of the future. Although this does not mean that we can ignore animal suffering, it does mean that animals do not have an interest in continuing to live and, so, we can continue to use them. Bentham stated:

> If the being eaten were all, there is very good reason why we should be suffered to eat such of them as we like to eat: we are the better for it, and they are never the worse. They have none of those long-protracted anticipations of future misery which we have. . . . [and] are never the worse for being dead.[13]

According to Bentham, animals do not care whether we use or kill them for our purposes as long as we do not make them suffer unduly in the process. He did not question the status of animals as property because he did not regard the ownership and use of animals for human purposes as per se objectionable. The primary issue for Bentham was not *whether* we used animals, but *how* we used them.

As I discuss in the following section, the property status of animals meant that Bentham's revolutionary call in favor of sentience turned out to be rather hollow. Although Bentham purported to reject the link between cognitive characteristics and moral status, he merely reintroduced it in another form.

II. CONVENTIONAL WISDOM AND ANIMAL WELFARE

Bentham's view is embodied in the principles of animal welfare that reflect our conventional wisdom about our moral obligations to animals. According to that conventional wisdom, we can use animals for our purposes, but, because animals can suffer, we must take their suffering

---

13. *Id.* at 282. *See infra* note 43 (discussing John Stuart Mill's views on differences between humans and other animals). Rights theorist Tom Regan comes close to Bentham's position when he argues that death is a greater harm for humans than for nonhumans, and that if we are faced with a "lifeboat" situation in which we can choose to save four humans or a million dogs, we ought to choose to save the humans because of this qualitative difference. *See* TOM REGAN, THE CASE FOR ANIMAL RIGHTS 324–25 (1983). For a discussion of Regan's position, see FRANCIONE, INTRODUCTION TO ANIMAL RIGHTS, *supra* note 8, at 215, n.61.

seriously and not treat them as mere things. Most of us agree that it is morally wrong to inflict "unnecessary" suffering on nonhumans and that we are obligated to treat animals "humanely." This notion is so uncontroversial that we have criminal laws, which originated in nineteenth-century Britain and are now ubiquitous, that purport to impose criminal penalties on those who fail to treat animals "humanely" or who inflict "unnecessary" or "unjustified" suffering on them.[14] In short, it seems that we have accepted Bentham's moral theory about the importance of sentience and implemented it in our law. And that is precisely the problem.

An examination of the conventions of animal welfare reveals confusion. If a prohibition against unnecessary or unjustified suffering of nonhumans is to have any meaningful content, it must preclude the infliction of suffering on nonhumans merely for our pleasure, amusement, or convenience. But the vast majority of the suffering and death that we impose on nonhumans can be justified *only* by our pleasure, amusement, or convenience and cannot, by any stretch, be characterized plausibly as "necessary."[15]

It is, for instance, not necessary to eat animals or animal products; indeed, animal products are increasingly believed to be detrimental to human health, and animal agriculture is unsound as an ecological matter. The best justification that we have for inflicting pain, suffering, and death on the over ten billion land animals that we kill and eat annually in the United States alone is that we enjoy the taste of meat and dairy. It is certainly not necessary to exploit animals for entertainment purposes or for recreational hunting. There is only one area in which a plausible necessity argument can be made—the use of nonhumans in experiments to find cures for serious human illnesses.[16] Although necessity claims in this context are suspect as well, it is the only use of nonhumans that cannot be summarily dismissed as nothing more than the infliction of suffering and death for trivial reasons.[17]

---

14. *See* FRANCIONE, INTRODUCTION TO ANIMAL RIGHTS, *supra* note 8, at 7–9.

15. *See id.* at 9–30 (discussing the supposed necessity of various animal uses).

16. *See id.* at 31–49 (discussing the supposed necessity of animal use in biomedical research and related contexts).

17. This is not to say that I regard the use of nonhumans in experiments as morally justifiable. I do not. *See id.* at 156–57. *See also* Gary L. Francione, *The Use of Nonhuman Animals in Biomedical Research: Necessity and Justification,* 35 J.L. MED. & ETHICS (forthcoming 2006) (arguing that the use of animals in experiments cannot be justified morally even if it can be argued that the use

In sum, we suffer from a sort of "moral schizophrenia" where animals are concerned. On the one hand, we claim to take animal suffering seriously and to regard unnecessary suffering as morally wrong. On the other hand, the overwhelming number of ways in which we use nonhumans—and the resulting suffering—cannot be regarded as necessary in any coherent sense. Many of us who live with nonhumans regard them as members of our families. Nevertheless, we turn around and stick forks into other nonhumans who are not relevantly different in any way from the animals we love.

Our moral schizophrenia about animals is related to their status as our property.[18] Although we claim to take animal interests seriously, animals necessarily remain as nothing more than things because they are commodities that we own and that have only the value that we choose to give them. In *Animals, Property, and the Law,* I argued that, although animal welfare laws seem to require that we balance human and nonhuman interests in determining the propriety of animal use or treatment, any supposed balance is meaningless because what we purport to weigh are the interests of property owners against the interests of their animal property. The result of this exercise is predetermined from the outset by the property status of the nonhuman.[19] The animal in question is always a "food animal," "game animal," "rodeo animal," "pet," or some other form of animal property that exists solely for our use and has no value except that which we give it.

Because animals are property, they are considered as having no inherent or intrinsic value, and we are generally permitted to ignore whatever interests they may have whenever it benefits us to do so. We may impose on them horrendous pain and suffering, clearly amounting to what would be regarded as torture if inflicted on humans, as long as it is regarded as necessary according to the norms that constitute the particular

---

is necessary in some situations). I do, however, regard our use of animals for food, entertainment, and hunting (uses that account for the vast majority of the suffering and death that we impose on nonhumans) as transparently trivial.

18. *See* FRANCIONE, INTRODUCTION TO ANIMAL RIGHTS, *supra* note 8, at 50–80 (discussing the property status of nonhumans).

19. *See generally* GARY L. FRANCIONE, ANIMALS, PROPERTY, AND THE LAW (1995) (discussing the failure of animal welfare laws to provide any significant protection to animals because of their status as property and the inability to balance in any meaningful way the interests of property against those of property owners).

form of institutionalized exploitation. For instance, cattle have an interest in not being castrated without anesthesia or branded with a hot iron—both very painful procedures—but these are regarded as "necessary" because they are "normal" agricultural practices. The "suffering" of property owners who cannot use their property as they wish counts more than the suffering of nonhumans. The requirement that we treat animals "humanely" and do not inflict "unnecessary" suffering is, in reality, nothing more than an injunction not to impose more pain and suffering than is required to facilitate particular animal uses in an efficient manner, and animal interests have no intrinsic value in our assessments.

Although we could certainly treat nonhuman animals better than we do now, their status as property militates strongly against any significant improvement.[20] Moreover, as I argued in *Rain Without Thunder: The Ideology of the Animal Rights Movement*,[21] there is no empirical evidence to indicate that animal welfare regulation will lead to the abolition of animal exploitation. Indeed, it appears as though animal welfare regulations do little to reduce actual animal suffering and have as their primary effect making humans feel more comfortable about exploiting nonhumans. We have had animal welfare laws for the better part of two hundred years, and we are exploiting more nonhumans today than at any point in human history.

In sum, although our conventional moral and legal thinking appears to reject the link between cognitive characteristics and moral status and to regard sentience alone as morally significant, the property status of animals rests squarely on the view that animals, unlike humans, do not have an interest in their lives because they are cognitively different from us. So although we reject the link in one sense, we accept it in another sense through the position that supposed cognitive differences justify our using animals in ways in which we do not use any humans. The result is that our moral and legal acceptance of the importance of sentience has not resulted in any paradigm shift in our treatment of nonhumans.

---

20. *See id.* at 14 (arguing that the status of animals as property makes better treatment difficult but not impossible). In the decade since I wrote *Animals, Property, and the Law,* there have been no significant improvements in animal welfare, at least in the United States, despite there being an extremely active and well-financed animal welfare movement. *See* Gary L. Francione, *Reflections on* ANIMALS, PROPERTY, AND THE LAW *and* RAIN WITHOUT THUNDER, 70 LAW & CONTEMP. PROBS. (forthcoming 2006).

21. GARY L. FRANCIONE, RAIN WITHOUT THUNDER: THE IDEOLOGY OF THE ANIMAL RIGHTS MOVEMENT (1996).

Indeed, some of the most shocking forms of animal exploitation, including intensive animal agriculture or what is called "factory farming," have developed in the past one hundred years—when we claimed to embrace a more enlightened view of the moral status of nonhumans and of our moral and legal obligations to them.

III. THE PROBLEMS OF SIMILAR-MINDS THEORY

The primary difference between the recent resurgence of the similar-minds approach represented by *GAP* and similar approaches and the view put forward by Bentham and incorporated into conventional animal welfare theory is that modern ethological research indicates that there may be *some* nonhumans whose minds may be sufficiently like ours in ways that Bentham and others did not recognize and who may thereby be entitled to greater moral and legal consideration. Perhaps it is time to take a closer look at the entire enterprise of linking the moral significance of nonhumans with cognitive attributes beyond sentience, rather than trying to determine whether some nonhumans have such cognitive attributes or have them in a way that makes them sufficiently similar to humans to merit moral and legal personhood.

As a preliminary matter, there is a sense in which the similar-minds theory is decidedly odd. Is there anyone who has ever lived with a dog or cat who does not recognize that these nonhumans are intelligent, self-aware, or emotional, even though they are more genetically dissimilar to us than are the great apes? My partner and I live with five rescued dogs. If someone were to question whether our canine companions had these mental characteristics, we would find that as odd as an inquiry about whether they had tails. This is not a matter of anthropomorphism, the ascription of human qualities where there is no empirical basis. There is simply no way that we can plausibly and coherently explain the behavior of these nonhumans without relying on concepts of mind. Nonhumans may not have intentional states that are predicative in the same way as are intentional states that involve symbolic communication, but they certainly do have cognitive states that are equivalent to beliefs, desires, etc.

Moreover, 150 years after Darwin, it is astonishing that we are so astonished that other animals may have characteristics thought to be uniquely human. The proposition that humans have mental characteristics wholly absent in nonhumans is inconsistent with the theory of evolution. Darwin maintained that there are no uniquely human characteristics: "[T]he difference in mind between man and the higher animals, great as it is, is certainly one of degree and not of kind."[22] That is, Darwin recognized that the differences between human and nonhuman minds are quantitative and not qualitative. He argued that nonhumans are able to think and possess many of the same emotional attributes as humans. This is not to say that there is not a significant difference in cognition between an animal that uses symbolic communication and one that does not; it is only to say that the difference is not qualitative in that one animal has a cognitive characteristic that has no equivalent in the other.

Although I believe that nonhumans do possess the characteristics that we regard as uniquely human, I also realize that there is controversy on this point, and, in any event, there are certainly differences between human minds and the minds of other animals who do not use language. There are, however, at least two reasons to reject the notion that nonhumans must be more than sentient to have full membership in the moral community. One difficulty is primarily practical and concerns whether similar-minds theory will result in any meaningful change even for those nonhumans who have cognitive characteristics very similar to our own. The other difficulty is primarily theoretical and concerns the failure of the theory to address the fundamental moral question of why any characteristic other than sentience is necessary in order to have full membership in the moral community.

A. Similar-Minds Theory: A Further Delay of Justice?[23]

It is likely that similar-minds theory will do nothing more than delay our confronting our moral and legal obligations to nonhumans for an indeterminate time while we purport to amass the empirical evidence necessary to conclude that at least some nonhumans have minds similar to those of humans. But even when there is absolutely no doubt about this

---

22. CHARLES DARWIN, THE DESCENT OF MAN 105 (Princeton Univ. Press 1981) (1871). *See also* JAMES RACHELS, CREATED FROM ANIMALS: THE MORAL IMPLICATIONS OF DARWINISM (1990) (discussing the moral implications of the common ancestry of humans and nonhumans).

23. For a further discussion of the ideas discussed in this section, see FRANCIONE, INTRODUCTION TO ANIMAL RIGHTS, *supra* note 8, at 117–19.

similarity, we ignore the evidence and continue our exploitation. For example, the similarities between humans and chimpanzees are unmistakable. Chimpanzee DNA is 98.5 percent the same as ours, and chimpanzees have a cultural and mental life very similar to our own. We have known about these similarities for a while now; indeed, the whole point of *GAP* was to present the overwhelmingly powerful case that there are no relevant differences between humans and the great apes for purposes of inclusion in the moral community. Nevertheless, we still continue to imprison chimpanzees in zoos and use them in biomedical experiments. Even Jane Goodall, who was described in *GAP* as a "person who has made people appreciate that chimpanzees are individuals with different personalities and complex social relationships,"[24] has declined to call for a complete ban on our use of these nonhumans.

A related problem is that the similar-minds theory does not specify the extent to which a nonhuman must possess a particular characteristic before we consider that nonhuman to be sufficiently "like us" for purposes of moral significance. For example, "[a] growing body of evidence seems to show that parrots, like chimps and dolphins, can master complex intellectual concepts that most human children are not capable of mastering until the age of 5."[25] We have historically regarded the ability to have abstract ideas as uniquely human and as indicative of a qualitative difference between humans and nonhumans. We know now that we may have been mistaken about this as parrots and other nonhumans also seem to have some form of abstract thought.[26] We are, however, still selling parrots in pet stores. How intelligent does the parrot have to be before we conclude that the parrot qualifies for membership in the moral community? Does the parrot have to have the conceptual ability of an eight-year-old? A twelve-year-old? Similarly, some chimpanzees have exhibited the ability to use and to manipulate human language; how extensive must their vocabulary and syntactical ability be before we conclude that humans and at least nonhuman primates have similar minds?

---

24. THE GREAT APE PROJECT, *supra* note 1, at 10.

25. William Mullen, *Parrots Don't Just Talk a Good Game*, CHI. TRIB., Nov. 7, 1997, § 1, at 1. *See also* HILLIX & RUMBAUGH, *supra* note 4 (discussing the cognitive characteristics of parrots).

26. It may, of course, be argued that the parrot (or, indeed, any nonhuman) does not have the ability to engage in abstract generalization but only the ability to form complex associations. *See* STEINER, *supra* note 9, at 30–31. But the ability to discriminate that is required in order to form complex associations would seem to involve some level of abstract thinking.

The problem with this game of special characteristics is that non-humans can never win. When we determine that parrots have the conceptual ability to understand and manipulate single-digit numbers, we demand that they be able to understand and manipulate double-digit numbers in order to be sufficiently like us. When a chimpanzee indicates beyond doubt that she has an extensive vocabulary, we demand that she exhibit certain levels of syntactical skill in order to demonstrate that her mind is like ours. The irony, of course, is that whatever characteristic we are talking about will be possessed by some nonhumans to a greater degree than some humans, but we would never think it appropriate to exploit those humans in the ways that we do nonhumans.

There is a legitimate concern that the similar-minds theory is really an *identical-minds* theory and that animals will never be regarded as entitled to full membership in the moral community unless their minds are exactly like ours. Even then, there is no guarantee that we will not discriminate against nonhumans. After all, in the nineteenth century, racists relied on phrenology, or the "science" of determining personality traits based on the shape of the head, to declare that people of color, Jews, and others had different minds. Thus, even having an identical mind is not sufficient if there is a reason and desire to discriminate. Given that there probably are differences between the minds of animals who use symbolic communication and those who do not, the similar-minds theory will only be a prescription for the continued oppression of nonhumans as we pursue the endless quest for an identity that may never be realized, particularly if we are motivated by a desire to continue to consume animal products.

B. Similar-Minds Theory: Begging the Question[27]

Even if similar-minds theory resulted in our recognizing the personhood of some nonhumans, such as the great apes or dolphins, what about the vast number of animals who will never demonstrate the ability to use human language or the other characteristics that we associate

---

27. For a further discussion of the ideas discussed in this section, see FRANCIONE, INTRODUCTION TO ANIMAL RIGHTS, *supra* note 8, at 111–27.

with human minds? Although the similar-minds approach claims that, as an empirical matter, we may have been wrong in the past and at least some nonhumans may have some of the aforementioned characteristics, it does not address the underlying—and fundamental—moral question: why is anything more than sentience necessary for nonhumans to have the right not to be treated exclusively as means to human ends?

Similar-minds theory begs the moral question from the outset by assuming that certain characteristics are special and justify differential treatment. For example, we claim that humans are the only animals (apart perhaps from some great apes) who can recognize themselves in mirrors. Even if that is true, what is the moral significance of this supposed fact? My rescued border collie may not be able to recognize herself in a mirror, but she can jump about six feet from a sitting position—something that I certainly cannot do, and, as far as I am aware, no other human can do either. Birds can fly without being in an aircraft; no human can. Fish can breathe underwater without the aid of a snorkel or air tank; no human can. The similar-minds theory begs the moral question from the outset because it assumes that *our* abilities are morally more valuable than *their* abilities. There is, of course, no justification for this position other than that *we* say so and it is in *our* interest to do so.

Moreover, even if all animals other than humans were to lack a particular cognitive characteristic beyond sentience, or possess that characteristic to a lesser degree or in a different way from humans, such a difference cannot serve to justify our treatment of nonhumans as things. It may be the case that differences between humans and nonhumans are relevant for other purposes. For example, no one maintains that nonhumans ought to drive automobiles or attend universities. However, any such differences have *no* bearing on whether we should eat nonhumans or use them in experiments, nor should they. This is clear in situations in which only humans are involved. Whatever characteristic we identify as uniquely human will be seen to a lesser degree in some humans and not at all in others. Some humans will have the exact same deficiency that we attribute to nonhumans. This deficiency may be relevant for some purposes, but it is not relevant to whether we enslave such humans or otherwise treat them as commodities with no inherent value.

Consider the characteristic of self-awareness. It would seem that *any* sentient being must be self-aware in that to be sentient means to be the sort of being who recognizes that it is *that* being, and not some other, who is experiencing pain or distress. Biologist Donald Griffin has observed that if animals are conscious of anything, "the animal's own body and its own actions must fall within the scope of its perceptual consciousness."[28] We nevertheless deny animals self-awareness because we maintain that they cannot "think such thoughts as 'It is *I* who am running, or climbing this tree, or chasing that moth.'"[29] Griffin maintains that

> when an animal consciously perceives the running, climbing, or moth-chasing of another animal, it must also be aware of who is doing these things. And if the animal is perceptually conscious of its own body, it is difficult to rule out similar recognition that it, itself, is doing the running, climbing, or chasing.[30]

He concludes that "[i]f animals are capable of perceptual awareness, denying them some level of self-awareness would seem to be an arbitrary and unjustified restriction."[31] As I have previously stated, "[w]hen a dog experiences pain, the dog necessarily has a mental experience that tells her 'this pain is happening to me.' In order for pain to exist, some consciousness—some*one*—must perceive it as happening to her and must prefer not to experience it."[32]

But even if we require self-awareness in the peculiarly humanocentric sense as the ability to have a "conscious experience . . . whose existence and content are available to be consciously thought about (that is, available for description in acts of thinking that are themselves made available to further acts of thinking),"[33] then many humans, such as the severely mentally disabled, lack self-awareness. A lack of the sort of self-awareness that we attribute to normal adult humans may be relevant for some purposes. We may, for instance, not want to allow a mentally disabled person to operate a motor vehicle. Nevertheless, lacking this sort of self-awareness has no bearing on whether we should, for instance, use such humans in painful biomedical experiments. For whatever

---

28. DONALD R. GRIFFIN, ANIMAL MINDS: BEYOND COGNITION TO CONSCIOUSNESS 274 (2001).
29. *Id.*
30. *Id.*
31. *Id.*
32. Francione, *Animals—Property or Persons?, supra* note 8, at 128.
33. PETER CARRUTHERS, THE ANIMALS ISSUE: MORAL THEORY IN PRACTICE 181 (1992).

characteristic we choose, there will be some humans who will have the characteristic to a lesser degree than some nonhumans and some humans who will not have it at all. The lack of the characteristic may be relevant for some purposes, but is irrelevant to whether we treat a sentient human as a thing all of whose fundamental interests may be ignored if it benefits us to do so.

As I discussed above, although Bentham ostensibly rejected the view that the moral status of nonhumans depends on their having minds similar to humans, he effectively reincorporated that view through the notion that we may continue to use and kill animals because they do not have an interest in their lives. Peter Singer, co-editor of *GAP*, does the same thing. He argues that although only sentience is needed for moral significance and we ought to take animal suffering seriously, it is permissible to continue to use animals because, with the possible exception of great apes, animals do not have a sense of the future and an interest in their lives.[34] According to Singer, "[a]n animal may struggle against a threat to its life,"[35] but that does not mean that the animal can "grasp that it has 'a life' in the sense that requires an understanding of what it is to exist over a period of time."[36] He concludes that "in the absence of some form of mental continuity it is not easy to explain why the loss to the animal killed is not, from an impartial point of view, made good by the creation of a new animal who will lead an equally pleasant life."[37] Like Bentham, Singer maintains that it is not the use per se of nonhumans that raises a moral issue but the suffering of the animals incidental to the use. He argues that it is possible to apply the principle of equal consideration—that we should treat similar interests similarly—to nonhuman interests in not suffering and that it

---

34. *See* PETER SINGER, ANIMAL LIBERATION 18–21, 228–30 (2d ed. 1990); FRANCIONE, INTRODUCTION TO ANIMAL RIGHTS, *supra* note 8, at 135–46 (discussing Singer's position). The view that animals do not have an interest in continued existence and, therefore, that animal use per se is not problematic is proposed by other theorists as well. *See* Gary L. Francione, *Equal Consideration and the Interest of Nonhuman Animals in Continued Existence: A Response to Professor Sunstein*, 2006 U. CHI. LEGAL F. (forthcoming 2006) (discussing the views of Cass R. Sunstein, who accepts the views of Bentham and Singer). *See also* Martha C. Nussbaum, *Beyond "Compassion and Humanity": Justice for Nonhuman Animals, in* ANIMAL RIGHTS: CURRENT DEBATES AND NEW DIRECTIONS, *supra* note 8, at 299, 314–15 (accepting the utilitarian view that the treatment of animals and not their use raises the primary moral issue in the context of killing animals for food).

35. SINGER, *supra* note 34, at 228.

36. *Id.* at 229.

37. *Id.*

is not necessary to abolish the property status of nonhumans in order to do so.

The position of Bentham and Singer that, as an empirical matter, animals do not have an interest in their lives rests on a problematic understanding of self-awareness. Any being that is sentient is necessarily self-aware.[38] Any being that is sentient necessarily has an interest in life because sentience is a means to the end of continued existence. To say that a nonhuman is sentient but does not have an interest in continued existence and does not prefer, want, or desire to live is peculiar.[39]

According to the Bentham/Singer view, a being, whether human or nonhuman, has an interest in continued existence only if the being has an autobiographical sense of self and can reflect on his or her life. However, there is no reason to link such a mental state with whether we treat someone as the resource of others. For instance, there are humans who experience transient global amnesia and have no sense of the past or the future but have a very distinct sense of self with respect to present events and objects. They are self-conscious but not in the same way as is a human adult without amnesia. That difference may be relevant for some purposes. We might not, for example, give someone without an autobiographical sense of self a scholarship to a university because such a person will probably not benefit from an education. No one would deny, however, that such humans have an interest in their lives. The characteristic of having transient global amnesia is not relevant to whether we treat such people as commodities whose fundamental interests may be sacrificed if it benefits us to do so.

In sum, the similar-minds approach is fundamentally misguided and, at best, will do nothing more than create new speciesist hierarchies in which we *may* move some nonhumans, such as the great apes or dolphins, into a preferred group[40] but continue to treat all other nonhumans as things that lack morally significant interests. The theory does not

---

38. *See supra* text accompanying notes 28–31.

39. *See* FRANCIONE, INTRODUCTION TO ANIMAL RIGHTS, *supra* note 8, at 137–38. Moreover, it is virtually impossible to explain a great deal of animal behavior without positing that animals anticipate the future. *See id.* at 139–40.

40. *See, e.g., Project R&R: Release and Restitution for Chimpanzees in U.S. Laboratories,* http://www.releasechimps.org ("No other species holds the unique position of chimpanzees—a species with so much that seems 'human.'"). Project R&R is a campaign of the New England Anti-Vivisection Society. [Ed. Note: This sentence has been removed from the website.]

explain why sentience is not a sufficient criterion for moral significance but merely assumes that some supposedly uniquely human characteristic is the ticket for admission to the moral community.

IV. HUMAN SLAVERY AND ANIMAL PROPERTY

If we were to abandon similar-minds theory altogether, including the Bentham/Singer version of the doctrine, and require only sentience for full membership in the moral community, we would have to abandon our treatment of nonhumans as our property. As I argue in *Introduction to Animal Rights,* while we do not protect humans from all suffering, we prohibit inflicting suffering on humans incidental to using them merely as the resources of others. We accord everyone, irrespective of his or her particular characteristics, a basic right not to be treated as the property of others.[41] We regard human slavery—even "humane" slavery—as unacceptable.

Bentham opposed human slavery, and, as I have discussed elsewhere, this arguably rested, at least in part, on his recognition that the principle of equal consideration could not be applied to slaves, who would always count for less than their owners did.[42] Bentham, however, failed to see that the same problem exists with animal property. To the extent that nonhumans have an interest in their lives, our use of them in situations where we would use no humans necessarily denies them equal consideration for this interest.

Moreover, even if it is plausible to maintain that nonhumans do not have an interest in continued existence, application of the principle of equal consideration to animal interests in not suffering—already difficult to do because of the need to make interspecies comparisons[43]—becomes

---

41. *See* FRANCIONE, INTRODUCTION TO ANIMAL RIGHTS, *supra* note 8, at 90–96.

42. *See id.* at 130–50 (discussing Bentham's views of slavery and their application to nonhumans). Similarly, Singer argues that we should not treat normal human adults as replaceable resources. *See id.* at 141. Although both Bentham and Singer, who are utilitarians, eschew moral rights, both appear to be at least rule-utilitarians, as opposed to act-utilitarians, when it comes to treating humans exclusively as resources.

43. *See id.* at 143. Indeed, such comparisons may be impossible. For example, John Stuart Mill, also a utilitarian, maintained that the pleasures of the human intellect have a much higher value than the sensations of nonhumans. According to Mill, "[i]t is better to be a human being

even more complicated when animals are viewed as human property. The property status of animals serves as what I have discussed elsewhere as a "two-edged sword wielded against their interests."[44] Property status stops us from perceiving animal interests as similar to ours in the first instance and subordinates animal interests to human interests even when human and animal interests are recognized as similar because the property status of animals is always a good reason to refuse them similar treatment.

There is no non-speciesist reason not to recognize that full membership in the moral community requires that we reject the slavery of nonhumans just as we rejected the slavery of humans. This would require that we abolish—and not merely regulate—our exploitation of nonhumans and that we stop bringing domestic animals into existence to serve as means to human ends.[45]

CONCLUSION

The similar-minds theory is not new. It has been around for a long time in the form of various attempts to link cognitive characteristics with moral personhood and has served as the primary theoretical vehicle to exclude nonhumans from membership in the moral community. We supposedly rejected this link when we accepted the principle that the ability to suffer is the only characteristic required for moral and legal significance. But the theory was reintroduced as the belief that nonhumans, unlike humans, have no interest in continued life, and this explains why we did not reject the property status of animals when we tried to apply the principle in moral and legal contexts. Although we claim to take animal interests seriously, we treat animals as nothing more than things.

Whether nonhumans have minds that are similar or identical to ours may be interesting from a scientific perspective, but it is wholly irrelevant

---

dissatisfied than a pig satisfied." John Stuart Mill, *Utilitarianism, in* THE BASIC WRITINGS OF JOHN STUART MILL: ON LIBERTY, THE SUBJECTION OF WOMEN, AND UTILITARIANISM 233, 242 (2002). This would suggest that there is a qualitative difference between humans and nonhumans that would militate in favor of human interests always prevailing.

44. Francione, *Animals—Property or Persons?*, *supra* note 8, at 122.

45. For a further discussion of the view that domestication cannot be justified, see FRANCIONE, INTRODUCTION TO ANIMAL RIGHTS, *supra* note 8, at 153–54.

from a moral perspective. If we take nonhuman interests seriously, we have no choice but to acknowledge that only sentience is relevant.[46] This requires that we go one step beyond Bentham and recognize that the property status of nonhumans means that we necessarily subscribe to a similar-minds theory that will result in our never giving animal interests serious, let alone equal, consideration. We should forget about the similar-minds theory. It is nothing but a prescription for confused thinking about the human/nonhuman relationship and a vehicle that will only serve to perpetuate our speciesist oppression of nonhumans. The efforts of animal advocates ought to be directed at promoting veganism and the incremental eradication of the property status of nonhumans.[47]

46. Professor Taimie Bryant also rejects the similar-minds approach and does not believe that particular human-like cognitive characteristics are necessary for moral status or legal protection. *See* Taimie L. Bryant, *Similarity or Difference as a Basis for Justice: Must Animals Be Like Humans to Be Legally Protected from Humans?,* 70 LAW & CONTEMP. PROBS. (forthcoming 2006). There are, however, significant differences in our approaches. In addition to rejecting cognitive characteristics beyond sentience as necessary for moral significance, as I have, she maintains that linking moral significance with sentience alone, as I do, is similarly problematic. She argues that a theory based on sentience is not sufficient to ensure protection for nonhumans because assessments of sentience are equally susceptible of being manipulated so that humans will inevitably be seen as having a qualitatively different level of sentience than nonhumans. This supposed difference will be used to exclude animals from the moral community just as supposed qualitative differences in other cognitive characteristics have been used. Although this use of sentience is surely possible, my theory rejects it from the outset in that I maintain that if a being is sentient at all, that being has interests and, if those interests are to be morally significant, the being must have a right not to be treated exclusively as the resource of humans. Bryant's view assumes that sentience is not necessary because we can create a system of duties that do not depend on whether the objects of those duties are sentient. To the extent that she maintains that such obligations are owed to non-sentient beings and do not merely concern those beings, I do not agree. In my view, we cannot owe a duty to a being that does not have interests, and non-sentient beings do not have interests.

47. For a discussion of incremental change at both the individual and social levels, see FRANCIONE, RAIN WITHOUT THUNDER, *supra* note 21, at 147–219. I have long argued that an animal advocate who agrees with the abolitionist or rights position ought to adopt a vegan lifestyle. On a social level, I have promoted abolitionist education and consumer boycotts. To the extent that advocates seek legislative or regulatory change as part of social change, they should pursue prohibitions that incrementally diminish property rights in nonhumans.

CHAPTER 4 / EQUAL CONSIDERATION AND THE INTEREST OF NONHUMAN ANIMALS IN CONTINUED EXISTENCE

A Response to Professor Sunstein

INTRODUCTION

The topic of this symposium—*Law and Life: Definitions and Decision-making*—provides an excellent opportunity to address some of the comments made by Professor Cass R. Sunstein in his review of my book, *Introduction to Animal Rights: Your Child or the Dog?*[1] A central argument in the book is that we cannot justify treating nonhumans as our property and using them for our purposes irrespective of how "humanely" we do so. Sunstein, on the other hand, maintains that it is morally permissible to use animals for human purposes, including uses that cannot be regarded as necessary, provided that we do not make animals suffer unduly in the process. The focus of animal advocacy, Sunstein argues, should be on prohibiting "the most indefensible practices"[2] rather than abolishing animal use, as I propose.

My difference with Sunstein over the proper focus for animal advocacy stems from our fundamental disagreement over whether animals

This essay was published originally in *The University of Chicago Legal Forum*, vol. 2006, pp. 231–252.

I wish to thank Anna E. Charlton for her comments on an earlier draft. Also, I am grateful for comments from Taimie Bryant, Darian Ibrahim, Jeff Leslie, Bonnie Steinbock, and the other participants at the Legal Forum Symposium at the University of Chicago on October 28-29, 2005. I acknowledge research support from the Dean's Research Fund of the Rutgers University School of Law—Newark.

1. Cass R. Sunstein, *Slaughterhouse Jive*, New Republic 40 (Jan 29, 2001), reviewing Gary L. Francione, *Introduction to Animal Rights: Your Child or the Dog?* (Temple 2000) (hereinafter *Introduction to Animal Rights*).

2. Sunstein, *Slaughterhouse Jive*, New Republic at 43 (cited in note 1).

have an interest in their lives—in other words, in their continued existence—distinct from, and in addition to, their interest in not suffering, which virtually no one disputes. If nonhumans do have an interest in their lives, then our *use* of them, and not just our *treatment* of them incidental to those uses, raises the primary moral issue. In this article I explore our disagreement.

In the following section, I describe in summary fashion the central ideas of my book and Sunstein's particular criticisms. I then discuss the view that animals do not have an interest in continued existence and other aspects of Sunstein's critique.

I. A BRIEF OUTLINE OF *INTRODUCTION TO ANIMAL RIGHTS*

In *Introduction to Animal Rights,* I argue that almost everyone agrees that it is morally wrong to inflict "unnecessary" suffering on nonhuman animals.[3] Indeed, this moral rule is so uncontroversial that it is embodied in anticruelty laws and other laws that purport to regulate our treatment of nonhumans.[4] If a prohibition on unnecessary suffering is to be meaningful, then it must at the very least rule out the infliction of animal suffering for purposes of mere human pleasure, amusement, or convenience. Nevertheless, the overwhelming amount of the suffering that we inflict on animals can be justified *only* by trivial human interests.[5] We not only use animals for purposes that cannot be considered as necessary, but we inflict significant pain and suffering on them in the process and accord them treatment that would be regarded as torture if we inflicted it on humans.

The use of animals for entertainment in circuses, movies, or rodeos, and in sport hunting cannot, by definition, be considered as necessary. The largest number of animals that we use—approximately 10 billion annually in the United States alone—is for food purposes. Not only is it not necessary to eat meat or dairy products for optimal health,[6] the evidence

---

3. Francione, *Introduction to Animal Rights* at xxii–xxiii (cited in note 1).
4. Id at 7–9.
5. For a discussion of the necessity of animal use, see id at 9–49.
6. Courts have explicitly recognized that prohibitions against "unnecessary" suffering or "needless" killing must be interpreted by reference to institutional uses that are not necessary, such as the use of animals for food:

points increasingly to animal foods being detrimental to human health.[7] Moreover, animal agriculture is unquestionably an environmental disaster in terms of the resources consumed by animals, as well as resulting air and water pollution, and erosion of topsoil.[8] We eat animals because we have traditionally done so and because we enjoy it; there is, however, no necessity involved. Our only use of nonhumans that is not transparently frivolous involves biomedical research intended to produce data that will be useful for important issues of human health. But even in this single context, claims of necessity are suspect.[9]

We suffer from a sort of "moral schizophrenia" where animals are concerned. We claim to take animal interests seriously, but we do not. I argue that our moral schizophrenia is in large part related to the property status of animals. Although we purport to accord moral significance to animal interests, the reality is that animals are nothing more than commodities with extrinsic value alone, and we regard them exclusively as means to our ends.[10]

Because animals are property, we do not even question whether it is necessary to use animals in the first place and we focus exclusively on treatment, purporting to "balance" human and nonhuman interests to determine whether treatment is "humane." The property status of animals, however, prevents us from balancing interests in a meaningful way because the interests of property owners, even when trivial, will almost always outweigh the interests of animals. The prohibition on unnecessary suffering turns out to be nothing more than a prohibition on

---

The flesh of animals is not necessary for the subsistence of man, at least in this country, and by some people it is not so used. Yet it would not be denied that the killing of oxen for food is lawful. Fish are not necessary to any one, nor are various wild animals which are killed, and sold in market; yet their capture and killing are regulated by law. The words "needlessly" and "unnecessarily" must have a reasonable, not an absolute and literal, meaning attached to them.

State v Bogardus, 4 Mo App 215, 216–17 (1877).

7. See Francione, *Introduction to Animal Rights* at 14 (cited in note 1).

8. See id at 14–17.

9. See id at 31–49 (discussing necessity claims concerning the use of animals in experiments). See also Gary L. Francione, *The Use of Nonhuman Animals in Biomedical Research: Necessity and Justification*, 35 J L Med & Ethics (forthcoming 2007) (same). I maintain even if there are some uses of animals in this context that may be described as "necessary," these uses cannot be justified morally.

10. See Francione, *Introduction to Animal Rights* at 50–80 (cited in note 1) (discussing the property status of animals). For a general discussion of the problems created by the property status of nonhumans, see Gary L. Francione, *Animals, Property, and the Law* (Temple 1995).

inflicting more suffering than is needed to use animals in an economically efficient manner for purposes that are, for the most part, justified by nothing more compelling than human pleasure, amusement, or convenience. This generally means as a practical matter that we ignore animal interests whenever it produces an economic benefit for humans.

By treating animals as property, we necessarily fail to accord moral significance to animal interests. Moral significance requires that we apply the principle of equal consideration—the requirement that like cases be treated alike—to animals.[11] Although there may be significant differences between humans and nonhumans, we recognize the important similarity that both are sentient and are unlike everything else in the universe that is not. We may not know whether insects are sentient, and we may not understand exactly how the minds of nonhumans work, but there is no serious doubt that most of the nonhumans whom we routinely exploit—the cows, pigs, chickens, rodents, fish, etc.—are capable of experiencing pain and suffering. All sentient beings are, by definition, similar in that they all have an interest in not suffering.

We do not protect humans from all suffering, but we prohibit treating humans exclusively as means to the ends of others, and we accord everyone a basic, pre-legal right not to be treated exclusively as a resource.[12] It is because we recognize this basic right that we regard human slavery as unacceptable even if it is "humane." So the question becomes: why do we not also extend this one right to nonhumans? Why do we not treat the interest of animals in not being used as resources as protected by a right, or, in other words, as not able to be compromised irrespective of consequential considerations? We cannot, I argue, provide an answer that does not beg the question and constitute *speciesism,* or the exclusion of nonhumans from the moral community based solely on species.[13]

Recognition that we cannot legitimately justify the institutionalized exploitation of nonhumans, which is based upon the property status of

---

11. See Francione, *Introduction to Animal Rights* at 81–86, 98–100 (cited in note 1) (discussing the application of the principle of equal consideration to animals).

12. See id at 90–96. Another way of expressing the same idea is to say that we recognize that all humans have "equal inherent value." See id at 96–98. By this, I mean only that any being whose interests are going to count in a meaningful way must have more than extrinsic value. To have only extrinsic value is to be a thing, a commodity. See also note 61 (discussing intrinsic value).

13. See Francione, *Introduction to Animal Rights* at 103–29 (cited in note 1) (discussing reasons advanced for denying animals the basic right not to be treated as things).

animals, requires that we *abolish* and not merely *regulate* that exploitation. We should care for those nonhumans whom we have caused to come into existence as our resources, but we should stop bringing domestic animals into existence because that practice simply creates false conflicts between humans and nonhumans and cannot be morally justified.[14]

The theory that I present in *Introduction to Animal Rights* requires only that animals be sentient in order to be members of the moral community. No other cognitive characteristic is required; indeed, it is precisely because we have erroneously linked moral significance with human-like characteristics that we treat animals as resources that exist solely for our use.[15] Finally, I argue that the abolition of institutionalized exploitation, rather than better regulation, is required by *any* theory—deontological or consequential—that regards animal interests as morally significant because animal interests will necessarily be discounted or ignored if animals are property.[16]

II. SUNSTEIN'S ARGUMENTS AND MY RESPONSES

In his review of my book, Sunstein makes three primary arguments. First, he maintains that I have not demonstrated that the use per se of nonhumans—as opposed to their ill-treatment—is morally objectionable, or that property status is inconsistent with according animals better treatment or recognizing their moral value.[17] Indeed, he maintains that property status "protects animals in important ways."[18]

Second, Sunstein expresses doubt that we can base a theory of animal rights on sentience alone.[19] He maintains that theories that focus on sentience are consequential and not deontological, and that rights

---

14. See id at 151–66 (exploring the implications of extending to nonhumans the right not to be resources).

15. See id at 116–29, 133–42 (discussing the relevance of cognitive characteristics beyond sentience to the moral status of nonhumans). See also notes 50–51 and accompanying text (discussing the view that nonhumans must have minds similar to those of humans in order to be morally significant).

16. See Francione, *Introduction to Animal Rights* at xxxiv, 146–48 (cited in note 1) (arguing that utilitarian theory, like rights theory, requires not treating animals as property).

17. See Sunstein, *Slaughterhouse Jive,* New Republic at 44–45 (cited in note 1).

18. Id at 44.

19. See id at 44–45.

theories ostensibly require that animals be moral agents in some relevant sense.

Third, he argues that even if nonhumans have rights, these rights may be overridden when the benefits of doing so are considerable just as human rights are subject to consequential limitations.[20]

In the following sections, I explore and respond to Sunstein's arguments.

A. Animals as Property and Equal Consideration

1. SUNSTEIN AND THE UTILITARIANS Sunstein does not believe that we have a moral obligation to stop using animals for human purposes even if these uses are not necessary.[21] For example, he asks whether, if "steps can be taken to ensure that animals raised for food are given decent lives[,] . . . would it be so clear that meat-eating is indefensible?"[22] He states that with respect to animal use generally, I have "not shown that human use of animals is morally unacceptable if the relevant animals are treated as well as possible and allowed, to the extent possible, to live decent lives."[23] Sunstein provides no detail on what he means by "to the extent possible" and does not address the fact that most exploiters claim that they already provide their animals "decent lives" consistent with their having the status of property and the economic realities entailed by that status.

Sunstein observes that Jeremy Bentham and Peter Singer, "strong advocates for animals and also utilitarians, do not object to meat-eating."[24] He recognizes that Bentham and Singer claim that nonhumans, unlike humans, are not self-aware, and, therefore, "what is important is their pains and pleasures while they are alive—not that they continue to live."[25]

---

20. See id at 45.
21. Sunstein claims that I "insufficiently" analyze the concept of necessity when I discuss necessary suffering because "[f]ew things are literally 'necessary.' When we say that something is necessary, we usually mean that it is clear that it should be done." Sunstein, *Slaughterhouse Jive*, New Republic at 43 (cited in note 1). Sunstein does not address the argument that a prohibition about unnecessary suffering is without meaning (however necessity is understood) if animal suffering and death can be justified only by human pleasure, amusement, or convenience.
22. Id at 44.
23. Id at 45.
24. Id at 44.
25. Sunstein, *Slaughterhouse Jive*, New Republic at 42 (cited in note 1).

Sunstein accepts this view, claiming that "Bentham was entirely right. Because animals can suffer, they should be protected, much more than they now are, against pain and distress."[26]

Sunstein agrees that the property status of animals "does violence to people's most reflective understandings of their relationships with other living creatures,"[27] but claims that property status "does not necessarily signify that animals will be treated as means or that their legal rights will amount to little in the real world."[28] He argues that equal consideration and the recognition of the intrinsic value of animal property are possible, even if difficult, and that any problems created by property status are contingent and not necessary. At several points in his review, Sunstein argues that although I am correct to point out the way in which we systematically ignore animal interests, I fail to recognize that we could treat animals better than we do even if they remain our property and that better regulation of institutionalized exploitation, rather than its abolition, ought to be our "current priority."[29]

Sunstein is correct to attribute the distinction between use and treatment, and the view that use per se does not raise a moral issue, to Bentham and Singer. The utilitarian position as articulated by Bentham and Singer is that the principle of equal consideration ought to apply to animals and that similar interests—and particularly the interest of animals in not suffering—ought to be treated similarly.[30] The utilitarians purport to reject the notion that animal suffering is not morally significant because animals lack some human-like characteristic, such as self-consciousness, rationality, or the ability to communicate in a symbolic language.[31] For instance, according to Bentham, animals had been "degraded into the class of *things*"[32] because they lacked certain human-like characteristics, such as the ability to think rationally or to use human language. He noted that:

---

26. Id at 45.

27. Id at 44.

28. Id.

29. Sunstein, *Slaughterhouse Jive*, New Republic at 43 (cited in note 1).

30. See Francione, *Introduction to Animal Rights* at 130–50 (cited in note 1) (discussing Bentham's arguments).

31. See id at 5–6, 133–34. For a further discussion of the views of Bentham and Singer concerning linking moral significance with human cognitive characteristics, see Francione, *Taking Sentience Seriously*, 1 J Animal L & Ethics 1 (2006).

32. Jeremy Bentham, *An Introduction to the Principles of Morals and Legislation* 310 (Hafner 1948).

a full-grown horse or dog is beyond comparison a more rational, as well as a more conversable animal, than an infant of a day, or a week, or even a month, old. But suppose the case were otherwise, what would it avail? the question is not, Can they *reason?* nor, Can they *talk?* but, Can they *suffer?*[33]

This is not to say that Bentham denied that there were empirical differences between humans and animals, or denied the relevance of these differences to our moral and legal obligations to animals. He discussed this in the context of why it is morally permissible to eat animals. Bentham was certainly aware that it is not necessary for humans to eat nonhumans, but he did not think that a moral issue is raised per se by the eating of meat because he believed that animals are not self-aware and have no sense of the future. Therefore, nonhumans have no interest in not being used for food. According to Bentham,

[i]f the being eaten were all, there is very good reason why we should be suffered to eat such of them as we like to eat: we are the better for it, and they are never the worse. They have none of those long-protracted anticipations of future misery which we have.[34]

He maintained that animals are "never the worse for being dead"[35] but that we have a moral obligation not to "torment them."[36] Therefore, because Bentham did not believe that animals have an interest in their lives, he did not challenge our use of animals per se, but only our treatment of them.

Singer, who further articulates Bentham's position, argues that we must treat similar interests in a similar way, but he maintains that most animals are not self-aware and have neither a "continuous mental existence" nor desires for the future.[37] An animal can have an interest in not suffering, but because "it cannot grasp that it has 'a life' in the sense that requires an understanding of what it is to exist over

---

33. Id at 311 n 1.
34. Id.
35. Id.
36. Bentham, *An Introduction to the Principles of Morals and Legislation* at 311 n 1 (cited in note 32).
37. Peter Singer, *Animal Liberation* 228 (Random House 2d ed 1990).

a period of time," the animal has no interest in continuing to live or in not being used as the resource or property of humans.[38] Animals do not care whether we raise and slaughter them for food, use them for experiments, or exploit them as our resources in any other way, as long as they have a reasonably pleasant life. According to Singer, because animals do not possess any interest in their lives per se, "it is not easy to explain why the loss to the animal killed is not, from an impartial point of view, made good by the creation of a new animal who will lead an equally pleasant life."[39]

Singer strongly condemns the practices of intensive agriculture because he believes that the amount of pain and suffering that animals experience under such conditions outweighs whatever benefits accrue to humans.[40] He claims to reject the notion that animals have value only as economic commodities, but he does not conclude that eating animals per se is morally unacceptable; rather, he maintains that it may be morally justifiable to eat animals "who have a pleasant existence in a social group suited to their behavioral needs, and are then killed quickly and without pain."[41] He states that he "can respect conscientious people who take care to eat only meat that comes from such animals."[42]

Although Sunstein purports to accept that sentience is the only characteristic required for the moral significance of animals, he, like Bentham and Singer, accepts that animal use per se is not morally objectionable. Sunstein does not explicitly endorse the view that animals do not have an interest in life. He does, however, maintain that Bentham was "entirely right"[43] in his analysis, and he acknowledges the view that animals do not have an interest in continued existence as central to Ben-

---

38. Id at 228–29.

39. Id at 229.

40. Singer's argument against intensive agriculture works only if one agrees with Singer's necessarily imprecise and subjective assessments of relative utilities. See Francione, *Introduction to Animal Rights* at 144–45 (cited in note 1).

41. Singer, *Animal Liberation* at 229–30 (cited in note 37).

42. Id at 230. For a further discussion of the view of Bentham and Singer that animals do not have an interest in life, see Francione, 1 J Animal L & Ethics 1 (cited in note 31). Other theorists, focusing particularly on the use of nonhumans for food, endorse the utilitarian view that it is the treatment and not the use per se of nonhumans that raises the primary moral question. See Martha C. Nussbaum, *Beyond "Compassion and Humanity": Justice for Nonhuman Animals*, in Cass R. Sunstein and Martha C. Nussbaum, eds, *Animal Rights: Current Debates and New Directions* 299, 314–15 (Oxford 2004).

43. Sunstein, *Slaughterhouse Jive*, New Republic at 45 (cited in note 1). Sunstein acknowledges that I "strongly disagree[ ]" with the view of Bentham and Singer about sentience and the interest

tham's view that animal use per se is not morally objectionable. More important, however, it is not possible to make sense of Sunstein's overall approach without attributing this view to him.

2. ANIMAL USE: AN INTEREST IN CONTINUED EXISTENCE The notion that animal use is not per se morally objectionable because animals do not have an interest in continued existence is problematic. Indeed, as I argue at length in *Introduction to Animal Rights,* it would seem that merely being sentient logically implies an interest in continued existence.[44] To be a sentient being means to have an experiential welfare. In this sense, all sentient beings have an interest not only in the quality of their lives but also in the quantity of their lives. Animals may not have thoughts about the number of years they will live, but by virtue of having an interest in not suffering and in experiencing pleasure, they have an interest in remaining alive. They prefer or desire or want to remain alive.

Sentience is not an end in itself; it is a means to the end of staying alive. Sentient beings use sensations of pain and suffering to escape situations that threaten their lives and sensations of pleasure to pursue situations that enhance their lives. Just as humans will often endure excruciating pain in order to remain alive, animals will often not only endure but inflict on themselves excruciating pain in order to live. For example, animals caught in traps have been known to gnaw off a limb to escape. Sentience is what evolution has produced in order to ensure the survival of certain complex organisms. To deny that a being who has evolved to develop a consciousness of pain and pleasure has no interest in remaining alive is to say that conscious beings have no interest in remaining conscious.

Moreover, and as I also discuss in *Introduction to Animal Rights,* even if we cannot know the precise nature of animal self-awareness, it appears that *any* being that is aware on a perceptual level must be self-aware and have a continuous mental existence.[45] Donald Griffin has observed that if animals are conscious of anything, "the animal's own body and its own

---

in continued existence, or the self-awareness of animals. See id at 42. But he does not address the arguments about continued existence that I make in *Introduction to Animal Rights.* Therefore, it is not clear in what respects he may feel that I have failed to address the utilitarian position.

44. See Francione, *Introduction to Animal Rights* at 137–42 (cited in note 1).

45. See id at 114–15.

actions must fall within the scope of its perceptual consciousness."[46] But we deny that animals are self-aware because we maintain that they cannot "think such thoughts as 'It is *I* who am running, or climbing this tree, or chasing that moth.'"[47] Griffin maintains that

> when an animal consciously perceives the running, climbing, or moth-chasing of another animal, it must also be aware of who is doing these things. And if the animal is perceptually conscious of its own body, it is difficult to rule out similar recognition that it, itself, is doing the running, climbing, or chasing.[48]

Griffin concludes that "[i]f animals are capable of perceptual awareness, denying them some level of self-awareness would seem to be an arbitrary and unjustified restriction."[49]

Although it is clear both as the result of evolution and confirming work by cognitive ethologists that animals other than humans possess cognitive characteristics that are at least equivalent to those thought to be unique to humans, I am unwilling to require that animals have minds that are similar to humans—beyond having the quality of being sentient—in order to be full members of the moral community.[50] As a practical matter, that is a game that animals can never win. However close their minds are to ours, the similarity will be insufficient to make them "like us." After all, we have for some time now recognized the remarkable similarity between humans and chimpanzees yet we still use them for experiments and display them at zoos.

As a theoretical matter, I object to what I have called "similar-minds" theory, or the view that the moral status of nonhumans is dependent on their having human-like cognitive characteristics.[51] I am content to acknowledge that even if nonhuman minds are similar to human minds,

46. Donald R. Griffin, *Animal Minds: Beyond Cognition to Consciousness* 274 (Chicago 2001).
47. Id.
48. Id.
49. Id.
50. See Francione, *Introduction to Animal Rights* at 116-19 (cited in note 1).
51. See Gary L. Francione, *Our Hypocrisy*, New Scientist 51 (June 4-10, 2005). See also Francione, *Introduction to Animal Rights* at 118-27 (cited in note 1) (discussing human and nonhuman cognitive characteristics); Gary L. Francione, *Animals—Property or Persons?*, in Sunstein and Nussbaum, eds, *Animal Rights* 108, 127-31 (cited in note 42) (same); Francione, 1 J Animal L & Ethics 1 (cited in note 31) (same).

there will still be differences because cognition in humans is very much a function of human language and nonhumans may not have intentional states that are predicative in the same way. Even if nonhumans are self-aware, that does not mean that they can recognize themselves in mirrors or keep diaries or anticipate the future by looking at clocks and calendars. Even if nonhumans have the ability to reason or think abstractly, that does not mean that they can do algebra.

There are, however, at least two related reasons why the lack of human-like varieties of cognitive characteristics cannot serve to provide a morally sound, nonarbitrary basis for justifying our continued use of nonhumans as human resources. First, any attempt to justify treating animals as resources based on their lack of human-like cognitive characteristics begs the question from the outset by assuming that these characteristics are special and justify differential treatment. My dog may not be able to recognize herself in a mirror, but she can recognize her scent on a patch of lawn that she regularly visits, and she can distinguish that patch from the ones used by my other canine companions. What makes recognition in a mirror better in a moral sense than recognition through scent? The answer, of course, is that *we* say so, but that is not a good argument for our treating animals as resources.

Second, even if all nonhumans lack a particular cognitive characteristic beyond sentience, or possess it to a different degree or in a different way from humans, there is no logical relationship between that lack or difference and our treatment of animals as resources. Differences between humans and nonhumans are undoubtedly relevant for some purposes, as are differences between humans. For example, a human who experiences transient global amnesia has no sense of the past or future but does have a sense of self with respect to the present. Such a person has an interest in her life and in not being treated exclusively as a means to the ends of others even if she does not have the same level of self-consciousness that is possessed by normal adults. In this sense, a person with this sort of amnesia is similarly situated to all other sentient humans who have an interest in being treated as ends in themselves irrespective of their particular characteristics. This disability may be relevant for some purposes, but it is irrelevant as to whether we treat her exclusively as a resource and disregard her fundamental interests, including her interests in not suffering and in continued existence, if it benefits us to do so.

Although some may be comfortable in saying that such humans count for less than do normal humans when it comes to deciding whether to take the liver from someone with amnesia to transplant into someone without amnesia, most are not. We recognize that apart from any other moral consideration, such reasoning leads to a sort of elitism that would justify our attaching greater moral value to the fundamental interests of the more intelligent, or to those who have whatever characteristic that we declare to be special. If we can use someone with amnesia as a forced organ donor to help someone without amnesia, why can't we kill and use the organs of someone who is less intelligent to save the life of someone more intelligent?

If nonhumans have an interest in life, we *cannot* apply the principle of equal consideration to animals who have the status of property because they have an interest in not being treated as resources just as humans have an interest in not being treated as slaves. More brutal forms of slavery are worse than less brutal forms, but we prohibit human slavery in general because all forms of slavery more or less allow the interests of slaves to be ignored if it provides a benefit to slave owners. Humans have an interest in not suffering the deprivation of their fundamental interests, including their interest in continued existence, merely because it benefits someone else, however "humanely" they are treated.[52] To the extent that we protect humans from being used exclusively as means to human ends and accord to all humans a right not to be treated as the property of others, and we do not accord this similar nonhuman interest the same sort of protection, we necessarily fail to apply the principle of equal consideration to animals.[53]

---

3. ANIMAL TREATMENT: THE PROBLEMS OF PROPERTY STATUS As far as issues of treatment—as opposed to use per se—are concerned, Sunstein maintains

---

52. See Francione, *Introduction to Animal Rights* at 89–90 (cited in note 1).

53. See id at 146. Others have recognized that the use of animals as resources is inconsistent with the principle of equal consideration. See, for example, David DeGrazia, *Taking Animals Seriously: Mental Life and Moral Status* 47 (Cambridge 1996) ("While equal consideration is compatible with different ethical theories, it is incompatible—if extended to animals—with all views that see animals as essentially resources for our use."). It is, however, not clear that DeGrazia grasps the implication of this view as he does not argue that we are obligated to abolish all animal exploitation rather than to better regulate it.

that the property status of animals is not a necessary impediment to our according animals better treatment and to our recognition that animals have "intrinsic value, and that animal well-being is a good in itself."[54] I certainly agree with Sunstein that we could give animals more consideration than we presently do even though they are our property, and I have never suggested otherwise. I do, however, think that he greatly underestimates how difficult this is to achieve in the real world. Indeed, in the decade since I first proposed in *Animals, Property, and the Law* that the property status of animals results in their receiving little or no protection under animal welfare laws,[55] there have been no significant improvements in animal welfare laws at least in the United States.[56] Moreover, as I argued in *Rain Without Thunder: The Ideology of the Animal Rights Movement,* there is no empirical evidence to support the suggestion that better regulation of animal exploitation leads eventually to the abolition of animal exploitation.[57]

Although we may accord animals better treatment, it is difficult to understand how we can comply with utilitarian theory and accord equal consideration to nonhumans that are property. The problems involved in making interspecies comparisons to determine whether interests are similar, for instance, would, as a practical matter and for a number of reasons, be insurmountable and would be present even if we focused only on the interest of animals in not suffering, and did not consider their interest in continued existence.[58] These problems are greatly exacerbated by the property status of animals, which acts as a blinder that effectively blocks even our perception of their interests as similar to ours because

---

54. Sunstein, *Slaughterhouse Jive,* New Republic at 45 (cited in note 1).

55. Consider Francione, *Animals, Property, and the Law* (cited in note 10).

56. See Gary L. Francione, *Reflections on* Animals, Property, and the Law *and* Rain Without Thunder, 70 L & Contemp Probs (forthcoming 2007).

57. See generally Gary L. Francione, *Rain Without Thunder: The Ideology of the Animal Rights Movement* (Temple 1996) (arguing that animal rights and animal welfare are very different approaches to the human-nonhuman relationship and that animal welfare understood as the regulation of animal use will not lead incrementally to the recognition of animal rights understood as the abolition of institutionalized animal exploitation).

58. See Francione, *Introduction to Animal Rights* at 143–44 (cited in note 1). Indeed, there is a tendency within utilitarian theory to accord the intellectual pleasures of humans a higher value than the cognitions of nonhumans. For example, according to John Stuart Mill, "[i]t is better to be a human being dissatisfied than a pig satisfied." John Stuart Mill, *Utilitarianism,* in *The Basic Writings of John Stuart Mill: On Liberty, The Subjection of Women, and Utilitariansim* 233, 242 (Modern Library 2002).

any limitation on property owners is understood to represent significant human "suffering." And even in those instances in which human and animal interests are recognized as similar, animals will lose in any balancing of interests because the property status of animals is always a good reason not to accord similar treatment unless to do so would benefit property owners.[59] The interests of slaves will never be viewed as similar to the interests of slave owners. The interests of animals that are property will never be viewed as similar to those of human property owners.

Although Sunstein claims that we can treat animal interests as morally significant even if animals remain human property, it would seem that any recognition that animals have "intrinsic value" and that respect for animal interests is a "good in itself" would necessarily require a departure from property status because we regard property as having only an extrinsic value. Our recognition of the intrinsic value of animals would require certain limitations on treatment that are not related to the instrumental value that such limitations would have to us as property owners.

4. PROPERTY STATUS: A BENEFIT? Sunstein claims that not only is the property status of animals not a necessary impediment to recognizing the intrinsic value of nonhumans, but that property status actually benefits nonhumans. Sunstein claims that the owners of "pets are unlikely to think that their animals are mere commodities"[60] and that these owners will likely regard themselves as having "the sorts of rights and duties that make sense for human beings entrusted with the care of living creatures."[61] Sunstein goes further and claims that "[t]he fact of ownership even protects animals in important ways" because owners are morally and legally obligated to protect their animals. Non-owners are also obligated to refrain from damaging the animal property of others, and "this

---

59. See Francione, *Animals—Property or Persons?* at 122 (cited in note 51). See generally Francione, *Animals, Property, and the Law* (cited in note 10) (further discussing the difficulty in balancing the interests of humans and animals with one another).

60. Sunstein, *Slaughterhouse Jive,* New Republic at 44 (cited in note 1).

61. Id. To the extent that owners of animals regard those animals as having a greater-than-market value, one might say that the owner regards the animal as having "intrinsic" value. That sense of "intrinsic" value, which concerns sentimental or idiosyncratic valuation by particular animal owners, is, however, different from the moral value that Sunstein refers to when he talks about our recognition as a general matter that animals have "intrinsic value, and that animal well-being is a good in itself." Id at 45.

makes it less likely that such harm will occur."[62] He argues that the well-being of domestic animals, and not benefit to humans, requires that we have the legal right and the duty to control the lives of these animals.

There are three responses to Sunstein's claims about these supposedly beneficial aspects of property ownership. First, Sunstein makes these observations with respect to only one aspect of the human-nonhuman relationship: the keeping by humans of nonhuman companions. Our relationship with our nonhuman companions is the one area in which at least some of us do not regard nonhumans as "mere commodities." Indeed, it is precisely because many of us regard our nonhuman companions as members of our families while sticking forks into other nonhumans, such as pigs, cows, chickens, etc., who are no different from our companions, that I regard our attitudes about animals as exhibiting moral schizophrenia.

Second, even in this limited context, which involves a small number of nonhumans relative to the number that we exploit, we cannot regard property status as beneficial to animals. We can certainly choose to treat our nonhuman companions well, but if we do not, their property status protects our decision. If we choose to keep our dog chained up in the backyard and ignore her except to bring her food or water, that is permissible. If we painfully discipline the dog to make her a more effective guard dog, that is also permissible. We can choose to take our healthy animal to our veterinarian and have her killed because she is no longer convenient to our lifestyle.

Although some of us treat our nonhuman companions well, more of us treat them poorly. In the United States, for instance, many dogs are dumped at a pound, transferred to a new owner, or abandoned. Some who claim to love their companion animals mutilate them senselessly by having their ears cropped, their tails docked, or their claws ripped out, which involves the painful partial removal of digits, in order to protect sofas and tables. The bottom line is that because animals are property, we are given great latitude as owners regarding how we value their interests.

Third, in arguing that property status is beneficial for nonhumans, Sunstein fails to address a central argument in *Introduction to Animal*

---

62. Id at 44.

Rights. If we took animal interests seriously, we would stop bringing domestic animals into existence in the first place.[63] We see every human use of nonhumans as presenting a choice similar to the one that we are confronted with in the hypothetical of whom to save in the burning house—the child or the dog?[64] Our moral discourse about the human-nonhuman relationship seeks to resolve conflicts between humans and animals. But we create these conflicts in the first place by bringing animals into existence for the sole purpose of killing them or otherwise using them exclusively as means to our ends. Moreover, the overwhelming proportion of our animal use involves human interests that are trivial relative to the animal interests at stake. If we recognize that animals have an interest in continued existence that is necessarily ignored by their status as our property and that there is no moral justification for our continued treatment of nonhumans as our property, we will abolish institutionalized animal exploitation and stop producing nonhumans for human purposes. We will thereby eliminate the overwhelming number of these false conflicts in which we are supposed to "balance" human and nonhuman interests—an act that is made impossible by the property status of nonhumans.

We should, of course, care for those domestic nonhumans who are here now as the result of our commodification of animals, but we should stop causing more, including dogs, cats, and other animals used as companions, to come into existence. Our remaining conflicts with nonhumans would involve wild animals, and the moral imperative would require that we apply the principle of equal consideration to resolve these conflicts. Difficult practical questions would remain, but the number of such questions would be substantially reduced.

---

63. See Francione, *Introduction to Animal Rights* at 153–54 (cited in note 1).

64. Sunstein claims that the subtitle of my book, *Your Child or the Dog?*, "is misleading and more than a little ridiculous; this is really not the kind of conflict that concerns Francione." Sunstein, *Slaughterhouse Jive*, New Republic at 42 (cited in note 1). I disagree with Sunstein in two respects. First, the hypothetical, which obviously invites the response that we would save the child over the dog, is often used to support the position that it is morally acceptable to use nonhumans for human purposes because the response shows that we accept that humans have greater moral value than nonhumans. A central argument of my book is that choosing the child over the dog does not entitle us to conclude anything about moral value or the legitimacy of our treatment of nonhumans as resources. See Francione, *Introduction to Animal Rights* at 157–60 (cited in note 1). Second, I maintain that because animals are property, we treat all questions involving animal use as involving a "conflict" between property owners and their property, and we thereby treat all situations as analogous to the example involving the burning house. See id at 153–54.

B. The Role of Sentience in Animal Rights Theory

Sunstein also claims that I take the "complicated and unusual step" of "merging the idea of animal welfare with the idea of animal rights, through the claim that animals have rights because they can suffer."[65] He doubts that this effort can succeed because "[t]he importance of suffering, under the utilitarian framework, is inextricably intertwined with the insistence on the overriding importance of consequences" and he is "not sure that [I] can insist on the centrality of suffering, and the right not to suffer, while also arguing that overall consequences do not matter."[66] Sunstein maintains that under the rights framework, "the insistence that consequences do not matter is inextricably intertwined with the claim that human beings are moral agents."[67] He concludes that he cannot see how I "can insist that consequences do not matter while refusing to say whether and in what sense animals are moral agents."[68]

I certainly agree with Sunstein that rights theories are usually based on moral agency. Immanuel Kant and John Rawls come to mind as prominent examples, and I discuss them and other rights theorists in *Introduction to Animal Rights* where I reject the notion that rights protection ought to be linked to moral agency.[69] Moral agency, like particular types of self-awareness, may be relevant for some purposes, but it is irrelevant as to whether the interest of a human or nonhuman in not being treated as a resource ought to be protected with a right. Again, we recognize this where humans are concerned. If a human cannot be considered as a moral agent, that characteristic may be relevant to whether we allow her to make binding contracts, but has absolutely no relevance to whether we use her as a coerced performer in a circus or enslave her for the benefit of moral agents.

---

65. Sunstein, *Slaughterhouse Jive,* New Republic at 44 (cited in note 1).
66. Id.
67. Id.
68. Id at 44–45.
69. See Francione, *Introduction to Animal Rights* at 122–25 (cited in note 1). In this sense, I agree with Tom Regan, who also argues that moral patients can be rightholders. See Tom Regan, *The Case for Animal Rights* 279–80 (California 1983). I disagree with Regan, however, to the extent that he rejects sentience alone as sufficient for status as a rightholder. I also disagree with Regan that death is a greater harm for humans than for nonhumans. Id at 324–25. See Francione, *Introduction to Animal Rights* at 215 n 61 (cited in note 1).

I also recognize that Singer and other utilitarians who purport to link moral significance with sentience alone reject rights. There is, however, no conceptual or logical connection between sentience and consequentialist theory. Moreover, as argued above, the equal consideration of the interests of animals that is sought by utilitarian theorists as the goal of animal welfare is impossible as long as animals are property. This is so both because animals have an interest in continued existence that is necessarily ignored as a consequence of property status, and because the interests of animals in avoiding suffering are almost certain not to receive equal consideration if animals are property. Therefore, if animal interests are to be morally significant—if the principle of equal consideration is going to apply to animals—then we must stop treating them as property even within the utilitarian framework. This would commit the utilitarian to the abolition of the property status of nonhumans, and not merely to the better treatment of our animal property, and would mean that both the utilitarian and the rights theorist are both committed to abolition of institutionalized exploitation.[70] This is less a merger of animal rights and animal welfare than it is a recognition that *any* theory that subscribes to the moral significance of animal interests requires the abolition of institutionalized animal exploitation, which necessarily precludes the equal consideration of interests.[71]

C. The Exploitation of Nonhuman Animals

Finally, Sunstein maintains that even if animals have inherent value and are entitled to moral consideration, it does not follow that we cannot exploit them. For example, Sunstein claims that I do not recognize that we regard it as acceptable to treat humans as means to ends in certain situations. Sunstein notes that "[w]hen you hire a plumber, a lawyer, an architect, or someone to clean your house, you are treating them as means, not as ends."[72] Sunstein fails to recognize a distinction that I drew explic-

---

70. Interestingly, Bentham rejected property status or slavery for humans, and Singer rejects the notion that we should treat normal humans as replaceable resources. That is, both arguably recognize that treating humans exclusively as resources precludes according them equal consideration. See note 77 and accompanying text.

71. See Francione, *Introduction to Animal Rights* at xxxiv, 148 (cited in note 1).

72. Sunstein, *Slaughterhouse Jive*, New Republic at 45 (cited in note 1).

itly in *Introduction to Animal Rights*—the distinction between treating another as a means to an end and treating another *exclusively* as a means to an end. I argued that although we can treat other humans as means to ends,

[t]here is a "red light" that . . . limits our use and treatment of humans. We can value our plumber as a means to the end of repairing our faucet, and it is all right to compensate a good plumber more highly than we do a lesser plumber. But if we no longer value the plumber as a plumber and moreover do not like her or value her in any other way, we cannot treat her solely as an economic commodity; we cannot enslave her in a forced labor camp; we cannot eat her, use her in experiments, or turn her into a pair of shoes.[73]

Our use of animals for food, clothing, entertainment, experiments, and the like goes qualitatively beyond the use the exploitation that most of us regard as permissible where humans are concerned.

Similarly, Sunstein maintains that even if nonhumans have rights, it does not follow that their rights cannot be overridden because it may be in their interests to override any rights that they have, as it is in the case of children, and because:

[w]hen the stakes are sufficiently high, government is permitted to override what would otherwise be rights, even constitutional rights. Free speech and freedom of movement can be restricted in times of war. In fact, an emergency is not required; you can be banned from writing graffiti on national monuments and even from trespassing on certain areas to carry your views to government officials. If consequences are relevant in the case of human beings, then they matter for animals, too.[74]

Sunstein maintains that I make too much of our moral intuition that we should not compel some humans to serve as nonconsenting subjects in biomedical experiments even if there were significant collective benefits.

---

73. Francione, *Introduction to Animal Rights* at 90 (cited in note 1).
74. Sunstein, *Slaughterhouse Jive,* New Republic at 45 (cited in note 1).

As to Sunstein's analogy to our control of children, I do not believe that children or nonhuman companions have rights to make choices that would endanger them. As to Sunstein's general point that rights may be overridden by consequences, I certainly agree that human rights are not absolute, and it is sometimes difficult to determine the scope of interests protected by a right. As a general matter, however, the defining characteristic of a respect-based right is that the interest that it protects cannot be compromised for consequential considerations alone.[75]

In *Introduction to Animal Rights,* I argue that there is a great deal of controversy about which interests should be protected by rights, but that the fundamental interest in not being treated as a resource must be protected by a right if the being in question is to be considered as a member of the moral community.[76] Indeed, although utilitarians generally reject moral rights, some have recognized a right to equal consideration, which may account for Bentham's rejection of human slavery and Singer's notion that normal humans should not be regarded as replaceable resources.[77] I maintain that the status of being a resource is inconsistent with equal consideration. A right to equal consideration must preclude being treated exclusively as a means to the ends of others and having one's fundamental interests in physical security, including and most importantly an interest in continued existence, subject to compromise for consequential reasons.

Sunstein fails to distinguish between the basic, pre-legal moral right not to be a resource and legal rights, which may be policy-based and subject to consequential limitation, or respect-based and less amenable to consequential limitation. For example, even if the prohibition on writing graffiti on national monuments is a consequential limitation on the right of free expression rather than a reflection of the speech/conduct

---

75. For a discussion of the distinction between respect-based and policy-based rights, see Francione, *Introduction to Animal Rights* at 190–91 n 17 (cited in note 1).

76. See id at 92–96.

77. See id at 132–37. I maintain that with respect to the institution of human slavery, Bentham and Singer, who are normally regarded as act-utilitarians, adopt at least a rule-utilitarian position and possibly recognize a right to equal consideration that is necessarily violated by treatment exclusively as a resource. Neither Bentham nor Singer maintains that we should inquire on a case-by-case basis whether utility will be increased if we enslave a particular person or treat a particular normal adult as a replaceable resource. Rather, both assume that the treatment of humans as resources is prohibited as a prima facie matter.

distinction that concerns the scope of the right, this is not a situation in which consequences are thought to justify treating the individual exclusively as a resource. Indeed, for Sunstein to regard such an example as relevant in this context indicates a certain distance on his part from the realities of animal exploitation.

The only situation in which consequences are offered to justify the treatment of humans exclusively as means to the ends of others and is thus analogous to the use of humans as nonconsenting subjects in biomedical experiments involves conscription, a practice that is rejected by many precisely because it involves treating the individual exclusively as a resource. Our deontological moral intuition is similar in both cases for precisely the same reason.

CONCLUSION

Ultimately, Sunstein maintains that our moral obligations are limited to ensuring that we ought to treat animals "as well as possible" and allow them "to the extent possible, to live decent lives."[78] He does not, however, explain what informs our understanding of what it means to treat our animal property "as well as possible" or what constitutes a "decent" life. His principle gives little direction that limits present use of animals and it does not pave a road to future reform. Indeed, Sunstein would not find a vivisector, factory farmer, or rodeo operator who would disagree with him on this point. They would and do argue that they treat their animals "as well as possible" and that their animals have "decent lives."

We have for the better part of 200 years accepted that we should treat animals "as well as possible," but, as the reality of animal use makes clear, that is a moral principle that lacks even a scintilla of meaningful content. As long as animals are property, we will be unable to recognize their intrinsic value. As long as we deny that nonhumans, like humans, have an interest in their lives, we will continue to focus our discussion about our moral obligations to animals in ways that very much miss the point and that will not result in any significant change in the prevailing paradigm.

---

78. Sunstein, *Slaughterhouse Jive,* New Republic at 45 (cited in note 1).

CHAPTER 5 / THE USE OF NONHUMAN ANIMALS
IN BIOMEDICAL RESEARCH
Necessity and Justification

Discourse about the use of animals in biomedical research usually focuses on two issues. The first, which I will refer to as the "necessity issue," is empirical and asks whether the use of nonhumans in experiments is required in order to gather statistically valid information that will contribute in a significant way to improving human health. The second, which I will refer to as the "justification issue," is moral and asks whether the use of nonhumans in biomedical research, if necessary as an empirical matter, can be defended as a matter of ethical theory.

If it is not necessary as an empirical matter to use animals in research, then there is no need to inquire about moral justification. Therefore, I examine the necessity issue first. The argument that it is necessary to use nonhumans in biomedical research, though flawed, is at least plausible, unlike our necessity arguments for other animal uses. I then discuss the justification issue and conclude that we cannot morally justify using nonhuman animals in research.

This essay was published originally in the *Journal of Law, Medicine & Ethics*, Summer 2007, pp. 241–48.

Copyright © 2007 Gary L. Francione. I appreciate the helpful comments that I have received from Anna E. Charlton and Darian Ibrahim and from participants at the Thomas A. Pitts Memorial Lectureship: Reflections on Emerging Technologies at the Centennial of Organ Transplantation, September 9–10, 2005, at the Medical University of South Carolina, where this essay was presented. I also acknowledge research assistance from Suzanna Polhamus and Erika Navarro and support from the Dean's Research Fund at the Rutgers University School of Law, Newark.

THE NECESSITY OF ANIMAL USE[1]

There are very few moral principles that are embraced by almost everyone. One such principle is that it is wrong to inflict "unnecessary" suffering on animals. This principle is so entrenched in our moral culture that the legal systems of the United States, Great Britain, and other countries purport to establish the principle as a legal standard in animal welfare laws. General animal welfare laws, such as anticruelty laws, prohibit the infliction of "unnecessary" suffering on animals without reference to particular uses although these laws often have explicit exemptions for certain uses, such as agriculture or hunting. Specific animal welfare laws regulate the treatment of animals in particular contexts, such as experimentation or slaughter. Many animal welfare laws are criminal laws, which indicates that we take the principle about unnecessary suffering so seriously that we are willing to punish those who violate it with the stigma of a criminal penalty.[2]

If a prohibition against unnecessary suffering of animals is to have any meaning, then it surely must preclude the infliction of suffering on animals merely for our pleasure, amusement, or convenience. Yet almost all of the suffering and death that we impose on nonhuman animals can be justified *only* by pleasure, amusement, or convenience. For example, the uses of animals for sport hunting and entertainment purposes cannot, by definition, be considered necessary. It is certainly not necessary for us to wear fur coats or use animals to test duplicative household products or toiletries.

---

1. For a further discussion of the necessity of various animal uses and of the material in this section, see G. L. Francione, *Introduction to Animal Rights: Your Child or the Dog?* (Philadelphia: Temple University Press, 2000): 1–49. Discussions of the necessity of animal use outside the context of research do not usually ask whether it is necessary to use animals at all for a particular purpose, but whether particular instances of pain or suffering are necessary even if the general use of animals in that context is not necessary. For reasons that I discuss later in this essay and in my other work (see, e.g., *id.*, at 50–80), that understanding of necessity is problematic. In the context of biomedical research, the necessity analysis focuses more on whether it is necessary to use animals at all for this purpose.
2. For a general discussion of animal welfare laws, including anticruelty laws and statutes such as the Animal Welfare Act, see G. L. Francione, *Animals, Property, and the Law* (Philadelphia: Temple University Press, 1995).

The largest number of animals that we use is for food—approximately 10 billion a year in the United States alone. In other words, we slaughter more than 27 million animals every day, or more than 1.1 million per hour, 19,000 per minute, or 300 every second. This is to say nothing of the billions more killed worldwide. These animals are raised under horrendous intensive conditions known as "factory farming," mutilated in various ways without pain relief, transported long distances in cramped, filthy containers, and finally slaughtered in the most unpleasant of circumstances. We also kill billions of fish and other sea animals annually.

It is not necessary in any sense to eat meat or animal products; indeed, an increasing number of health care professionals maintains that animal foods may be detrimental to human health. Moreover, respected environmental scientists have pointed out the tremendous inefficiencies and resulting costs to our planet of animal agriculture. For example, animals consume more protein than they produce. For every kilogram (2.2 pounds) of animal protein produced, animals consume an average of almost 6 kilograms, or more than 13 pounds, of plant protein from grains and forage. It takes more than 100,000 liters of water to produce one kilogram of beef and approximately 900 liters to produce one kilogram of wheat. It takes only one-sixth of an acre of land to supply a vegetarian with food for a year; it takes three and three-quarters acres to supply a meat eater. Therefore, an acre of land can feed approximately 20 times more vegetarians than meat eaters. Animal agriculture is responsible for the devastation of our topsoil and the consumption of enormous amounts of other resources, such as water and energy, and results in a considerable amount of water pollution and generation of greenhouse gases. Our only justification for the pain, suffering, and death inflicted on these billions of nonhuman animals is that we enjoy the taste of flesh and other animal products.

In short, we suffer from a sort of "moral schizophrenia" where nonhumans are concerned. We claim to embrace the principle that unnecessary suffering is wrong, but most of our animal uses cannot be defended as necessary in any meaningful sense.

The only uses of animals that cannot be dismissed out of hand as transparently frivolous involve using nonhumans in biomedical research intended to produce data that will be useful for important issues of human health and disease. It is important to understand that this is only a small segment of the many activities that constitute vivisection, and much animal use in this context has more to do with corporate profits and the endless barrage of consumer products that fuel those profits than with compelling claims of human health.[3] In any event, it is at least plausible to claim that the use of animals for testing and developing procedures and cures is necessary to obtain certain desirable and significant benefits (given that the use of human subjects requires informed consent), and that this animal use at least ostensibly involves something other than pleasure, amusement, or convenience. Those who defend the use of nonhumans for this purpose also claim that they use nonhumans only where an alternative is not available, use the fewest number of animals possible, and expose those animals to the least amount of pain and suffering consistent with the scientific objectives of the use. Therefore, they argue that our use of animals for this purpose, and the pain, suffering, and death that we inflict incidental to it, are necessary in a way that cannot be claimed for our other uses of nonhumans.

As a preliminary matter, it is interesting to note that the use of animals for scientific purposes was a primary focus of the British animal protection movement of the 19th century and the American movement in the 20th century. For example, the two most prominent recent American campaigns—involving Edward Taub's deafferentation experiments at the Institute for Behavioral Research and the experiments at the Head Injury Clinical Research Laboratory at the University of Pennsylvania—both concerned vivisection.[4] This is not to say that animal advocates have not promoted vegetarianism, or opposed hunting or the use of animals in entertainment or for fur. It is only to observe that vivisection has been a major concern of animal advocates, even though it at least appears to present more difficult issues of necessity than do these other uses of animals and involves fewer animals. As a result, there are more laws in both the United States and Great Britain that purport to regulate vivisection than any other animal use; however, I have elsewhere questioned

---

3. For a discussion of the variety of uses of nonhumans in vivisection, including product testing and education, see Francione, *supra* note 1, at 45-49. I do not discuss experiments intended to address health concerns of domestic nonhuman animals as I argue that if we took animal interests seriously, we would not continue to facilitate the production of domesticated nonhumans for human use. See Francione, *supra* note 1, at 153-154.

4. For a discussion of these campaigns, see Francione, *supra* note 2, at 72-78, 179-183.

the efficacy of such laws.[5] The emphasis by animal advocates on vivisection may have to do with the fact that this use of animals involves a relatively small and specialized portion of the population; therefore, the criticism of vivisection is less threatening to the general public than is advocacy of vegetarianism and is easier to use for purposes of fundraising campaigns. Indeed, many animal advocates continue to eat animal products or engage in other forms of animal exploitation, and vivisection is a more comfortable issue for them.

I do not share the view of some animal advocates that we have learned nothing useful from vivisection, although I do maintain that claims about what we have learned are greatly exaggerated. However, I also believe that there are serious problems with claims of necessity, as well as the claim that researchers take seriously the moral imperative to inflict only that suffering necessary for a particular scientific purpose.

First, animals are almost always used to develop medical procedures or therapies; therefore, it is difficult to make any accurate factual representation about the actual causal role that animal use has played in any particular medical discoveries. Since animals are always used as models of disease or to test procedures or drugs, we cannot claim with any certainty to know that procedures or discoveries that are attributed to animal use would not have occurred in its absence.

Second, because of the biological differences between human and other animals, there is always a problem extrapolating the results of animal experiments to humans. Although the uncertainty of extrapolation affects all biomedical research involving animals, it is particularly problematic in the context of the use of animals for testing purposes, which usually involves predicting how humans will react to exposure over a lifetime to small quantities of a substance based on how nonhumans respond to large quantities over a short period. The problem of extrapolation is compounded by the fact that there is no species of animal that has reactions identical to those of humans.

Third, the data produced by animal use are often unreliable. For example, results from toxicity tests using animals can vary dramatically depending on the method that is used. It is not uncommon for an inhalation study of a chemical to result in the development of cancer when

---

5. *Id.*, at 165–250.

oral administration of the same substance does not. Moreover, variations in acute and chronic toxicity tests may also be quite dramatic. These variations occur from laboratory to laboratory, within the same species of animal, and between species of animals.

Fourth, any claim of necessity assumes there is no other way to solve human health problems. That is, even if animal experiments are causally related to the production of data relevant to human health matters, it does not follow that animal experiments are the only, or the most efficient, way to solve those health problems. Animal research is costly, and it may plausibly be argued that, if the money were spent in other ways, the end result might be better. For example, the considerable expenditure on AIDS research using animals has produced little of use to humans suffering from AIDS and most of what has resulted in longer and better lives for those suffering from HIV and AIDS has come from clinical trials with humans.[6] It is certainly plausible to claim that if the money spent on in-vivo research were instead spent on public safe-sex education campaigns, needle exchanges, and condom distribution, the rate of new HIV cases would drop dramatically. The choice to use animal experiments to address the problem is, in many ways, as much a political and social decision as a scientific one. Animal experiments are considered an acceptable way of solving the AIDS problem whereas needle exchanges, condom distribution, and safe-sex education are politically controversial. Moreover, there are strong institutional incentives that militate against the use of alternatives to in-vivo research such as computer models. Animal use is familiar to experimenters who are often reluctant to embrace new and unfamiliar technologies. But the fact that vivisection may be more politically, socially, or institutionally acceptable than other ways of addressing health problems does not, of course, mean that it is more effective.

Fifth, there is empirical evidence that challenges the notion that animal experiments contribute positively to human health and indicates that, in many instances, they have actually been counterproductive. Numerous examples illustrate this point. For example, although studies concluded by the early 1960s that a correlation between lung cancer and cigarette smoking existed, the failure to develop an animal model of lung

---

6. J. Bailey, "Non-human Primates in Medical Research and Drug Development: A Critical Review," *Biogenic Amines* 19, no. 4–6 (2005): 235–255, at 247–248.

cancer led researchers to reject the validity of the theory that smoking caused lung cancer.[7] Similarly, polio experiments involving monkeys resulted in misleading conceptions of the disease in humans and this delayed prevention.[8] By the early 1940s, it was clear that asbestos caused cancer in humans, but since animal experiments did not confirm the dangers of asbestos, this substance remained unregulated in the United States for decades.[9] Although it is admittedly difficult at the outset of an experiment to know whether animal use will produce useful or nonuseful data, the existence of these counterproductive results should cause even the strongest defenders of animal use to be more skeptical about its necessity.

Sixth, even if we accept that some use of animals is empirically necessary in cases involving serious issues of human health, there is a great deal of vivisection that does not fit into this category and where animal use can only be described as trivial and unnecessary and, in some cases, downright bizarre. For example, psychological journals are rich with examples of animal use that are hard to defend even if we accord only minimal importance to animal interests.[10] Moreover, a great deal of animal use for testing indisputably frivolous or duplicative products cannot plausibly be characterized as necessary.

Seventh, in making any claim that we need to use animals to find cures for human diseases, we must at least consider that a great deal of that disease appears to be related to a clearly unnecessary use of animals—our eating of animal products. Indeed, much in-vivo research purports to concern illness caused by wholly unnecessary and often very destructive human behavior. This matter implicates issues of moral justification, but it is also relevant to claims of empirical necessity.

Eighth, the claim that researchers inflict only the amount of pain or suffering required for the particular use is open to serious question. In

---

7. H. LaFollette and N. Shanks, "Animal Experimentation: The Legacy of Claude Bernard," *International Studies in the Philosophy of Science* 8, no. 3 (1994): 195–210, at 204.

8. See Bailey, *supra* note 6, at 249.

9. P. E. Enterline, "Asbestos and Cancer," in L. Gordis, ed., *Epidemiology and Health Risk Assessment* (New York: Oxford University Press, 1988): 82–84.

10. See, e.g., H. Çetinkaya and M. Domjan, "Sexual Fetishism in a Quail (*Coturnix japonica*) Model System: Test of Reproductive Success," *Journal of Comparative Psychology* 120, no. 4 (2006): 427–432; J. A. Jenkins, P. Williams, G. L. Kramer, L. L. Davis, and F. Petty, "The Influence of Gender and the Estrous Cycle on Learned Helplessness in the Rat," *Biological Psychology* 58 (2001): 147–158.

the first place, most of the nonhumans that are used in experiments—rats and mice—are not even covered by the Animal Welfare Act, which means that the data necessary to support such a claim are not available. More importantly, however, the information that we have about animal pain and suffering comes from the reports of those who do the experiments and there have been multiple instances in which researchers do not regard even invasive procedures to be painful or to cause distress in animals.[11]

In sum, it can be argued that there is a difference between most of our animal use, which does not involve any sort of necessity, and vivisection for health and disease purposes, which involves arguably plausible but questionable claims of necessity. Nevertheless, I will assume that there are at least some uses of nonhumans in this context that are necessary in that certain important benefits for humans would not be obtained but for the use of nonhumans (given limitations on the use of humans), and where researchers really do impose only that level of pain and suffering required for the purpose. It is necessary now to consider whether vivisection, even if arguably necessary in certain limited situations, is morally justifiable.

THE JUSTIFICATION OF ANIMAL USE

Even if the use of nonhumans in experiments may be considered necessary in that there are data that we can only get from using them as experimental subjects, and even if we could get all the data we need from using nonhumans, it would still be more efficacious to use humans as experimental subjects. The use of humans would not involve the extrapolation and other problems that make animal research problematic.

Humans and nonhumans alike have an interest in not being used in biomedical experiments. We accord all humans a right not to be used as non-consenting subjects in such experiments.[12] When we say that humans have a "right" not to be used for these purposes, this means simply

---

11. M. T. Phillips, "Savages, Drunks and Lab Animals: The Researcher's Perception of Pain," *Society and Animals* 1 (1993): 61–81.

12. For a further discussion of the basic right of humans not to be treated exclusively as means to the ends of others, see Francione, *supra* note 1, at 90–98, 156–157.

that the interest of humans in not being used as non-consenting subjects in experiments will be protected even if the consequences of using them would be very beneficial for the rest of us. The question, then, is why do we think that it is morally acceptable to use nonhumans in experiments but not to use humans?

As a historical matter, there are three primary reasons that have been advanced for claiming that it is morally acceptable to use nonhumans in situations in which we would not regard it as permissible to use any humans.[13] The first reason is that animals are not sentient. For example, French philosopher René Descartes (1596–1650) maintained that animals are nothing more than automatons, or robots, created by God. According to Descartes, animals do not possess souls, which are required for consciousness, and, therefore, they cannot experience pain, pleasure, or any other sensation or emotion. Descartes also pointed to the fact that animals do not use verbal or sign language as an indication of their lack of consciousness. If Descartes were correct, then we could no more speak sensibly about animals having interests than we could about clocks having interests, and it would be absurd to talk about our having any moral or legal obligations to animals.

I do not think that anyone, with the exception of a few philosophers who enjoy academic controversy for its own sake, maintains any longer that animals are not sentient.[14] Indeed, the entire foundation of anticruelty laws and statutes like the Animal Welfare Act is that animals are sentient and, therefore, do have interests in not suffering.

The second reason is that, although animals are sentient and have an interest in not suffering, they lack "souls" or are otherwise the "spiritual inferiors" of humans and God has granted us permission to use them for our purposes. This belief has not only served historically as an important part of our justification for exploiting nonhumans, but it is of contemporary relevance in a world that increasingly embraces fundamentalist religious ideologies. Although I certainly think that the morality of animal use can be examined even within such ideologies, I also think that such a discussion is tangential to the topic at hand because most scientists and

---

13. For a further discussion of the reasons that have been offered to justify animal use, see *id.*, at 103–129.

14. For a discussion of modern philosophers who apparently adopt the Cartesian position, see *id.*, at 104–106.

researchers who defend animal experiments do not rely on religious jus-
tifications, at least not explicitly.

The third and primary reason is that, although animals are sentient
and have an interest in not suffering, we can ignore that interest when
it benefits us to do so because animals lack some characteristic supposedly unique to humans—most usually a cognitive characteristic—and
are thereby the "natural inferiors" of humans. That is, there is some qualitative cognitive distinction between humans and nonhumans that supposedly justifies our treating animals exclusively as means to our ends.
The list of characteristics that are supposedly possessed only by humans
includes self-consciousness, reason, abstract thought, emotion, the ability to communicate with symbolic language, and the capacity for moral
behavior.

The notion that humans have mental characteristics that have no
equivalents in nonhumans is arguably inconsistent with the theory of
evolution. Darwin maintained that there are no uniquely human characteristics: "[T]he difference in mind between man and the higher animals, great as it is, is certainly one of degree and not of kind." Animals
are able to think and possess many of the same emotional responses as do
humans: "[T]he senses and intuitions, the various emotions and faculties, such as love, memory, attention, curiosity, imitation, reason, &c., of
which man boasts, may be found in an incipient, or even sometimes in a
well-developed condition, in the lower animals." Darwin noted that "associated animals have a feeling of love for each other" and that animals
"certainly sympathise with each other's distress or danger."[15]

Cognitive ethologists and others have confirmed that animals, including mammals, birds, and fish, have at least the equivalent of the cognitive characteristics once thought to be uniquely human.[16] Nonhumans
are intelligent and are able to process information in sophisticated and

---

15. C. Darwin, *The Descent of Man, and Selection in Relation to Sex* (Princeton: Princeton University Press, 1981): at 105, 76, 77.
16. See, e.g., M. Bekoff and D. Jamieson, eds., *Readings in Animal Cognition* (Cambridge: MIT Press, 1996); D.R. Griffin, *Animal Minds: Beyond Cognition to Consciousness* (Chicago: University of Chicago Press, 2001); M.D. Hauser, *The Evolution of Communication* (Cambridge: MIT Press, 1996); M.D. Hauser, *Wild Minds: What Animals Really Think* (New York: Owl Books, 2001); C.A. Ristau, ed., *Cognitive Ethology: The Minds of Other Animals: Essays in Honor of Donald R. Griffin* (Hillsdale, N.J.: Lawrence Erlbaum Associates, 1991); S. Savage-Rumbaugh and R. Lewin, *Kanzi: The Ape at the Brink of the Human Mind* (New York: Wiley, 1994).

complex ways. They are able to communicate with other members of their own species as well as with humans; indeed, there is considerable evidence that nonhuman great apes can communicate using symbolic language. The similarities between humans and animals are not limited to cognitive or emotional attributes alone. Some argue that animals exhibit what is clearly moral behavior as well.[17] There are numerous instances in which animals act in altruistic ways toward unrelated members of their own species and toward other species, including humans.

Although it certainly appears that animals other than humans possess characteristics purported to be unique to humans, I recognize that there is debate on this point and that there are, in any event, differences between human minds and the minds of nonhumans in that the latter do not use symbolic communication. However, as a matter of logic and sound reasoning, we cannot justify our exploitation of nonhuman animals by pointing to their supposed lack of humanlike varieties of particular cognitive characteristics, or, indeed, of any characteristic beyond sentience, or subjective awareness.[18]

Any attempt to justify treating animals as resources based on their lack of cognitive characteristics claimed to be uniquely human begs the question from the outset by assuming that certain human characteristics are "special" and justify differential treatment. Although there are things that only humans can do (although not all humans may be able to do them), there are things that only nonhumans can do. Humans alone may be able to write symphonies, do calculus, or recognize themselves in mirrors, but only nonhumans can fly or breathe underwater without assistance. What makes our characteristics special is, of course, that *we* say so. But apart from this obviously self-interested position, there is no reason to conclude that characteristics thought to be uniquely human can serve as a nonarbitrary justification for treating animals as our laboratory tools. These characteristics can serve this role only after we have *assumed* their moral relevance.

---

17. For example, Frans de Waal states that "honesty, guilt, and the weighing of ethical dilemmas are traceable to specific areas of the brain. It should not surprise us, therefore, to find animal parallels. The human brain is a product of evolution. Despite its larger volume and greater complexity, it is fundamentally similar to the central nervous system of other mammals." F. de Waal, *Good-Natured: The Origins of Right and Wrong in Humans and Other Animals* (Cambridge: Harvard University Press, 1996): at 218.

18. I argue that sentience alone is sufficient for full membership in the moral community, which involves the right not to be treated as a resource. See Francione, *supra* note 1, at 92–100, 116–119.

Moreover, even if all animals other than humans lack a particular characteristic beyond sentience, or possess it to a different degree or in a different way than do humans, there is no logically defensible relationship between the lack or lesser degree of that characteristic and our treatment of animals as resources. Differences between humans and other animals may be relevant for other purposes. No one argues that we ought to let nonhuman animals drive cars or vote or attend universities. These differences, however, have no bearing on whether it is morally justifiable to treat animals as human property and use them as non-consenting subjects in experiments. This is clear when we consider the moral status of humans. Whatever characteristic we identify as uniquely human will be seen to a lesser degree in some humans and not at all in others. Some humans will have the exact same deficiency that we attribute to animals, and although the deficiency may be relevant for some purposes, most of us would reject this deficiency as providing a moral justification for using humans in biomedical experiments.

Consider, for instance, the characteristic of self-consciousness, which many have regarded as the most important of the supposed uniquely human traits.[19] Peter Carruthers defines self-consciousness as the ability to have a "conscious experience . . . whose existence and content are available to be consciously thought about (that is, available for description in acts of thinking that are themselves made available to further acts of thinking)."[20] But many humans, such as the severely mentally disabled, do not have self-consciousness in that sense. We do not, however, regard it as permissible to use them as we do laboratory animals. The fact that the mentally disabled human may not have a particular sort of self-consciousness may justify differential treatment in some respects. It may, for instance, be relevant to whether we give her a job teaching in a university, or allow her to drive a car. But it has no relevance to whether we treat her exclusively as a resource and use her in painful experiments or as a forced organ donor if it benefits us to do so.

Many have argued that because nonhuman animals have no sense of justice, and that only humans can respond to moral obligations or claims of right, we can have no moral obligations to animals and can exclude

---

19. I maintain that any being who is sentient is necessarily self-aware. *Id.*, at 114, 137–142.

20. P. Carruthers, *The Animals Issue: Moral Theory in Practice* (Cambridge: Cambridge University Press, 1992): at 181.

them from the moral community. This is a reciprocity theory in that it maintains that animals cannot respond to our moral claims, including our claims of right, so they cannot have any rights. There are two versions of this reciprocity thesis. The first version, which originated with the Stoics, is that humans can extend justice only to other rational beings because rational beings alone can understand the requirements of justice and participate in the community formed by rational beings. Immanuel Kant (1724-1804) accepted this view and maintained that we cannot have moral duties to beings other than rational beings. More recently, John Rawls, author of the influential book, *A Theory of Justice,* maintains that we are required to include in the moral community only those who "are capable of having (and are assumed to acquire) a sense of justice, a normally effective desire to apply and to act upon the principles of justice, at least to a certain minimum degree."[21] According to Rawls, "it does seem that we are not required to give strict justice" to animals because they lack the capacity for a sense of justice.[22] Similarly, Carl Cohen argues that we can exclude animals from the moral community because they are not "capable of exercising or responding to moral claims."[23]

A second version of this reciprocity theory, which originated with the Epicureans and was followed by philosopher Thomas Hobbes (1588-1679), maintains that moral rights and duties flow from an imaginary or hypothetical social contract between beings who can agree on rules that govern behavior.[24] Since animals are incapable of making or responding to moral claims, they cannot participate in the formation of any social contract, and, therefore, we have no moral obligation not to harm them. Rawls, who also defends a contractual view of justice, maintains that the social contract is based on what rational humans, who knew that they were going to be members of a society, would agree to before they knew what position they would occupy in that society. He argues that, because animals cannot participate in such an arrangement, "it does not seem possible to extend the contract doctrine so as to include them in a natural way."[25]

---

21. J. Rawls, *A Theory of Justice* (Cambridge: Belknap Press, 1971): at 505.

22. *Id.,* at 512.

23. C. Cohen, "The Case for the Use of Animals in Biomedical Research," *New England Journal of Medicine* 315 (1986): 865-870, at 866.

24. See Francione, *supra* note 1, at 122-123.

25. See Rawls, *supra* note 21, at 512.

Again, there are many human beings who are not able to exercise or respond to moral claims. Assuming that moral rights and duties are properly viewed as arising from a hypothetical social contract—a very significant assumption—there are plenty of humans who lack the capacity to participate in such contractual arrangements. The ability to respond to or make moral claims may be useful for some purposes, such as deciding whether to allow someone to make a binding contract or whether to appoint a guardian to look after her interests. But these characteristics are wholly irrelevant to whether a human should be treated as the resource of others.

Peter Carruthers, who also defends a contractual view of moral rights and duties, argues that animals lack the rational agency to participate in forming the social contract, and, like Rawls, concludes that they have no moral status.[26] But Carruthers specifically addresses the problem of what to do with humans who also lack the rational agency to participate in the social contract. He argues that for two reasons we can accord such humans moral status without extending moral status to animals. The first is a slippery slope argument: "[I]f we try to deny moral rights to some human beings, on the grounds that they are not rational agents, we shall be launched on a slippery slope which may lead to all kinds of barbarisms against those who *are* rational agents."[27] Carruthers does not argue that all humans deserve to have moral rights, but rather that we risk denying rights to "normal" humans if we start making such distinctions among humans. He argues that this approach depends on the fact that there are no "sharp boundaries" between an adult who is not very intelligent and one who is severely mentally disabled, or between a normal elderly person and an extremely senile one, but that there are such "sharp boundaries" between humans and animals.[28]

There are, however, at least two difficulties with Carruthers' first argument. First, his view that the boundary between a normal elderly person and an extremely senile one is less sharp than that between an extremely mentally disabled human adult and a normal chimpanzee is dubious. Second, his protection for mentally disabled or senile humans depends on our inability to make distinctions among humans without the threat

---

26. See Carruthers, *supra* note 20, at 98–121.

27. *Id.*, at 114.

28. *Id.*, at 114–115.

of excluding "normal" humans from the moral community. Although there are certainly going to be cases where it is difficult to draw the line, it is also the case that we can distinguish between rational humans and those who are unequivocally non-rational. If we had a rule that defined a non-rational human as having an IQ less than twenty and administered that rule fairly, then it would seem that Carruthers would be committed to saying that it would be acceptable to deny moral status to such humans.

The second reason Carruthers gives for according moral status to all humans, including non-rational ones, is that social instability would result were we to deny moral status to such humans because "many people would find themselves psychologically incapable of living in compliance" with such an arrangement.[29] Again, there are two objections to Carruthers' theory. First, if the stability of the society were not threatened by excluding such beings from the moral community, then it would be perfectly acceptable to treat such humans as resources and to deny them moral status altogether. For example, no significant social instability resulted in Germany as a result of the Nazi view about the undesirability of the mentally disabled and their use in biomedical experiments. Second, if social stability is threatened by denying moral value to animals, then Carruthers would presumably have to make his theory accommodate animals, which only reveals that Carruthers' reasoning is merely an endorsement of the moral values of the status quo. Carruthers has failed to advance a solution to the problem faced by the contract theorist, who wishes to include within the moral community those humans unable to understand or consent to the social contract but to exclude all nonhumans because they are unable to participate in the contract, other than stipulating that only humans are intended to be beneficiaries of the contract.

Some people argue that membership in a species whose "normal" members have a special characteristic is enough to mandate that all members of that species should be treated as having the special characteristic, whether or not they actually have it. Carl Cohen argues that humans "who are unable, because of some disability, to perform the full moral functions natural to human beings are certainly not for that rea-

---

29. *Id.*, at 117.

son ejected from the moral community. The issue is one of kind."[30] This argument, however, begs the question since the problem is how to distinguish humans from other animals by some characteristic that may be shared by some animals but that is not possessed by all humans. We do not solve that problem by pretending that all humans have the special characteristic that animals supposedly lack when some humans in fact do not possess it.

In sum, reliance on cognitive characteristics beyond sentience to justify the use of nonhumans in experiments requires either that we assume that these characteristics are morally relevant or that we ignore the fact that we do not regard the lack of such characteristics as morally relevant where humans are concerned. We are left with one and only one reason to explain our differential treatment of animals: We are human and they are not, and species difference alone justifies differential treatment. But this criterion is entirely arbitrary and no different from maintaining that, although there is no special characteristic possessed only by whites, or no defect possessed by blacks that is not also possessed by whites, we may treat blacks as inferior to whites merely on the basis of race. It is also no different from saying that, although there is no special characteristic possessed only by men or no defect possessed only by women, we may treat women as inferior to men based merely on sex.

CONCLUSION

The vast majority of our uses of nonhuman animals cannot be characterized as "necessary" in any coherent sense of that word. The use of nonhumans in biomedical research may involve a plausible claim of necessity although, as I argued, any such claim is problematic in a number of respects. But such a claim, even if justified, cannot serve to provide a satisfactory moral basis for this use of animals.

---

30. See Cohen, *supra* note 23, at 866.

CHAPTER 6 / ECOFEMINISM AND ANIMAL RIGHTS

A Review of *Beyond Animal Rights: A Feminist Caring Ethic for the Treatment of Animals**

INTRODUCTION: RIGHTS, HIERARCHIES, AND ECOFEMINISM

For the past several years, Josephine Donovan and Carol J. Adams, together with Marti Kheel, Kenneth Shapiro and Brian Luke, have been arguing that animal rights provides an inadequate basis for the liberation of nonhumans from the often barbaric and virtually always exploitative way in which we treat them.[1] They have argued that rights are patriarchal and that rights theory perpetuates human hierarchy over animals. They claim to go "beyond" animal rights by importing a concept central to much recent feminist writing—the ethic of care—into the debate about animals.

The ethic of care is located within the view known as "ecofeminism," which maintains that "the patriarchal conceptual framework that has maintained, perpetuated, and justified the oppression of women in Western culture has also, and in similar ways, maintained, perpetuated, and

This essay was published originally in the *Women's Rights Law Reporter,* vol. 18, pp. 95–106 (1996).

© 1996 by Gary L. Francione. I gratefully acknowledge comments from Anna Charlton, Priscilla Cohn, and Drucilla Cornell. This essay is dedicated to Stratton, who sat here while I wrote.

*Josephine Donovan and Carol J. Adams, eds., *Beyond Animal Rights: A Feminist Caring Ethic for the Treatment of Animals* (New York: Continuum 1996). ISBN 0-8264-0836-2. $24.95.

1. BEYOND ANIMAL RIGHTS: A FEMINIST CARING ETHIC FOR THE TREATMENT OF ANIMALS (Josephine Donovan & Carol J. Adams eds., 1996) [hereinafter BEYOND ANIMAL RIGHTS]. *See also* ANIMALS AND WOMEN: FEMINIST THEORETICAL EXPLORATIONS (Carol J. Adams & Josephine Donovan eds., 1995) [hereinafter ANIMALS AND WOMEN]. Luke and Kheel also have chapters in ANIMALS AND WOMEN, as does the author. *See* Gary L. Francione, *Abortion and Animal Rights: Are They Comparable Issues?, in* ANIMALS AND WOMEN, at 149. A number of essays in BEYOND ANIMAL RIGHTS are reprints.

justified the oppression of nonhuman animals and the environment."[2] The solution is to eschew the rights approach, which "tends to be abstract and formalistic, favoring rules that are universalizable or judgments that are quantifiable"[3] in favor of focusing "upon the particulars of a given situation"[4] and employing "an ethic that 'makes a central place for values of care, love, friendship, trust, and appropriate reciprocity—values that presuppose that our relationships to others are central to our understanding of who we are.'"[5] Ecofeminists reject universalizable judgments because general standards supposedly facilitate patriarchy and dualisms in which women and animals are marginalized as the less-valued "other" in these dualisms. Some ecofeminist writers reject rights theory because it generally values inanimate nature less than it does nonhumans or humans.[6]

I have elsewhere argued that animal rights theory is the *only* way to alter the status of animals as property, or "things," and thereby eliminate the person/thing dualism that is the foundation of all institutionalized exploitation.[7] We can use animals for food, in experiments, for clothing or entertainment only because animals are *things;* they have *no* interests that cannot be "sacrificed" if it is thought (correctly or mistakenly) to be in the interests of humans. This is precisely what it *means* to be property.

---

2. Deane Curtin, *Toward an Ecological Ethic of Care (1991), in* BEYOND ANIMAL RIGHTS, *supra* note 1, at 60. I do not mean to suggest that all versions of ecofeminism actually endorse the application of the ethic of care presented in BEYOND ANIMAL RIGHTS, *supra* note 1, or that ecofeminism is necessarily committed to an ethic of care (as presented) as a theoretical matter. For the most part, however, most ecofeminist writers seem to accept that the ethic of care is a foundational element of ecofeminism.

3. Josephine Donovan & Carol J. Adams, *Introduction* to BEYOND ANIMAL RIGHTS, *supra* note 1, at 15.

4. *Id.* at 16.

5. Curtin, *supra* note 2, at 61 (quoting Karen Warren, *The Power and the Promise of Ecological Feminism,* 12 ENVTL. ETHICS, 125, 143 (1990)).

6. *See generally* Marti Kheel, *The Liberation of Nature: A Circular Affair (1985), in* BEYOND ANIMAL RIGHTS, *supra* note 1, at 17.

7. *See* GARY L. FRANCIONE, RAIN WITHOUT THUNDER: THE IDEOLOGY OF THE ANIMAL RIGHTS MOVEMENT (1996) [hereinafter FRANCIONE, RAIN WITHOUT THUNDER]; GARY L. FRANCIONE, ANIMALS, PROPERTY, AND THE LAW (1995) [hereinafter FRANCIONE, ANIMALS, PROPERTY, AND THE LAW]. *See also* Gary L. Francione, *Animal Rights and Animal Welfare,* 48 RUTGERS L. REV. 397 (1996) [hereinafter Francione, *Animal Rights and Animal Welfare*]; Gary L. Francione, *Animals, Property and Legal Welfarism: "Unnecessary" Suffering and the "Humane" Treatment of Animals,* 46 RUTGERS L. REV. 721 (1994) [hereinafter Francione, *Animals, Property and Legal Welfarism*].

Rights theory requires the *abolition* of the institutionalized exploitation of animals. Ecofeminism assumes the legitimacy of institutionalized exploitation as part of the normative context in which the ethic of care is to be applied. I concede that rules often provide only indeterminate normative guidance and that other values (including the ethic of care) may be useful or necessary to decide particular situations. But the ethic of care is relevant to deciding whether we should eat *this particular animal* or use *this particular animal* in an experiment only if the institutional exploitation of animals in science and agriculture is accepted as a general matter.

To put the matter simply, we must decide whether we are going to eat animals as a matter of social practice, whether we are going to use them in experiments and for clothing and entertainment. We must decide whether animals are beings who have no interests, a *logically* necessary prerequisite to any institutionalized exploitation. For example, we could not have had human slavery without first deciding that it was morally permissible to treat slaves as "things," as human property, rather than as persons who have at least some interests that are protected from being traded away for consequential reasons alone (in this case, benefit for the slaveowners).

It would be absurd to say in the face of human slavery that the ethic of care could have supplanted rights and that we could have decided how to deal with slaves on a case by case basis, eschewing general notions and relying instead on the "relational ontology" that emphasizes "contextual relations" and the "particulars of a given situation" over general standards. The slave *is* a social construction involving the notion of a human all of whose interests may be ignored if it is in the interests of the slaveowner to do so. Similarly, "food" animals, "laboratory" animals, "rodeo" or "circus" animals assume various social constructs of the "animal" other and all of these characterizations normatively assume that an "animal" *is* a "thing" that we can use for our "benefit."[8] If such a normative characterization lacks some moral justification, then it represents nothing more than a restatement of the hierarchy of humans over animals. In the absence of any such justification, the dualism that ecofeminists supposedly reject is very much alive and well.

---

8. *See generally* FRANCIONE, ANIMALS, PROPERTY, AND THE LAW, *supra* note 7; Francione, *Animals, Property, and Legal Welfarism, supra* note 7.

The theory of animal rights says that we can no longer treat animals as "things," or as property.[9] Rights theory is far less concerned with what rights animals would have were they no longer regarded as property, but is concerned more with the basic right of animals not to be regarded as property in the first place. The general rules of rights theory are quite determinate and need no filling in: acceptance that at least some nonhumans are the sorts of beings who should not be treated instrumentally, i.e., that they should not be treated as beings who have *no* interests that cannot be sacrificed for human benefit, means that we can no longer justify the institutions of exploitation that *necessarily* assume the instrumental status of all animals. Rights theory protects what I have called the "minimal conditions of 'personhood'" in that to say that a being has any rights at all is to say that being is a *person,* a member of the moral community. "Things" that have an instrumental existence alone *cannot* be members of the moral community. That is precisely what it means to be a "thing," or to be property. Whatever else a "person" may be, the concept of "personhood" *requires* some notion that the being designated as a "person" has basic interests that cannot be disregarded simply because it is convenient or otherwise beneficial to do so.

In the context of feminist theory, Drucilla Cornell has made similar arguments about the importance of a deontological core that serves to delimit the "person." In *The Imaginary Domain,* Cornell argues that it is necessary to protect certain conditions that make possible the "minimum degree of individuation" that Cornell regards as necessary (but not sufficient) "for the equivalent chance [of women] to transform . . . [themselves] into individuated beings who can participate in public and political life as equal citizens."[10] Cornell claims that only universalizable standards can protect these necessary conditions for personhood.[11] Cornell's position is that only by employing some rights-type deontological protection for the minimum conditions of individuation can we have a truly meaningful feminist theory.[12]

---

9. *See generally* FRANCIONE, RAIN WITHOUT THUNDER, *supra* note 7; Francione, *Animal Rights and Animal Welfare, supra* note 7.
10. DRUCILLA CORNELL, THE IMAGINARY DOMAIN: ABORTION, PORNOGRAPHY & SEXUAL HARASSMENT 4 (1995).
11. *See id.* at 13–20.
12. *See id.* at 4–5, 18.

The ecofeminists jettison rights theory although some deontological notion is necessary to protect the concept of "personhood," whether of animals or humans. Rights theory seeks to abolish the hierarchical characterization of nonhumans as "things" in a "person/thing" dualism. The ecofeminists claim to reject hierarchy, but merely substitute a different way of dealing with the nonhuman "thing," rather than abolishing altogether the elite and hierarchical structure that makes institutionalized animal exploitation possible in the first instance.

There can be no doubt that the ethic of care is an important and useful notion for attempting to achieve the "unified sensibility" of feeling and thought necessary to overcome admittedly patriarchal misuses of reason.[13] Unfortunately, the essays in the Adams/Donovan collection apply the ethic of care in a simplistic and superficial way that merely begs the question against animal rights, rather than providing any sort of alternative approach. The result is a confused and confusing collection of essays that do not, as the title promises, move *beyond* animal rights to embrace a more progressive approach, but rather, defend a quite reactionary view that is consistent with, and relied upon, by those who exploit nonhuman animals.

Beyond Animal Rights is a collection of essays most of which are reprinted. In general, the essays are theoretical and focus on the supposed defects of rights theory and the ways in which the ethic of care can remedy these defects. Several essays discuss specific issues, such as vegetarianism and pet ownership.[14] One essay discusses various psychological experiences that accompany an ethic of care.[15]

In this review, I will first discuss the notion of animal rights as a theory that provides a baseline of protection for nonhumans. I will then distinguish between issues involving whether a being ought to be considered a member of the moral community as an initial matter (the question of *inclusion)* and issues involving what rights particular persons, or members of the moral community, ought to have (questions concerning the *scope*

---

13. *See* Robin Morgan, *Metaphysical Feminism, in* THE POLITICS OF WOMEN'S SPIRITUALITY: ESSAYS ON THE RISE OF SPIRITUAL POWER WITHIN THE FEMINIST MOVEMENT 387 (Charlene Spretnak ed., 1982).

14. *See, e.g.,* Curtin, *supra* note 2; Rita C. Manning, *Caring for Animals (1992), in* BEYOND ANIMAL RIGHTS, *supra* note 1, at 103.

15. *See* Kenneth Shapiro, *The Caring Sleuth: Portrait of an Animal Rights Activist (1994), in* BEYOND ANIMAL RIGHTS, *supra* note 1, at 126.

of rights). Finally, I will argue that the ecofeminist critique of rights theory merely begs the question against rights theory insofar as it holds that we can continue to treat animals as "things" as a general matter. Questions about the scope of rights in society may be complicated by the fact that rules are indeterminate as a general matter. The ethic of care may help us to make indeterminate standards more definite, but the ethic of care cannot go "beyond" animal rights if it accepts the legitimacy of institutionalized animal exploitation.

ANIMAL RIGHTS AND ANIMAL WELFARE

In the United States alone, over eight billion animals are consumed yearly for food. These animals are usually reared in extremely confined conditions known as "factory farming" or "intensive agriculture."[16] They are subjected to extraordinary suffering throughout their lives, and the conditions of slaughterhouses today are only marginally better than those of the 19th century. Millions of animals are used yearly in experiments and for testing new consumer products; these uses often involve the burning, scalding, irradiation, or cutting of animals who receive no anesthesia or post-procedure analgesia.[17] Millions of animals are killed for sport and entertainment. For example, every Labor Day, the town of Hegins, Pennsylvania sponsors an event in which eight thousand pigeons are released from small traps and shot at close range for "fun." Many of the pigeons are not killed by the bullets, and the town employs young children who kill the wounded animals by wringing their necks or repeatedly smashing the animals on the pavement or against a wall.[18]

Concern about animal use has historically been limited to ensuring the supposedly "humane" treatment of animals, and to preventing the imposition of "unnecessary" suffering. This position, known as the *animal welfare* view, assumes the legitimacy of treating animals exclusively as means to human ends as long as certain "safeguards" are employed.[19] The

---

16. *See generally* JIM MASON & PETER SINGER, ANIMAL FACTORIES (rev. ed. 1990).

17. *See generally* PETER SINGER, ANIMAL LIBERATION (2d ed. 1990).

18. *See* FRANCIONE, ANIMALS, PROPERTY, AND THE LAW, *supra* note 7, at xiii–xv.

19. *See generally* FRANCIONE, RAIN WITHOUT THUNDER, *supra* note 7, at 7–14 (generally discussing animal welfare).

late 1970s marked the emergence of the *animal rights* movement, which "retained the animal welfare tradition's concern for animals as sentient beings that should be protected from unnecessary cruelty," but "added a new language of 'rights' as the basis for demanding" the *end* of animal exploitation.[20] "To oversimplify the matter a bit, the welfarists seek the *regulation* of animal exploitation; the rightists seek its *abolition.*"[21]

As a general matter, "[r]ights are moral notions that grow out of respect for the individual. They build protective fences around the individual. They establish areas where the individual is entitled to be protected against the state and the majority *even where a price is paid by the general welfare.*"[22] That is, to say that I have a right of liberty means that my interest in my liberty will be protected from incursion, unless I engage in conduct that is determined by a jury to constitute a crime, or in the situation of military conscription. In virtually all other circumstances, my interest in my liberty will be protected even in (and especially in) the face of an assertion that although innocent of any wrongdoing, my liberty interest should be violated because others—perhaps many others—will benefit from the violation of my right. The justification for human slavery involved the view that the basic liberty interests of some humans could be sacrificed to benefit the owners of the slaves; the justification for racism and sexism similarly involve treating the fundamental interests of people of color and women in an instrumental way to facilitate the interests of whites or of males generally. Rights notions are intended to place limits on the instrumental treatment of persons, and to ensure that certain fundamental interests *cannot* be sacrificed for the general welfare.

The theory of animal rights maintains that at least some nonhumans possess rights that are normatively similar to those possessed by humans.[23] Animal rights ensure that relevant animal interests are accorded the same type of protection accorded to human interests protected by claims of fundamental rights, and that these animal interests may

---

20. *See* JAMES M. JASPER & DOROTHY NELKIN, THE ANIMAL RIGHTS CRUSADE: THE GROWTH OF A MORAL PROTEST 5 (1992).

21. *See* FRANCIONE, RAIN WITHOUT THUNDER, *supra* note 7, at 1.

22. Bernard E. Rollin, *The Legal and Moral Bases of Animal Rights, in* ETHICS AND ANIMALS 106 (Harlan B. Miller & William H. Williams eds., 1983).

23. *See* FRANCIONE, RAIN WITHOUT THUNDER, *supra* note 7, at 1–4, 14–20.

not be sacrificed simply to benefit humans, no matter how "humane" the exploitation or how stringent the safeguards from "unnecessary" suffering.[24]

RIGHTS THEORY AND PERSONHOOD

Our treatment of nonhuman animals reflects a distinction that *we* make between humans, most of whom we unproblematically regard as *persons,* and nonhumans, whom we regard as *things.* Although we may regard some animals as having certain "interests," we regard *all* of those interests to be tradable, dependent on *our* judgment that the sacrifice of the interest(s) will *benefit* us. This trade is generally permissible even when the animal interest involved is significant and the human interest is admittedly trivial, as is the case of the use of animals for "entertainment" purposes such as pigeon shoots, rodeos, or circuses. Animals are not persons in either moral theory or under the law: they are *property* in that they exist solely as means to human ends. They have no interests that cannot be sacrificed, even when the "benefit" to be gained by humans is mere amusement at the cost of great pain or death to the animal. That is precisely what it means to *be* property.

"Persons" are precisely those beings who have interests that *cannot* be traded merely for consequential reasons alone. Some of these persons, such as corporations, are *de jure* persons alone in that their personhood exists solely because they are creations of a legal system. But what is common to *every* person is that they have at least some interests, although not necessarily all the same interests, that are protected (by moral theory or law or both) even if trading away those interests will produce consequences that are deemed to be desirable.

All "persons" *must* have at least one interest that is protected from being sacrificed merely for consequential purposes: the interest in continued existence. Without this all other interests would be meaningless. This point may be understood by referring to a concept discussed by philosopher Henry Shue in his book, *Basic Rights.*[25] According to Shue, a basic

---

24. *See id.*
25. HENRY SHUE, BASIC RIGHTS: SUBSISTENCE, AFFLUENCE, AND U.S. FOREIGN POLICY (1980).

right is not a right that is "more valuable or intrinsically more satisfying to enjoy than some other rights."[26] Rather, a right is a basic right when "any attempt to enjoy any other right by sacrificing the basic right would be quite literally self-defeating, cutting the ground from beneath itself." Shue states that "non-basic rights may be sacrificed, if necessary, in order to secure the basic right. But the protection of a basic right may not be sacrificed in order to secure the enjoyment of a non-basic right." The reason for this is that a basic right "cannot be sacrificed successfully. If the right sacrificed is indeed basic, then no right for which it might be sacrificed can actually be enjoyed in the absence of the basic right. The sacrifice would have proven self-defeating."[27] Shue emphasizes that basic rights are a prerequisite to the enjoyment and exercise of non-basic rights, and that the possession of non-basic rights in the absence of basic rights is nothing more than the possession of rights "in some merely legalistic or otherwise abstract sense compatible with being unable to make any use of the substance of the right."

Although Shue identifies several basic rights, the most important of these is the "basic right to physical security—a right that is basic not to be subjected to murder, torture, mayhem, rape, or assault."[28] While acknowledging that it is not unusual in a given society that some members of at least one ethnic group receive less physical protection than others, Shue argues that "few, if any, people would be prepared to defend in principle the contention that anyone lacks a basic right to physical security."[29] If a person does not enjoy the basic right to security, and may be killed at will by any other person, then it is difficult to understand what *other* rights that person might enjoy. Most of the time, discussions about rights occur in the context of discussions of human rights. These discussions are not concerned with whether we should be able to kill and eat *people,* or whether we should be able to use *people* in experiments to which they have not given their informed consent, or whether we should be able to use *people* in rodeos, or exhibit *people* in zoos. It is assumed—at least under the law of most countries and at least in the moral views of most people—that people have certain rights, or, at least, that they have

26. *Id.* at 20.
27. *Id.* at 19.
28. *Id.* at 20.
29. *Id.* at 21.

certain interests that cannot be compromised simply because it will benefit others to do so.

Shue is certainly correct in noting that we always assume that humans have basic rights to physical security, whether or not there are social differences in terms of the actual distribution of the right. In other words, recognition of the basic right of physical security is a right *as a matter of law* irrespective of whether the state enforces this right in an evenhanded manner. In the case of animals, however, the situation is precisely the opposite. We talk informally about the rights of animals, but animals do not have the basic legal right of physical security, and they cannot possess it *as a matter of law*. Because animals are regarded as the property of their human owners, animals can be killed for food, used in experiments, and exploited in numerous other ways for no other reason than that the owner of the animal regards it as a "benefit" to do so. Moreover, because animals do not have the basic legal right of physical security (or any other basic rights), it is senseless to talk about animals having true legal rights at all.

Animal rights theory seeks to move at least some nonhumans from the "thing" side of the "person/thing" dualism over to the "person" side. There are at least two reasons to offer in favor of this move. First, there is no characteristic or set of characteristics that is possessed by all humans (whom we regard as persons) that is not possessed by at least some animals. To put the matter a different way, those who support animal exploitation argue that animals are *qualitatively* different from humans so animals can be kept on the "thing" side of the "person/thing" dualism; animal rights advocates argue that there is no such difference because at least some nonhumans will possess the supposedly "exclusive" characteristic while some humans will not possess the characteristic. Nor is it enough to argue that species difference is itself morally relevant; after all, to rely on species *alone* as morally relevant is to assume what needs to be proved by those who hold such a view, and is morally indistinguishable from using race, sex, sexual orientation, or ability to determine membership in the moral community of persons. In other words, there is no reason to exclude animals from the progressive concept of personhood that has been developed.[30]

---

30. This is essentially the approach employed in James Rachels, Created From Animals: The Moral Implications of Darwinism (1990).

There is another related, more "positive," reason to view animals as persons. Although there will undoubtedly be borderline cases, it is clear that at least some animals possess the characteristics that we normally associate with personhood. For example, in *The Case for Animal Rights*, Tom Regan argues that theoretical and empirical considerations indicate that at least some animals possess beliefs, desires, memory, perception, intention, self-consciousness and a sense of the future. The attribution of at least several of these mental states reveals that it is perfectly sensible to regard certain nonhumans as psychophysical individuals who "fare well or ill during the course of their life, and the life of some animals is, on balance, experientially better than the life of others."[31] Because animals have desires, beliefs, and the ability to act in pursuit of their goals, they may also be said to have preference autonomy, an important characteristic for the attribution of rights.[32]

CONFUSING ISSUES OF INCLUSION IN THE CLASS OF RIGHTHOLDERS WITH THE SCOPE OF RIGHTS

A common misconception is that animal advocates argue that animals should have the *same* rights as humans. As far as I am aware, *no* rights advocate maintains this view. Moreover, the criticism itself indicates a fundamental confusion about rights theory. In many ways, animal rights theory is about the *inclusion* of nonhumans on the "person" side of the "person/thing" dualism. This matter of inclusion is to be distinguished from the matter of the *scope* of any rights that animals may have once we move them from one side to the other. I have elsewhere used the example of human slavery to illustrate this point. Although human slaves in the United States were regarded under the law as "persons" for purposes of criminal liability, they were, for virtually all other purposes, both *de jure* and *de facto* "things." This status as a "thing" is a *logical* consequence of the institution of human slavery which treated all slave interests— including Shue's basic right of physical security—as tradable as long as

---

31. TOM REGAN, THE CASE FOR ANIMAL RIGHTS 82 (1983).
32. Preference autonomy may be a sufficient but not necessary condition for purposes of inclusion in the moral community.

there were perceived benefits for slaveowners. Slaves had no rights of association; slave families were routinely broken up, and slaves could be killed or tortured for what was essentially the pleasure or amusement of slaveowners.

To include slaves in the class of persons—moving them from the "thing" side of the "person/thing" dualism to the "person" side—is not necessarily to say anything about the *scope* of particular rights that the liberated slaves may have. Indeed, the move entails the exclusion of only one sort of exploitation: the institutionalized commodification of human beings in which their basic right of physical security, the prerequisite for their having rights *at all,* can be violated by others for consequential reasons. Other considerations will govern the *scope* of rights that these "new" persons may have. For example, the abolition of human slavery only began, and did not end, a discussion about what additional rights—other than the right not to be slaves—should be accorded to former slaves.

Similarly, when we move at least some nonhumans from the "thing" side over to the "person" side, we have said nothing about the *scope* of rights that they will have. All we have done—through the *inclusion* of animals on the "person" side—is to recognize that species *alone* is an insufficient justification for treating nonhumans as "things." Species may be significant when we determine the *scope* of particular rights. For example, it would be absurd to discuss the rights of animals to drive or to vote or the right of an animal to get a scholarship to attend college. But the inability of nonhumans to adhere to rules of the road, choose intelligently among political rivals, or do calculus are all *irrelevant* to the basic notion of *personhood:* after all, we accept that some adult humans will be unable to perform basic functions but we still do not place them on the "thing" side of the "person/thing" distinction. We may very legitimately award a math scholarship to Jane rather than Simon based on Jane's better ability to do mathematics. As long as Simon has had a fair opportunity to develop his mathematical abilities, using Jane's intelligence as a criterion for determining the distribution of the particular resource in question (educational benefits) is fair. But Jane's greater intelligence does not justify Jane's treating Simon as her slave or otherwise placing Simon on the "thing" side of the equation.

There is, however, one sense in which including animals as members of the class of "persons" is very different from including additional humans within that class. If we acknowledge that Simon is not a "thing," the protection that we have given to Simon is at the same time quite significant (after all, the basic right to physical security is a prerequisite to all other rights), but also the very bare minimum that is needed to distinguish Simon from being a *thing*. Saying that Simon is included in the class of persons says nothing about the scope of rights that he may have other than to say that we will protect Simon's right to *be* a person in that we will at least recognize *de jure* that Simon's basic right to physical security will be protected from being traded away for consequential reasons.

If, however, we recognize that animals are not "things," i.e., that their basic right to physical security cannot be sacrificed merely because we think the consequences justify the sacrifice, then we can no longer justify the institutionalized exploitation of animals for food, experiments, clothing, or entertainment. These forms of institutionalized exploitation necessarily assume that animals are things whose interests are contingent on human desires. Once we recognize that animals are not "things," we can no longer justify the use of animals in experiments any more than we could humans. We have at least *de jure* ruled out the institutional use of coerced humans in biomedical experiments. Although many people will tolerate the payment of low wages to workers, few would similarly tolerate human *slavery*.

A primary result of according personhood status to at least some nonhumans would be to require the abolition of institutionalized animal exploitation. Once we recognize that animals are no longer "things," then we can no longer treat them as beings whose fundamental interests in their own lives may be sacrificed because we enjoy the taste of meat, or because we enjoy shooting pigeons or because we enjoy the feel or look of fur or leather. That is, according personhood status to animals does not mean that we simply get more serious about whether a particular form of slaughter to produce meat is more "humane," or that we take animal interests more seriously in determining whether a particular experiment involving animals is "necessary." It means that we accept that the use of animals for food or science or entertainment or clothing represents forms of institutionalized exploitation that are *logically* inconsistent with the personhood of animals.

ECOFEMINISM AND THE ACCEPTANCE OF INSTITUTIONALIZED EXPLOITATION

It is now easy to understand the fundamental confusion that pervades virtually all of the essays contained in *Beyond Animal Rights*. The ecofeminist position is that the ethic of care is meaningful to discussions about whether to include animals within the moral community as an initial matter. To put the matter another way, the essayists argue that the ethic of care does not *require* an end to institutionalized exploitation. And a number of the writers included in this volume are explicit on this point.

For example, Deane Curtin argues for a "contextual moral vegetarianism" position that "responds to particular contexts and histories"[33] and is "based on actual interests in the narrative context of lived experiences."[34] Although Curtin expresses support for vegetarianism, she argues that a broad range of considerations inform the "contextual relations" that will determine whether vegetarianism is appropriate in a particular case.[35] In short, Curtin argues that although vegetarianism is morally desirable, there are a variety of circumstances in which it may be acceptable to eat animals although it would not be acceptable to inflict similar harms on *any* human being. For instance, Curtin argues that the killing of animals as part of cultural tradition may be morally acceptable under an ethic of care, especially in circumstances in which the humans have some way "of expressing spiritually the idea 'we are what we eat,' even if they are not vegetarian."[36] The limiting principle of contextual moral vegetarianism turns out to be *precisely* what it is under traditional animal welfare theory: people should not inflict "pain that is completely unnecessary and avoidable" and "[t]he injunction to care . . . should be understood to include the injunction to eliminate needless suffering wherever possible, and particularly the suffering of those whose suffering is conceptually connected to one's own."[37] This once again establishes a hierarchy where

---

33. Curtin, *supra* note 2, at 69.
34. *Id.* at 64.
35. She explicitly recognizes that rights theorists provide that rights can be overridden in light of particular considerations, but she claims that contextual moral vegetarianism requires even greater flexibility. *See id.* at 69, 75 n.28.
36. *Id.* at 71.
37. *Id.* at 71–72.

one's own suffering is the standard by which all other suffering is measured. Curtin explicitly acknowledges that contextual moral vegetarianism allows for more meat consumption than would be permitted under a rights theory—even a rights theory that allowed for some consideration of particular contexts to determine whether *prima facie* rights should be overridden in a particular case.

Josephine Donovan praises utilitarian moral theory (upon which animal welfare is based) as having "the virtue of allowing some flexibility in decision-making" that is characteristic of the relational ontology of the ethic of care.[38] Utilitarian moral theory emphasizes "that an awareness of consequences can and should influence the evaluation of an individual's fate in any given situation."[39] One such "virtue" of the "flexibility" of utilitarianism is that under certain circumstances, the use of animals in experiments may be permissible. Kenneth Shapiro, another contributor to the collection, is also the editor of *The Journal of Applied Welfare Science*, which publishes articles about more "humane" ways of using animals in experiments and for food.[40] To promote "humane" exploitation is necessarily to have taken a *normative* position about the moral permissibility of the institutionalized exploitation of vivisection or meat production in the first place—a position that is explicitly at odds with rights

---

38. Josephine Donovan, *Animal Rights and Feminist Theory (1990)*, in BEYOND ANIMAL RIGHTS, *supra* note 1, at 39. Although ecofeminists often praise utilitarian moral theory relative to rights theory, they generally ultimately reject both the utilitarian theory of Peter Singer and the deontological theory of Tom Regan as patriarchal and hyperrational. In the animal rights movement, it is common to lump both utilitarian and rights views together as "animal rights" positions. For a discussion of the resulting theoretical and strategic difficulties that have resulted from this combination of consequential and non-consequential views, see FRANCIONE, RAIN WITHOUT THUNDER, *supra* note 7.

39. Donovan, *supra* note 38, at 39.

40. *See* Shapiro, *supra* note 15. Shapiro argues that the rights approach is "revolutionist" and "creates an attitude more hateful than caring." *Id.* at 144.

 Shapiro promotes the use of a six-step "pain scale" to be used by experimenters to evaluate the invasiveness of their research. At the lower end of the scale is level 2, which represents "[l]aboratory experiments and certain field studies involving mild pain/distress and no long-term harm," includes "frequent blood sampling," "intramuscular injection, skin-scraping," "[n]egative reinforcement" such as "mild electric shock" and "brief cold water immersion," "[f]ood deprivation" that does not result in more than a 10% weight loss, "water deprivation slightly exceeding particular species' requirements (e.g., deprivation in rats of less than 18 hours)" and "[p]rocedures involving anesthetized animals with mild post-operative pain/distress and no long-term harm." Kenneth J. Shapiro & Peter B. Field, *A New Invasiveness Scale: Its Role in Reducing Animal Distress*, 2 HUMANE INNOVATIONS & ALTERNATIVES IN ANIMAL EXPERIMENTATION 43, 44–45 (1988).

theory, which regards as morally impermissible any exclusively instrumental treatment of a rightholder.

Rita Manning recognizes that riding horses is potentially hazardous to horses and that breeding them for human amusement is morally problematic.[41] Nevertheless, applying the ethic of care, she concludes that it is morally acceptable to continue to breed, purchase and ride horses "both because horses make wonderful friends and because they are unique parts of the natural world."[42] Manning claims that the end of domestication would be a tragedy "for the many animals who flourish" in domestic service to humans as "willing partners."[43] These notions, of course, are hierarchical and normative in that Manning regards horses as "friends" *for us.* There is no notion that horses need to be bred to serve some need *of theirs* for "friendship." Moreover, we do not need to breed or ride horses for them to be a part "of the natural world"—we need only leave extant wild horses alone. Finally, Manning offers absolutely no evidence for the claim that horses are "willing partners." Like Curtin, Manning urges that the ethic of care is similar to the animal welfare ethic and requires that "we actively seek to avoid risk of injury insofar as we can."[44] Manning fails to demonstrate that there is anything *necessary* about the practice of continuing to breed domesticated animals solely for human amusement or because people like Manning regard horses as "exemplars of majestic values: beauty, dignity, strength, courage, speed, endurance, and agility."[45] What this really means, of course, is that *some* horses are "exemplars" for *us.* Not all horses are considered beautiful or they may not display the characteristics that *we* value. Manning also discusses the importance of the "ritual" involving "the economic transaction involved in buying a horse: the prepurchase exam, the bill of sale, the check."[46] Manning praises the "ritual" recognition of the animal's property status as conveying "a new sense of responsibility toward the animal."[47] Manning fails to recognize that in making these comments, she *assumes* that animals are commodities who obtain meaning as the result of economic

---

41. *See* Manning, *supra* note 14, at 113.
42. *Id.*
43. *Id.*
44. *Id.* at 114.
45. *Id.* at 113.
46. *Id.* at 115.
47. *Id.*

transactions. Moreover, she fails to explain how the prospective buyer or seller gains any "new sense of responsibility" if the horse fails to pass the prepurchase exam because of a serious "defect" that renders the horse nothing more than a profit-making object. Manning expresses doubt about whether one is "acting to further the interests of an animal by killing it and eating it," but states that under an ethic of care, "it is possible to give an animal care that is sensitive to its interests up to the moment of slaughter."[48] Donovan remarkably (and inaccurately) praises Manning's position as going "beyond just respecting the rights of another."[49]

These are just several examples from many that are found throughout the book. In even these selected few we see that all the authors ostensibly accept as legitimate the institutionalized exploitation of nonhumans. That is, the nonhuman "other" that is involved is a "laboratory animal," a "food" animal, or some "exemplar of majestic value." All of these "others," are, however, socially constructed "things," or means to ends. They are *not* persons, and this is precisely the problem. Like classical animal welfare, which places humans in a hierarchical position over animals, ecofeminism places humans in a hierarchical position over nonhumans in that nonhumans *still remain things in an ecofeminist ontology.* To the extent that animal interests are valued in an ecofeminist ontology, those interests may be sacrificed if the aggregation of consequences militates in that direction. This sort of proposal, urged throughout *Beyond Animal Rights,* is no different *structurally* from the fundamental premise of animal welfare ideology—that animals may be treated as "things" as long as such treatment is "necessary." The ecofeminist notion of what constitutes "necessity" may be and probably *is* more generous than its counterpart in animal welfare ideology. But the end result is that the ideology of both animal welfare and ecofeminism retains the hierarchy of human over non-human: the non-human is treated differently from the human in that the latter is regarded as a "person" while the former is regarded as a "thing." This is explicitly in contrast to rights theory, which eliminates the "thing" status of at least some animals. Ironically, ecofeminism *systematically* devalues animal interests because it regards

---

48. *Id.* at 119.
49. Josephine Donovan, *Attention to Suffering: Sympathy as a Basis for Ethical Treatment of Animals (1994), in* BEYOND ANIMAL RIGHTS, *supra note 1, at 161.*

the *categorical* rejection of institutionalized exploitation as itself a hierarchical position.

Donovan, Adams, and their colleagues also suggest that relationships between and among humans should not be governed by rights but by an ethic of care, although the ecofeminists do not seriously suggest that "contextual relations" can justify the use of *humans* for food or in scientific experiments to which they had not consented.[50] None of the writers suggest that rape may be morally permissible dependent on "contextual relations." None of the writers suggest that the morality of human slavery is dependent on "contextual relations." So, although these essays purport to reject the hierarchy of patriarchal ethics, and to offer the ethic of care as an alternative, the ethic of care is applied in significantly different ways depending on whether we are talking about humans or animals. When we apply the ethic of care to human beings, we assume from the outset that human beings have at least some interests that *cannot* be compromised *irrespective of context.* When we apply the ethic of care to animals, we assume that *all* animal interests can be violated if the "context" justifies it. The feminist ethic of care and animal welfare theory *both* accept the notion of animals as "things" and accept the legitimacy of the resulting hierarchy.

One of the first theorists to apply the ethic of care to animals was Nel Noddings in her 1984 book, *Caring.*[51] Noddings very explicitly accepted the legitimacy of the institutionalized exploitation of nonhumans, and the superiority of human beings.[52] But Noddings failed to recognize that accepting institutionalized exploitation as the normatively acceptable context in which an ethic-of-care analysis is to be applied merely restates and further reifies the very same hierarchical distinction between human persons and things that Noddings explicitly rejects. Her differential treatment of nonhuman others represented otherwise the very *speciesism* that animal rights theory seeks to abolish by recognizing the minimal conditions necessary for nonhuman personhood. Noddings claimed that we

---

50. Donovan suggests that it may be permissible to sacrifice the interests of humans, but does not pursue this notion. *See* Donovan, *supra* note 38, at 39. Brian Luke explicitly rejects sacrificing the interests of humans. *See* Brian Luke, *Justice, Caring, and Animal Liberation (1992), in* BEYOND ANIMAL RIGHTS, *supra* note 1, at 80.

51. NEL NODDINGS, CARING: A FEMININE APPROACH TO ETHICS & MORAL EDUCATION (1984).

52. *Id.* at 148–59.

can have ethical relations with animals but, apart from justifying the infliction of pain, these relations are dependent on our choice and animals have no right to their lives because that is something we must confer.[53] The ecofeminists do not eliminate personhood status for humans (or the abstract standards that constitute absolute prohibitions against rape and infringements of the female person). They reject it only for nonhumans.

An ethic of care can help to inform our relationship with others only *after we have already recognized that animals may not be treated exclusively as means to human ends,* which is the central point of animal rights theory. That is, an ethic of care can help once we have accepted the personhood of nonhumans and have included them within the scope of our moral community. Rights theory seeks to undermine the status of animals as property, and to require the inclusion of at least some nonhumans in the class of potential rightholders. To the extent that the question is whether nonhumans should be *included at all* in the class of potential rightholders, the ethic of care has little to offer, and this matter of inclusion is the central concern of animal rights theory. An ethic of care cannot coherently suffice to *require* that inclusion, and, as such, the ethic of care falls short of, and does not transcend, rights theory.

Other feminist theorists who have written about the ethic of care clearly recognize that such an ethic only makes sense *when it is applied to situations involving extant rightholders.*[54] Adams, Donovan, Luke, Shapiro, and their ecofeminist colleagues fail to understand this important limitation, and as a result, their attempt to apply the ethic of care as a replacement for rights theory fails. Far from going "beyond" animal rights, the views expressed in these essays beg the question against animal rights, and, indeed, these essays illustrate fundamental confusion about the role of deontological notions in moral reasoning.[55] Unfortunately, the

---

53. *Id.* at 153. For the most part, ecofeminists refer to Noddings as a central figure in developing the ethic of care and they endorse her views. Although Curtin criticizes certain views held by Noddings, Curtin nevertheless endorses a "contextual" approach that systematically undervalues animal interests. *See* Curtin, *supra* note 2, at 68.

54. *See, e.g.,* CAROL GILLIGAN, IN A DIFFERENT VOICE, xv–xxvii (1982, preface 1993).

55. I do not mean to suggest that these ecofeminist writers are the only ones to beg the question in this way. For example, David DeGrazia argues that the principle of equal consideration as applied to nonhumans means that we may no longer "see animals as essentially resources for our use." DAVID DEGRAZIA, TAKING ANIMALS SERIOUSLY 47 (1996). But DeGrazia then goes on to argue that certain forms of institutionalized exploitation may be consistent with the notion of

authors merely create a *different* sort of hierarchy that accords greater weight to feminist concerns, but still draws a sharp dividing line between human and nonhuman.

The confusion implicit in the ecofeminist analysis (as represented in this volume) is seen clearly in the four reasons offered in the introduction to *Beyond Animal Rights* concerning the supposed inadequacy of rights theory.

First, the ecofeminists claim that rights theory provides *less* protection than does the ethic of care.[56] But as we have seen, rights theory abolishes the hierarchy that permits animals who are relevantly similar to humans to be treated as non-similar, as "things." Although rights theory *does* require that animals who are regarded as persons be relevantly similar to human "persons," even with this limitation, rights theory eradicates the status of the "thingness" of at least *some* animals (including most of the domestic animals that we use for food or in experiments), whereas the ethic of care retains the "thingness" status for *all* animals except those who are the recipients of our care in particularized "relational contexts." The normative legitimacy of the institutionalized exploitation of all *other* animals is accepted. The ethic of care structurally provides the same level of protection to animal interests as does animal welfare: animals are not *entitled* to any sort of baseline minimum protection (that is what it means to be a "thing"), and any protection that they receive depends on a particular context.

Moreover, the ecofeminist position misunderstands the notion of the minimum conditions for personhood. The "similarity" that is required for the personhood of animals is merely that the animals have that level of complex consciousness that justifies an attribution of personhood to human persons. That is, a nonarbitrary application of the minimum level of complex consciousness required to say that a human, such as an

---

equal consideration. The problem that DeGrazia misses is that *all* forms of institutionalized exploitation *assume* that animals are "resources" in that they are deemed to possess *no* interests that cannot be traded away if it is deemed to be in the interests of humans.

56. The ecofeminists claim that rights theory "requires an assumption of similarity between humans and animals, eliding the differences. In reality, animals are only with considerable strain appropriable to Cartesian man." Donovan & Adams, *Introduction, supra* note 3, at 14–15. This suggests that rights theory relies on some criterion that will provide less protection to animals than that provided by ecofeminism, which supposedly does not require or rely upon these similarities.

infant or mentally disabled human, is a person, would lead us to the con-clusion that a healthy adult dog possesses all of the relevant characteris-tics of personhood. This assertion does not mean that the *scope* of animal rights is the same as human rights, just as the scope of rights of some people may legitimately be treated differently from the scope of rights of others. All that is required for the personhood of at least some animals is merely the recognition that the "thingness" status of at least some nonhumans is arbitrary and unjustifiable. No further similarity is required.

Second, the ecofeminists criticize rights theory for ignoring that ani-mals, and especially domestic animals, exist in a relationship of depen-dency with humans. They claim that rights theory is atomistic and fos-ters the ontology of "a society of equal autonomous agents."[57] To the extent that the ecofeminist position accepts the legitimacy of the institu-tions of exploitation that create the dependence of animals on humans, the position merely begs the question and their objection to the animal rights view becomes meaningless. To the extent that the ecofeminists see rights as *necessarily* atomistic, they again betray their confusion over the question of whether (at least some) animals are properly viewed as "things" with no protectable interests (the matter of inclusion) with the question of what *other* rights animals should have (the matter of scope). Rights theory certainly can have an atomizing effect at the level of dis-cussing the scope of animal *or* human rights, and can foster mythologies of independence that actually serve to oppress those who fare less well under such mythologies. But at the level of whether to include animals in the moral community *at all,* the decision to reject the "thingness" sta-tus of animals is clearly not atomistic and does not assume a mythology of independence or autonomy. If anything, this decision is an actualiza-tion of the communitarian goal of enlarging the moral community of persons based on the recognition that a wide variety of beings possess the characteristics that have led us to apply the concept of personhood to groups other than white males.

Third, the ecofeminists claim that the rights position is hyperrational and that it devalues emotion. This position appears to have two parts. One part is that male theorists, notably Peter Singer and Tom Regan, themselves devalue the role of emotion in moral life. This claim about the

---

57. *See id.* at 15.

moral psychology of Singer and Regan is—even if true—less interesting than the claim, also advanced by the ecofeminists, that rights are some-how *inherently* patriarchal or hierarchical.[58] This second (and more inter-esting) claim is simply *wrong*. We have seen that to the extent that we are speaking of the right to be included in the moral community *at all*, this right is *anything but* patriarchal or hierarchical. Unlike the ecofeminist position, the rights position eliminates the "thingness" of nonhumans and thereby diminishes the force of the normatively constructed dual-ism that has been used to justify the human oppression of nonhumans, just as the rights view diminishes the force of the male/female dualism.

Fourth, the ecofeminists claim that the rights view is characterized by an approach that is "abstract and formalistic, favoring rules that are uni-versalizable or judgments that are quantifiable."[59] There is no doubt that the determinate value of rules is suspect as a general matter. There is also no doubt that rules may be used in an oppressive way. But the right of inclusion in the moral community is a right that is *necessary for the very concept of personhood.* The rule says merely: do not treat persons as things. The rule establishes the moral community whose interests *must* be taken seriously and gives minimal deontological protection to the members of this community in order for them to *remain* a part of that commu-nity. Personhood (whether of humans or nonhumans) requires that cer-tain interests be protected *as a matter of basic moral rules.* Without such rules, that define what I have called the "minimum conditions of person-hood," and that feminist scholar Drucilla Cornell calls the "minimum conditions of individuation"—which *necessarily* involve deontological notions—there can be no *persons*. The notion of personhood imposes limits on the interest-balancing process. When we seek to apply the "re-lational ontology" required by the ethic of care to, say, a matter involv-ing our human children, there are a number of options, such as killing our children, that are ruled out from the outset and ruled out *as a matter of rules.* Similarly, if we seek to apply the ethic of care in male-female re-lationships, the "relational ontology" excludes from the outset the use

---

58. Even on this point, it appears as though the ecofeminists fail to perceive the subtlety of the rights position. For example, Tom Regan maintains that, "'philosophy can lead the mind to wa-ter but only emotion can make it drink.'" Patrice Greanville, *The Search for a New Global Ethic,* ANIMALS' AGENDA, Dec. 1986, at 40 (quoting Tom Regan).

59. Donovan & Adams, *Introduction, supra* note 3, at 15.

of battery or rape. These options are excluded as a matter of a *rule* that forbids that conduct whether or not we "care" about the victim. These "baselines" that inform the application of the ethic of care in human situations are ignored in these essays when nonhumans are involved, and that is precisely what speciesism is.

Finally, the ecofeminist critique of rights ignores that at least some deontological notions are necessary in any coherent normative scheme. Unless there are *some* beings within the system whose interests are protected against being traded away for consequential reasons alone, there can be no "persons" within that system. Even utilitarianism requires a notion of "personhood" that has some deontological elements or else innocents can be "sacrificed" for the common good, a notion that even some who consider themselves utilitarians reject. Similarly, a Marxist may very well reject as bourgeois many *conceptions* of rights, but even a Marxist must set some limits—and these limits are clearly deontological notions—on the interests of the individual that may be sacrificed for the common good. A failure to do so is precisely what led to Stalin's massacre of millions of peasants in the collectivization of Russia in the 1930s.

Once *any* normative system acknowledges, as all must, that there must be some "persons" within the system, the only question is whether the characteristics of personhood as we come to understand and develop them through public discourse are applicable to other beings on the "thing" side of the person/thing dualism.

CONCLUSION

The ecofeminist critique of rights is based in part on the rejection of dualism that places animals and nature on the "thing" side of the person/thing dualism. But the ecofeminist position still allows for the objectification of animals as "things" that have no interests that cannot be ignored if there is human benefit in doing so. The ethic of care is applied in a context in which there is a *preexisting* denial of personhood that renders absurd the attempt to apply an ethic of care. The position defended in *Beyond Animal Rights* is analogous to saying that it is hierarchical to endorse a general deontological or rights-based standard that abolishes and prohibits slavery altogether, but that it would eliminate hierarchy to apply the ethic of care in particularized situations involving slaves and in which we simply assumed the legitimacy of the institution of slavery. The position is also analogous to claiming that it would be hierarchical to have a general prohibition against rape that did not permit that conduct under *any* circumstance.

The ethic of care may help us to negotiate life's moral hazards, but there must be limits to the balancing of interests inherent in the "relational ontology" of ecofeminism. Those limits are set by general rules that protect certain animal interests from being balanced away, just as the fundamental interests of human beings are protected. In this sense, "caring" is simply not enough.

❖ ❖ ❖

Postscript (2008): This essay relied on Regan's theory of rights, including his notion of preference autonomy as an important characteristic for the attribution of personhood. However, as I indicated in the essay, I considered that preference autonomy may be sufficient but not necessary for inclusion in the moral community. In any event, my view, as expressed in *Introduction to Animal Rights: Your Child or the Dog?* and the more recent essays in this book, is that only sentience is required for nonhumans to possess the basic right not to be treated as a thing.

CHAPTER 7 / COMPARABLE HARM AND
EQUAL INHERENT VALUE
The Problem of the Dog in the Lifeboat

INTRODUCTION

In *The Case for Animal Rights,* Tom Regan posits the following hypothetical: five survivors—four normal adults and one normal dog—are on a lifeboat. There is room in the boat only for four, and one of the occupants must be thrown overboard. Regan maintains that his rights theory provides an answer to the problem. Although death is a harm for the dog, Regan argues, death would be a qualitatively greater loss, and, accordingly, a greater harm, for any of the humans: "To throw any one of the humans overboard, to face certain death, would be to make that individual worse-off (i.e., would cause *that* individual a greater harm) than the harm that would be done to the dog if the animal was thrown overboard."[1] It would, on Regan's view, be morally obligatory to kill the dog. Further, Regan claims even if the choice is between a million dogs and one person, it would still be obligatory under rights theory to throw the dogs overboard.

This notion of comparable harm is not unique to Regan although different theorists use it in different ways. Other theorists who subscribe to

This essay was published originally in *Between the Species,* Summer & Fall 1995, pp. 81–89.

Copyright © 1995 by Gary L. Francione. I gratefully acknowledge helpful comments received from Anna Charlton, Esq., co-director of the Rutgers Animal Rights Law Center, Priscilla Cohn, Professor of Philosophy at Pennsylvania State University, Tom Regan, Professor of Philosophy at North Carolina State University, and Steve Sapontzis, Professor of Philosophy at California State University. This essay is dedicated to my canine companions, Bandit, Stratton, Emma, Tedwyn, and Robert, who will always have a safe place in my lifeboat.

1. Tom Regan, *The Case for Animal Rights* (Berkeley & Los Angeles: University of California Press, 1983), p. 324.

some version of animal rights share Regan's view. For example, Joel Feinberg argues that although animals have rights, the rights position is consistent with holding "that an individual human life as such is a thing of far greater value than an individual animal life as such."[2] This view is also shared by those who work outside the rights paradigm; indeed, one of the few points of similarity between Regan's rights theory and the utilitarian theory of Peter Singer is that although both rely heavily on normative notions of equality, both appeal to the notion that some beings have qualitatively different and ultimately more valuable experience for purposes of resolving conflicts between beings who have moral standing. For example, Singer argues that "we can make sense of the idea that the life of one kind of animal possesses greater value than the life of another; and if this is so, then the claim that the life of every being has equal value is on very weak ground."[3]

Reliance on notions of comparable value and harm by Regan, Feinberg, and Singer has occasioned critical reactions by friend and foe alike. For example, philosopher S. F. Sapontzis, who argues in favor of including animals as members of the moral community, takes issue with the hierarchical status of humans implied by the notion of comparable harm. Humans undoubtedly can experience things that animals cannot, but the opposite is true as well: "We cannot enjoy the life of a dog, a bird, a bat, or a dolphin."[4] Accordingly, we cannot use species alone to make judgments of relative harm to resolve conflicts between humans and nonhumans without being guilty of the very speciesism that is the foundation of animal exploitation.

Peter Carruthers, who rejects the moral standing of animals, similarly bases his argument in very large part on Regan's and Singer's willingness to argue that human experience is such that humans generally suffer greater harm than do animals when humans are foreclosed from satisfying opportunities. Carruthers argues that we have a common-sense moral view that human life cannot be weighed against animal life that is so strong that even Regan and Singer affirm the validity of this view.

2. Joel Feinberg, "Human Duties and Animal Rights," in *Rights, Justice, and the Bounds of Liberty* (Princeton, N.J.: Princeton University Press, 1980), p. 203.

3. Peter Singer, *Practical Ethics* (Cambridge: Cambridge University Press, 1979), p. 90.

4. S. F. Sapontzis, *Morals, Reason, and Animals* (Philadelphia, Pa.: Temple University Press, 1987), p. 219.

Carruthers maintains that the moral theory that is most comfortably consistent with this common-sense view is some form of contractualism that would exclude animals from the moral community because animals are not rational agents.[5]

Ironically, one of Regan's most vocal critics is Singer, who asks "can a theory that tells us that all subjects-of-a-life (including dogs) have equal inherent value be reconciled with the intuition that it is the dog that must be sacrificed?"[6] Singer argues that because Regan maintains that, in the lifeboat example, his theory would allow for the killing of a million dogs as well, Regan's theory would permit more animal use than Singer explicitly acknowledges would be permitted at least in theory under utilitarianism. Singer denies that individual capacities (intelligence, awareness) play a role in his assessments about the morality of imposing pain on animals although Singer's construction of "interests" is heavily dependent on those capacities. Singer thinks that dependence on these capacities may cut in favor of the animal (i.e., we ought to attach greater interest to the animal's interest in avoiding pain or suffering because the animal may feel greater fear than a human because of different cognitive capacities), but that is irrelevant. The point is that whether it does cut in favor of the animal or not is an empirical question, and Singer's theory allows for those capacities to matter and cannot delimit only those whose application will favor nonhumans. Singer explicitly relies on capacities in resolving issues about the morality of killing animals. This leads him to the view that since most farm animals, in Singer's view, are incapable cognitively of grasping that they have a "life," they can be consumed by humans if they are raised entirely outside of the practices known collectively as "factory farming" or as "intensive agriculture," and if they are slaughtered painlessly.[7]

The use of comparable-harm analysis presents serious difficulties for any theory that seeks to expand in any significant way the protection accorded to nonhumans. These difficulties affect both deontological and consequentialist theories (albeit in different ways). I will, for the most part, confine my remarks to Regan's theory in which the notion of com-

5. Peter Carruthers, *The Animals Issue: Moral Theory in Practice* (Cambridge: Cambridge University Press, 1992), p. 9.

6. Peter Singer, "Ten Years of Animal Liberation," *New York Review of Books*, January 17, 1985, p. 49.

7. Peter Singer, *Animal Liberation*, 2d ed. (New York: New York Review of Books, 1990), pp. 228–30.

parable harm is central. I will first set out the context in which Regan develops his views on comparable harm. I will then explore the implications of the notion of comparable harm for rights theory. I will argue that Regan's resolution of the lifeboat example is inconsistent with a radical egalitarian theory, but I will suggest a reading of Regan's theory that places the lifeboat example in a different theoretical context.

EQUAL INHERENT VALUE AND COMPARABLE HARM

The central part of Regan's rights argument begins with his introduction of the postulate that moral agents have a distinct moral value—inherent value—that is separate from any intrinsic value such as pleasure or preference satisfaction. This notion of inherent value is presented by Regan as the primary alternative to the utilitarian notion that individuals are receptacles whose value may be determined by aggregating the intrinsic value that attaches to their experience. Inherent value is also an alternative to perfectionist ethics. Moral agents with inherent value must possess that value equally or else the notion of inherent value may collapse into one of the "pernicious"[8] perfectionist theories of justice "according to which what individuals are due, as a matter of justice, depends on the degree to which they possess a certain cluster of virtues or excellences, including intellectual and artistic talents and a character that expresses itself in the performance of heroic or magnificent deeds."[9] Perfectionist theories are objectionable not only because they provide "the foundation of the most objectionable forms of social, political, and legal discrimination" but also because "[w]hether individuals have the talent necessary to acquire the favored virtues (e.g., ability to do higher mathematics) is beyond their control."[10]

The attribution of equal inherent value to at least some moral patients (all normal mammals aged one year or more) is required because both agents and patients are subjects-of-a-life; that is, agents and patients are conscious, and possess a complex awareness (including beliefs and desires and an ability to pursue and satisfy them) and psychophysical

---

8. Regan, *supra,* p. 234.
9. *Idem,* pp. 233–34.
10. *Idem,* p. 234.

identity over time. Agents and patients may be harmed or benefited and have a welfare in that their experiential life fares well or ill for them, independently of the utility that they have for others or the interest that others have in them. Being a subject-of-a-life is not only a sufficient condition for having inherent value but is also a criterion that allows for the intelligible and nonarbitrary attribution of equal inherent value to moral agents and moral patients, including nonhumans. Regan stresses that there is no nonarbitrary way to separate moral agents from moral patients and that there is no nonarbitrary way of differentiating nonhuman moral patients from their human counterparts.

Regan's respect principle, a predistributive formal principle, requires that we treat those who have inherent value in ways that respect that value and holds that no individual with inherent value may be treated solely as a means to an end in order to maximize the aggregate of desirable consequences. From the respect principle we may derive the harm principle, which holds that, as a *prima facie* matter, harming the interests of a subject-of-a-life is showing disrespect for the inherent value of the moral agent or patient. In light of the *prima facie* nature of the obligations imposed by the harm principle, it is necessary to determine under what circumstances inflicting harm on moral agents or patients will be permitted. It is in this context that the notion of comparable harm becomes relevant.

Regan distinguishes two types of harm: harms that are inflictions and harms that are deprivations. "Acute or chronic physical or psychological suffering is the paradigm of a harm understood as an infliction."[11] Deprivations involve "*losses* of those benefits that make possible or enlarge the sources of satisfaction in life."[12] According to Regan, "[w]hatever the category, not all harms are equal."[13] Harms are comparable "when they detract equally from an individual's welfare, or from the welfare of two or more individuals."[14] Similarly, harms may not be comparable in those instances in which there are differential effects on the welfare of morally relevant beings. Although we may assume that there is a "strong presumption" that "like harms have like effects," the realities of individual

---

11. *Idem*, p. 94.
12. *Idem*, p. 97.
13. *Idem*, p. 303.
14. *Idem*, p. 304.

variability require recognition that like harm may detract differently from individual welfare and may not be counted as comparable.[15]

This notion of comparable harm is the foundation for the two general principles that Regan uses to resolve conflicts. The "miniride" principle, which assumes that the morally innocent individuals involved will be harmed in a *prima facie* comparable way, holds that in such situations (and in the absence of special considerations) we should choose to override the rights of the few rather than to override the rights of the many.[16] The "worse-off" principle, which assumes that the morally innocent individuals involved will suffer non-comparable harm, holds that in such situations (and in the absence of special considerations) we should choose to override the rights of the many when the "harm faced by the few would make them worse-off than any of the many would be if any other option were chosen."[17]

So, the notion of comparable harm (and its related concepts) plays a significant role in Regan's theory, since it specifies the circumstances under which harm may be inflicted on subjects-of-a-life, all of whom possess equal inherent value. In this context, Regan discusses the admittedly exceptional case of the four humans and the dog (or a million dogs) in the lifeboat. The dog has inherent value; indeed, according to Regan, the dog has inherent value that is *equal* to that possessed by her human co-passengers. Both the dog and the humans have a *prima facie* right not to be harmed. The decision to throw the dog overboard is not speciesist, Regan argues, because the decision to sacrifice the dog is not based on species membership but rather, "on assessing the losses *each individual* faces *and* assessing these losses *equitably.*"[18] There is no aggregating of harms in that the rights view would require throwing one million dogs overboard to save the four humans. Although the dogs are subordinated to the humans, this does not mean that there should be any "*routine* subordination of the less virtuous by those who are more virtuous, so that the latter may develop their virtues optimally. The rights view disallows such subordination."[19] The lifeboat case is an exceptional case and

---

15. *Loc. cit.*
16. *Idem,* pp. 305–07.
17. *Idem,* p. 308.
18. *Idem,* p. 325.
19. *Loc. cit.*

"[w]hat the rights view implies should be done in *exceptional* cases . . . cannot fairly be generalized to unexceptional cases."[20]

HARM AS AN EMPIRICAL MATTER, "ROUTINE" SUBORDINATION, AND THE "EXCEPTIONAL" CASE

From the above description of certain aspects of Regan's theory, it is clear that Regan very explicitly rejects any sort of perfectionism in favor of radical egalitarianism. Regan's postulate of equal inherent value is, according to Regan's own description, "categorical" and "admitting of no degrees."[21] That is, Regan rejects the notion that individuals can have different degrees of inherent value: "If moral agents are viewed as having inherent value to varying degrees, then there would have to be some basis for determining how much inherent value any given moral agent has."[22] A theory of differing levels of inherent value would risk reliance on some version of perfectionism, which Regan rejects.

In addition, the attribution of equal inherent value to moral agents *and* moral patients alike rests on the notion of the subject-of-a-life, which Regan also recognizes as categorical.[23] Indeed, the concept must be categorical; if beings could possess status as a subject-of-a-life to varying degrees, then it might be possible that only moral agents—and not moral patients—would have that status. But Regan rejects this notion in favor of an egalitarian criterion that "does not assert or imply that those who meet it have the status of subject of a life to a greater or lesser degree, depending on the degree to which they have or lack some favored ability or virtue (e.g., the ability for higher mathematics or those virtues associated with artistic excellence). One either *is* a subject of a life, in the sense explained, or one *is not*. All those who are, are so equally."[24]

In order to be a subject-of-a-life, a being need only be sentient, possess beliefs and desires (and an ability to act in pursuit of desires and goals), perception, memory, a psychophysical identity over time, emotional life, and experiential welfare that is better or worse depending

---

20. *Loc. cit.*
21. *Idem*, p. 244.
22. *Idem*, p. 236.
23. *Idem*, p. 244.
24. *Idem*, pp. 244–45.

on what happens to that being. Because both moral agents and moral patients are subjects-of-a-life, "one cannot *nonarbitrarily* maintain that how much inherent value moral patients have depends on the degrees to which they possess the virtues in question or on how much utility for others they have."[25]

Although both equal inherent value and the criterion used to attribute that value to moral agents *and* moral patients are categorical, the concept of harm apparently is not categorical, in that Regan allows supposed differences between humans and nonhumans to rebut the "strong presumption" that "like harms have like effects." As between the human and nonhuman occupants of the lifeboat, the same harm is deemed to be qualitatively different. Regan defends his theory of comparable harm in three ways. First, he maintains that there is, as an empirical matter, a difference between the harm suffered by the human and the same harm suffered by a nonhuman. Second, he argues that perfectionist ethical theories would permit "the *routine* subordination of the less virtuous by those who are more virtuous."[26] Third, he argues that "prevention cases, including lifeboat cases, *are* exceptional cases."[27]

I want to discuss briefly the empirical nature of harm determinations, the notion of "routine" subordination, and the problem of identifying "exceptional" circumstances.

(A) HARM AS AN EMPIRICAL MATTER Regan regards both the postulate of equal inherent value and the criterion used to attribute that value to moral agents and patients (all subjects-of-a-life) as categorical and admitting of no degrees whatsoever. Harm, however, is different. Although there is obvious overlap, we can, as an empirical matter, identify at least two types of harm—inflictions and deprivations—and we may, also as an empirical matter, judge that different rightholders may be affected in different ways by the same type of harm.

The problem with regarding harm as an empirical matter is that it involves a different analysis from that involved in the formulation of Regan's theoretical postulates. Not only is it difficult as an empirical

25. *Idem*, p. 240.
26. *Idem*, p. 325.
27. *Loc. cit.*

matter to make some of the assessments that need to be made to compare harms, but, more important, any such consideration of supposed empirical facts about harm in this regard is inconsistent with what it is necessary to *disregard* in the formulation of those theoretical postulates. Regan carefully constructs his postulate of equal inherent value so that it *excludes* any notion of individual characteristics or what may be thought to be virtues in a perfectionist theory. Similarly, his subject-of-a-life criterion excludes any notion of individual characteristic or virtue apart from those characteristics—sentience, beliefs, desires, psychophysical identity over time—that are constitutive of subject-of-a-life status. In light of the obvious empirical differences among human beings, and between humans and animals, Regan could have developed a concept of "subject" that reflected those differences. But he avoided these characteristics in favor of categorical theoretical notions that disregarded as irrelevant the existence of these empirical differences.

If the status of being a subject-of-a-life is, as Regan argues, an all-or-nothing proposition, then all such subjects must be equal for purposes of deciding at least those conflicts that involve interests protected under the rights theory. If all rightholders have inherent value because to accord them differential value would lead to perfectionism, and if moral agents and patients alike have this equal value because to accord them differential value would lead to perfectionism, then accepting a theory of comparable harm based at least in part on the presence or absence of certain virtues may be the same as arguing that the being who is harmed less has an inherent value that is different from, and less than, the one harmed more. Indeed, in Singer's theory, the different quality of experience is used primarily to determine the relative value of different beings and not to differentiate the varying degrees of harm suffered by beings with the same inherent value.[28]

(B) "ROUTINE" SUBORDINATION Part of the difficulty surrounding the notion of comparable harm is related to ambiguity involving precisely what constitutes "routine" subordination and when we have an "exceptional" case. When Regan says that the lifeboat example does not involve the "routine" subordination of one subject-of-a-life to another, he means

---

28. Singer, *supra* n. 3, pp. 88–90.

that the principle that we should favor humans over the dog is not one that we should apply save in "exceptional" circumstances. A routine subordination in unexceptional cases would likely represent some form of perfectionism. Indeed, Regan argues that the postulate of equal inherent value is acceptable because it avoids the "wildly inegalitarian implications of perfectionist theories."[29] Moreover, Regan rejects any attempt to argue that moral patients (including nonhumans) have less inherent value than moral agents on the grounds that such an argument would require, *inter alia,* reliance on perfectionist notions such as intellect or artistic ability, etc.[30]

The problem is that even if the lifeboat example is the only or the primary example of the "exceptional" case, it still represents a form of perfectionism. If, for example, *all* cases were lifeboat (or otherwise "exceptional") cases, and all of these exceptional cases involved normal, healthy humans and normal, healthy dogs, then the prescription for resolving those cases would require that we regard the harm to the dogs as incomparable to the harm suffered by the humans because of a supposed excellence enjoyed by the latter to a greater degree: humans have a qualitatively greater opportunity for satisfaction that is foreclosed by action that is detrimental to them.

Regan argues that *even* in the lifeboat case, the decision to kill the dog is not based on any appeal to perfectionist theories but, rather, is based on consideration of the equal inherent value and equal *prima facie* right not to be harmed. Although Regan may be correct to argue that his resolution of the lifeboat example does not appeal explicitly to perfectionism as advocating the *routine* subordination of rightholders, his resolution does appeal to a supposed human "excellence" (the ability to pursue opportunities for satisfaction). But to say that this virtue may be appealed to only in exceptional cases is nevertheless to say that *in that class of cases,* there is routine subordination based on a supposed virtue possessed by one *class* of rightholders.

(C) "EXCEPTIONAL" CIRCUMSTANCES The third problem involved in using comparable-harm analysis involves delineating those circumstances in

---

29. Regan, *supra,* p. 247.
30. *Idem,* p. 240.

which the analysis will apply. Although Regan talks of "exceptional" circumstances, it appears as though the miniride and worse-off principles are intended to be principles to resolve conflict as a general matter. And, in morality, conflict is the rule and not the exception. To the extent, then, that comparable-harm analysis is to be applied in *any* situation of conflict between or among rightholders, the result in the lifeboat situation portends difficulties for an animal rights theory. The use of a putative human excellence to justify the killing of the dog in the lifeboat example opens the door to perfectionist ethical theory in that *any* such consideration, it seems, detracts from the notion of equal inherent value, which rests, at least in part, on the notion that possession of inherent value depends only on the status of the individual as a subject-of-a-life with consciousness, complex awareness, and a psychophysical identity over time. To the extent that we regard harms to normal, healthy rightholders as incomparable, we depart from the presumption that Regan establishes that we should assume that like harms have like effects on rightholders.

Even if, however, the comparable-harm analysis applies only to truly "exceptional" cases, it is difficult to know exactly what cases are covered. For example, Sapontzis argues that it is improper to use animals in medical experiments except when animal use (and perhaps the use of comatose or terminally ill humans) is "necessary for and greatly outweighed by some clear and present, massive, desperately needed good."[31] How close is this situation to the lifeboat example? Does it qualify as an "exceptional" case? If so, it would seem that even a rights advocate could justify using animals (or "marginal" humans) based on the differential "excellence" possessed by normal humans whose use for the purpose would foreclose more opportunities for satisfaction.

The preceding discussion indicates that a reliance on comparable-harm analysis is problematic not only because it may entail speciesist conclusions. Let us return to the lifeboat. There are five survivors—all human. Four of the survivors possess some sort of extraordinary talent—one is a gifted musician, one a genius mathematician, etc. The fifth survivor is a normal, healthy adult who works at a minimum wage job and possesses no special skill or talent. If we can depart from the assumption that like harms have like effects when the fifth passenger is a dog, why not

---

31. Sapontzis, *supra*, p. 224.

assume that the like harm of death will have a different impact on the four talented survivors than it will on the fifth untalented survivor because death for the former will foreclose opportunities for satisfaction in a way that it will not for the latter?

"EXCEPTIONAL" CIRCUMSTANCES AND BASIC RIGHTS

There is, however, an important sense in which the real difficulty with the lifeboat example is that Regan mentions it *at all*. Although Regan thought that his general theory of animal rights provided an answer for the lifeboat situation, he may have made the mistake of confusing a question concerning the rights that animals would have in a situation in which animal *rightholders* had a conflict with human rightholders with a general theory that concerned only the question of whether animals had a single right not to be treated *solely* as means to ends.

It is my view that Regan never intended *The Case for Animal Rights* as an exhaustive analysis of every issue—including how to resolve conflicts between rightholders—that flowed from the recognition that animals have rights. Regan's primary focus was on the violation of animal rights through their treatment *solely* as means to human ends in institutionalized exploitation represented by factory farming, vivisection, and animal use for clothing and entertainment. That is, Regan argued that animals ought to be included in the class of rightholders, and that in order for membership in this class, it is necessary that we recognize the *basic right of animals not to be treated as property*, or, as Regan puts it, not to be treated *exclusively* as means to human ends.

Although the notions of "basic" and "absolute" rights are discussed in much philosophical literature, its most lucid presentation for present purposes may be found in the analysis presented by Professor Henry Shue in his book, *Basic Rights*.[32] According to Shue, a basic right is not a right that is "more valuable or intrinsically more satisfying to enjoy than some other rights."[33] Rather, a right is a basic right when "any attempt to

---

32. Henry Shue, *Basic Rights: Subsistence, Affluence, and U.S. Foreign Policy* (Princeton, N.J.: Princeton University Press, 1980).
33. *Idem*, p. 20.

enjoy any other right by sacrificing the basic right would be quite literally self-defeating, cutting the ground from beneath itself." Shue states that "non-basic rights may be sacrificed, if necessary, in order to secure the basic right. But the protection of a basic right may not be sacrificed in order to secure the enjoyment of a non-basic right." The reason for this is that a basic right "cannot be sacrificed successfully. If the right sacrificed is indeed basic, then no right for which it might be sacrificed can actually be enjoyed in the absence of the basic right. The sacrifice would have proven self-defeating." Shue emphasizes that basic rights are a prerequisite to the enjoyment and exercise of non-basic rights, and that the possession of non-basic rights in the absence of basic rights is nothing more than the possession of rights "in some merely legalistic or otherwise abstract sense compatible with being unable to make any use of the substance of the right."[34]

In order for animals to enjoy any rights *at all,* it is first necessary that they stop being regarded as "things" which, as a matter of law and (some) moral theories, *cannot* have rights. For example, the law regards animals as property, and "'[l]egal relations in our law exist only between persons. There cannot be a legal relation between a person and a thing or between two things.'"[35] Property "cannot have rights or duties or be bound by or recognize rules."[36] Regan's enterprise may be understood as an argument in favor of the single, basic right not to be regarded as property. A right to be treated as a moral and legal *person* is perhaps the most basic right in that personhood is a necessary condition of having relations *at all* in any normative system that distinguishes between persons and things.

Regan's theory of animal rights is similar to theories about the abolition of human slavery, which concerned the basic right of human beings not to be regarded as the property of others. Those who opposed slavery argued that it was morally wrong to treat human beings exclusively as means to the ends of other humans. But the abolitionist position did not entail what particular rights would be possessed by the lib-

---

34. *Idem,* pp. 19–20.
35. C. Reinold Noyes, *The Institution of Property* (New York: Longmans, Green & Co., 1936), p. 290, n.13 (quoting *Restatement of the Law of Property* (St. Paul, Minn.: American Law Institute, 1936)). *See also* Gary L. Francione, *Animals, Property, and the Law* (Philadelphia, Pa.: Temple University Press, 1995).
36. Jeremy Waldron, *The Right to Private Property* (Oxford: Clarendon Press, 1988), p. 27.

erated slaves—other than the basic right not to be regarded as property. Regan is concerned about institutionalized animal exploitation, and it is this concern that led him to reject "routine" subordination and to use of the miniride and worse-off principles in only "exceptional" circumstances.

An important part of Regan's theory is that all forms of institutionalized exploitation of animals violate the respect and harm principles because they fail to treat individuals as possessing equal inherent value, and rely on some form of utilitarian or perfectionist thought. For example, a slave owner could not rely on the worse-off or miniride principles to complain of harm when a slave was liberated against the owner's will. In this sense, then, Regan might have a way of distinguishing exceptional or extraordinary cases from most others in that some involve institutionalized animal exploitation that Regan would argue is from the outset violative of animal rights. Regan's theory would conceptually prevent there being a conflict from the outset in such situations. Regan could argue consistently that rights theory conceptually prevents our making any sort of comparable-harm determination in the context of animal use (or the use of "defective" humans) to find a cure for the most serious epidemic. Such animal use would entail institutions that are inherently exploitative of animals because they regard animals solely as means to human ends. This option is not open to Singer, who, if he is to be consistent, must inquire as to whether any exploitation—institutionalized or not—is justified by the principle of utility. For Singer, all cases are lifeboat cases. For Regan, exceptional cases *exclude* the institutionalized treatment of rightholders solely as means to the ends of others.

If this interpretation of Regan is correct, then two things are now clear. First, it was wholly unnecessary for Regan even to discuss the lifeboat example. Regan applies the miniride and worse-off principles to the lifeboat example, which, by Regan's own and explicit account, indicates that we are dealing with a situation in which there is no institutionalized exploitation operative, so the case does not concern the matter that is the primary subject of Regan's analysis. Regan's resolution of the lifeboat example is not required by his overall theory because the lifeboat example concerns a very different context—the resolution of a conflict between two rightholders—from the one that occupies Regan's attention throughout *The Case for Animal Rights*—the inclusion of nonhumans in the class of rightholders. Regan thought that his general theory provided an answer to the lifeboat situation, and this may have resulted from confusing issues concerning *conflicts* between rightholders with issues concerning membership in the *class* of potential rightholders.

Second, to the extent that Regan's (unnecessary) resolution of the problem *requires* the use of some form of perfectionism, such a requirement *is* problematic for Regan's overall theory, but not for the reasons pointed to by his critics. Regan could say that although all beings with inherent value possess that value equally for purposes of not treating any being exclusively as a means to an end in institutionalized exploitation, these beings do not possess the same value for purposes of resolving conflicts between rightholders. This reflects our intuition that it may be permissible to award Mary a scholarship if she is better in math than Johnny, but that it is not permissible to enslave Johnny for Mary's use simply because he is less intelligent than she.

The problem is that in light of Regan's analysis of the lifeboat example, it would seem that he is committed to resolving virtually *every* human/animal conflict in favor of the human. This does not, as some have suggested, mean that he is on a slippery slope back to vivisection. On the contrary, Regan can claim that the respect principle is always violated in cases of institutionalized exploitation. But it does give nonhumans a somewhat pyrrhic victory. Animals may no longer be regarded as property, but their interests will nevertheless not prevail most of the time because the characteristics upon which we relied to justify their property status will now be used to resolve any conflict that they may have *as rightholders* with a human rightholder.

Once animals are no longer treated as property, then it will become necessary to determine what particular rights are or should be possessed by animals. At this juncture, it may be *permissible* to take the presence or absence of certain virtues to resolve conflicts between or among rightholders. It is, however, problematic to say that rights theory *requires* that we throw the dog—or a million dogs—overboard, just as it would be problematic to say that a human rights theory about the abolition of human slavery requires that we always throw overboard the human with the least intelligence.

Perfectionism in the context of deciding issues or conflicts involving at least basic rights raises serious problems for any theory that rests on a notion of radical equality. My ability to do mathematics may legitimately be used to decide whether I get a math scholarship; that ability is irrelevant to whether, in a situation of famine, I should get the one remaining crust of bread. Respect for my basic or fundamental rights (however understood) should not, on a radical egalitarian view, depend on my virtues, which are, in any event, out of my control for the most part. To the extent that Regan links even basic rights (other than the right not to be property) with the possession of certain "virtues," he allows for differential consideration of equal inherent value. Such differential consideration would not justify using animals in experiments or otherwise relegating them to property status, but it might very well mean that animals will continue to lose in virtually every situation in which their "rights" were found to conflict with those of humans.

In order for Regan to escape this difficulty, he needs a theory about basic rights *other* than the right not to be property. Once individuals are determined to possess equal inherent value, then any conflict involving basic or fundamental rights ought to be decided without reference to any particular "virtue," which is what comparable-harm analysis prescribes.[37] Alternatively, Regan needs a theory about why the basic right not to be property is different from other basic rights. Regan would have to defend the notion that the harm of being treated exclusively as a means to an end is somehow different in a morally significant way from the harm of being deprived of *other* basic rights. One possible option is for Regan to argue that the right not to be property is the most basic of all rights because as long as a being is characterized as property, that being will be unable to enjoy those other rights as protected interests if virtually *all* interests are considered as tradable. The problem is that Regan never addressed this issue and never explicitly recognized that his theory was more about the abolition of animal slavery than a general theory of rights that animals would possess once they were no longer regarded as human property. Moreover, it is not clear that such a difference would be significant morally in comparison to deprivation of other basic rights, such as a minimal right of physical security or minimal subsistence.

---

37. It may also be the case that inflictions should be treated differently from deprivations. Although there may be a good deal of overlap here, it seems that inflictions concern harms that are more related to basic rights.

CONCLUSION

In sum, the observation that Singer, Carruthers, and others have made of Regan's theory—that the lifeboat example sinks, as it were, the whole theory because it allows for a necessary compromise of the categorical nature of Regan's concepts of equal inherent value and subject-of-a-life—is incorrect. Regan's overall rights theory is not threatened by his compromise of his categorical concepts as long as the "exceptional" circumstances in which this compromise can occur are limited to those that are identified exclusively by reference to those categorical concepts. That is, "exceptional" circumstances can *never* include institutionalized exploitation so, irrespective of the emergency, such as a plague, performing animal experiments (a form of institutionalized exploitation) would always be deemed to violate the respect principle. Regan can retain comparable-harm analysis, but he cannot, it seems, accept any sort of "perfectionism," even in the exceptional case, insofar as basic rights are concerned.

Regan's resolution of the lifeboat example was unnecessary because it did not concern the general context of his theory, which involved only the basic right not to be treated *exclusively* as a means to an end. The lifeboat example concerns a conflict *between* rightholders. To the extent that in such situations Regan would *require* choosing the human interest over the animal interest, it is problematic for his theory because it would mean that animals, although no longer property, will virtually never prevail in any conflict with human rightholders.[38]

❖ ❖ ❖

Postscript (2008): In this essay, I argued that Regan's theory of comparable harm does not present an insurmountable problem for Regan's overall

---

38. It appears as though Regan may have modified his intuition about the lifeboat example. Although he has not addressed the specific issue, in a reply to Singer's comments, he described the lifeboat example and asked whether it would "be wrong to throw the dog overboard in these dire circumstances?" and not whether it would be obligatory to do so. He argues that the judgment may very well rely on the moral agent's assessment of the differing capacities of the lifeboat occupants. Letter from Tom Regan to the Editor, *New York Review of Books*, April 25, 1985. But that is very different from saying that it is obligatory to throw the dog overboard.

theory as long as the exceptional circumstances to which he refers excludes institutionalized exploitation. I have, however, come to the view that Regan may not be able to rely on such an exclusion.

To the extent that Regan applies his worse-off principle in any situation of conflict to favor humans based on the notion that death is a greater harm to humans than to animals because it forecloses more opportunities for satisfaction, it would seem that there is a morally relevant qualitative distinction between humans and nonhumans that would justify a non-categorical formulation of Regan's subject-of-a-life and equal-inherent-value postulates. For Regan, being a subject-of-a-life is not only a sufficient condition for having inherent value, but is also a criterion that allows for the intelligible and non-arbitrary attribution of equal inherent value to moral agents and moral patients, including nonhumans. He stresses that there is no non-arbitrary way to separate moral agents from moral patients and that there is no non-arbitrary way of differentiating nonhuman moral patients from their human counterparts.

If the harm of death to the human is always greater because of species, then there is arguably a non-arbitrary way of differentiating humans from nonhumans. Therefore, if Regan argues that we are morally required to choose to kill a million dogs in order to save one human because death is a qualitatively greater harm to the human, it would seem that he has opened the door to the argument that institutionalized animal use can be justified at least in exceptional circumstances.

As I discuss in the essay and in subsequent writing, the choice of a human over a nonhuman in any conflict situation based on some supposedly qualitative cognitive difference (such as death being a greater harm to the human) is speciesist. To the extent that this choice is required, it is not only speciesist, but it ensures that nonhumans will never prevail in any conflict with humans.

As I discuss in *Introduction to Animal Rights: Your Child or the Dog?*, we may, in the lifeboat or burning-house situation, decide to favor the human over the nonhuman not because death is a lesser harm to the nonhuman, but because we do not know what death means to the nonhuman and we have a better idea what it means to the human. We might, therefore, rely on this—a matter of epistemological limitation on our part and not any empirical claim that death is a lesser harm to humans—as the tie-breaker. We might also flip a coin. We might also decide to choose the nonhuman for some other reason, such as that the human in question is very old and the nonhuman in question is very young. In no case, however, would I think it appropriate to invoke any notion that humans are "higher" animals. Indeed, this is ultimately the problem with Regan's analysis. To the extent that he maintains that humans are "higher" animals in that, as a matter of empirical fact, death is a greater harm to humans, and, as a normative matter, this difference is morally relevant, then, it would seem difficult to be able to confine this analysis only to the exceptional situation of the lifeboat. It would ostensibly be relevant earlier in the analysis when Regan claims that there is no non-arbitrary way to distinguish between moral agents and moral patients for purposes of saying that the respect principle, which prohibits instrumental treatment, applies to all subjects-of-a-life.

In sum, Regan's notion that death is a qualitatively different and greater harm for humans based only on species presents serious difficulties for Regan's theory of animal rights and for his view that we should abolish institutionalized exploitation. In many respects, Regan's view comes uncomfortably close to the position defended by Bentham and Singer that animals do not have an interest in continued life. Regan's position is different in that, unlike Bentham and Singer, he maintains that death is a harm for nonhumans whereas Bentham and Singer deny this (Singer maintains that nonhuman great apes and, perhaps, a few other species may also have an interest in life). But Regan's notion that nonhumans have a qualitatively or presumptively different and lesser interest in life does provide for a non-arbitrary way to justify attribution of different degrees of inherent value, which could be used to justify the use of nonhumans and, therefore, plays a similar theoretical role to the notion proposed by Singer and Bentham.

In the preface to the second edition of *The Case for Animal Rights* (2004), Regan attempts to deal with the problem of the dog in the lifeboat by making three points. First, he relies on the argument that I made in 1995 in the preceding essay—that the lifeboat situation excludes the rights violations inherent in institutionalized exploitation. But, as I have argued above, that answer does not address the problem in a satisfactory manner. Second, and quite remarkably, Regan argues that certain forms of institutionalized exploitation, such as the domestication of nonhumans (the dog in the lifeboat), do not necessarily involve coercion or violate the rights of nonhumans. Finally, Regan claims that whether death fore-closes more opportunities for satisfaction for a human or nonhuman is a matter of case-by-case analysis, and not a matter of species, but he re-tains what is tantamount to a species-based distinction in that the ex-ample that he mentions in which the dog would prevail over the human involves an irreversibly comatose human for whom death is *no* loss. But Regan cannot avoid a species-based distinction unless he purports to sup-port a case-by-case analysis that would, for instance, ask whether a men-tally disabled (but not comatose) human has fewer opportunities for sat-isfaction than a normal dog.

Finally, although this essay focused on Regan's theory of rights and his subject-of-a-life concept, my view, as expressed in *Introduction to Ani-mal Rights: Your Child or the Dog?* and in my other work, is that sentience alone is a necessary and sufficient condition for full membership in the moral community.

REFERENCE GUIDE TO SELECTED TOPICS

As this book comprises chapters that were published as individual essays rather than as a single book, I have chosen to provide the following reference guide to the broad themes of these essays rather than a traditional index. This reference guide is exhaustive neither of the topics covered nor the individuals discussed in the book, and does not necessarily provide every reference to those topics and individuals included. Moreover, there will be inevitable overlap among these broad themes.

—Gary L. Francione

OUR EXPLOITATION OF NONHUMAN ANIMALS

Our thinking about nonhuman animals is confused. For example, we simultaneously treat some nonhumans as members of our families and others as our food. Our "moral schizophrenia" about nonhumans is discussed at pp. 25–28, 135, 150, 163, 172.

Humans have historically justified their exploitation of nonhumans on three grounds. These are discussed at pp. 3, 28–29, 131n10, 178 (the Cartesian theory of animal automatons); pp. 3–4, 52n74, 178–79 (religious grounds); and pp. 4, 10–14, 29–30, 52–61, 123–25, 137–45, 157–60, 179–85, 210–29 (cognitive differences between humans and nonhumans).

THE ANIMAL WELFARE POSITION

The animal welfare position, which holds that we may use nonhumans for human purposes, is the prevailing contemporary framework that governs our relationship with nonhumans. This position maintains that although we may use nonhumans, we have a moral and legal obligation to treat them "humanely" and not to inflict "unnecessary" suffering on them. See pp. 1, 5–9, 30–36, 67–68, 133–34, 149, 171, 191–92.

However, the overwhelming amount of animal use by humans cannot plausibly be described as "necessary." See pp. 7, 36–37, 68–69, 100–101, 149–50, 171–72.

Vivisection involves the use of nonhuman animals in experiments or for other purposes related to science and is arguably our only use of nonhumans that is not transparently trivial. The necessity of animal use for this purpose is discussed at pp. 37, 172–77; the moral justification for vivisection is discussed at pp. 64, 177–85.

Nonhuman animals are our *property*; they are things that we own. They have only the value that we accord to them. As a result, animal welfare, both as a social theory and as applied through animal welfare laws, fails to provide any significant protection for animal interests. The problems presented by the property status of animals and the failure of animal welfare are discussed throughout the book, but particularly at pp. 7–9, 19, 37–44, 69–71, 72–106, 135–37, 145–46, 150–52, 154, 160–64, 166, 193–96.

Ethical theory concerning nonhuman animals seeks to clarify how we should resolve conflicts between humans and nonhumans. These conflicts are, for the most part, ones we create because we regard animals as property and bring them into existence so that we can treat them as our resources. See pp. 13–14, 63–66, 152, 164.

Animals are property in the same way that humans who were enslaved were property. The law failed to protect human slaves just as it fails to protect nonhuman animals. See pp. 9, 46–51, 52–53, 61–63, 104–106, 128, 145–46, 166n70, 168, 196–98.

The animal welfare position reflects the view that animals do not care *that* we use them, but only *how* we use them. According to this position, nonhumans do not have an interest in continuing to live, but only have an interest in not suffering. This view is espoused by Bentham, Singer, and, arguably, by Sunstein, and is described at pp. 6, 53–54, 133, 143–44, 153–57 (Bentham); pp. 18–20, 54–55n81, 143–44, 153–57 (Singer); and pp. 153–57 (Sunstein). Regan defends the related position that death is a lesser harm for humans than for nonhumans. See pp. 13–14, 165n69, 210–29.

"New welfarism," like classical welfarism, promotes the regulation of animal treatment, but seeks to go beyond traditional welfare theory and to provide greater protection for animal interests or to abolish animal use through incremental regulation. See pp. 2, 14–21, 106–16, 186–209.

Animal advocacy groups have effectively formed "partnerships" with animal exploiters by promoting supposedly "humane" animal products, by focusing on animal welfare reforms that effectively make animal exploitation more economically efficient, and by making animal exploitation more socially acceptable. See pp. 15–16, 72–96, 108–10, 126–27.

THE ANIMAL RIGHTS/ABOLITIONIST POSITION

"Animal rights," properly understood, means the *abolition* of animal use and not the *regulation* of animal treatment. This theme runs throughout the book, but is discussed particularly at pp. 1–2, 13, 21–23, 25, 62–63, 65, 70, 106–16, 127–28, 146, 148, 151–52, 164, 166, 188, 191–92.

To treat animals as "persons" does not mean that we treat them in all respects as we treat humans, but rather, that we apply the principle of equal consideration and treat human and similar nonhuman interests in a similar way. However, if animals are property, the principle of equal consideration will have no meaningful application to their interests because animals will be regarded as "things" without protectable interests. See pp. 12, 18–20, 44–66, 105–106, 143–46, 151, 153–64, 166, 168, 189–90, 193–98.

A right is a way of protecting an interest. A right protects an interest even if the consequences of violating the interest would benefit others. See pp. 20, 49, 168, 177–78, 192.

Although there is a great deal of disagreement about what human interests ought to be protected by a right, there is general agreement that all humans, irrespective of their particular cognitive characteristics, have a basic, pre-legal moral right not to be treated as the property of others. The basic right not to be treated as property, or the right to equal consideration of one's fundamental interests, is discussed at pp. 12, 49–52, 70, 145, 151, 168–69, 189, 193–98, 221–22.

To say that a nonhuman has a basic right not to be treated as property is another way of saying that nonhumans, like humans, have intrinsic or inherent value that precludes their being treated as our property or as commodities with only extrinsic or conditional value. See pp. 23, 50n71, 60–61n97, 67–71, 103–105, 135–36, 151n12, 162, 210–29.

If a nonhuman animal is sentient, or subjectively aware, we should accord that nonhuman the basic moral right not to be treated as our property. No other cognitive characteristic is required. Nonhumans do not have to have minds that are similar to human minds to be full members of the moral community. See pp. 10–14, 54–61, 123–25, 129–47, 152, 157–60, 165–66, 179–85.

The theory of animal rights denies the welfarist position that animals do not have an interest in continued existence and only have an interest in not suffering. See pp. 10–11, 13–14, 54–57, 144, 157–60, 165–66.

Recognizing the right of nonhumans not to be treated as property requires that we stop bringing domestic nonhumans into existence and that we leave nondomesticated nonhumans alone. To the extent that we have conflicts with the latter, we should apply the principle of equal consideration to resolve such conflicts. See pp. 13, 63–66, 128, 146, 152, 164.

The moral baseline of the animal rights/abolitionist movement is veganism, which involves not eating, wearing, or using animal products. Just as someone who opposes human slavery should not own slaves, a person who objects to animal exploitation should not consume animal products. See pp. 16–17, 65, 101, 107–16, 122, 127–28, 147.

ANIMAL LAW

"Animal law" has become a specialty legal practice. For the most part, this practice, and most law school courses that focus on the doctrines promoted thereby, reinforce the property status of animals. See pp. 116–21, 123.

From 1990 until 2000, Anna Charlton and I operated the Animal Rights Law Clinic at Rutgers University School of Law in Newark, New Jersey. This was the first time in the history of American legal education that students received academic credit for working on actual cases involving animal issues at the same time that they studied the philosophical foundations of the abolitionist approach to animal rights. See pp. xv, 121–23.

❖ ❖ ❖

Hundreds of individuals, including philosophers, lawyers, and animal advocates are discussed and cited throughout the book. The following are those whose views are of particular relevance: